THE REALITY OF FAITH

THE REALITY
OF FAITH

*A Way Between Protestant Orthodoxy
and Existentialist Theology*

by

H. M. KUITERT

Translated by Lewis B. Smedes

WILLIAM B. EERDMANS PUBLISHING COMPANY
Grand Rapids, Michigan

TABLE OF CONTENTS

INTRODUCTION

- From antimetaphysical theology to the essence of faith
- "Realitas fidei": objective and subjective genitives
- The practical side

INTRODUCTION

The subject of this book is the antimetaphysical trend of modern theology.

One can, of course, use any of several designations other than "antimetaphysical" to capture the central issues of theology in our time. But the word antimetaphysical—besides getting at the main motive behind modern theology—is broad enough to catch many of the more specific issues in its net.

For instance, it includes the program of demythologizing, which is itself focused on the narrower question of New Testament interpretation. It also embraces the problem of whether theology is the product of religious projection, a problem of anthropology. From a somewhat different point of view, the word antimetaphysical is big enough in scope to allow us to discuss the nature of theological language—the problem of whether language about God describes something about the person using the language or whether it describes a state of affairs outside the person using it. These areas of discussion are all related to one basic drive in modern theology, a drive to be rid of metaphysics.

This makes it clear that we must face up to the nature of faith. We must ask what the relationship is between *fides quae* and *fides qua,* between what is believed and the act of believing. Are both of these significant? Or is only the subjective action, the dynamics of faith, important? If the "thing believed" is truly significant, what is its relation to the dynamic action called believing? Furthermore, we must ask about the significance of the definitions (or images) that people give to the object of their faith: does genuine faith depend on its concepts or images? Or can a person have authentic faith apart from the accuracy of the concepts that faith forms of its object? Can faith, perhaps, function without any concepts at all?

In mentioning these more specific areas of concern, we have

suggested some of the problems in theology that the broad term
antimetaphysical includes. Somewhere in the background of these
and other issues lies a single driving motive behind modern
theology—the desire to rid itself of metaphysics and metaphysical
theology.

There are also some practical reasons for using the general
and negative term antimetaphysical. It permits us to cover a good
deal more ground than we could if we limited ourselves, let us
say, to the question of demythologizing. We want to dig into the
history of theology to find the roots of the modern trend. We are
allowed to ask about the influence of modern philosophy on
theology. And, not least significantly, the word antimetaphysical
demands that we face up to the question of the scientific character
of theology, the question of whether dogmatic statements can
legitimately lay claim to being statements with scientific validity.
This last question forces us to come to grips with the question
of whether dogmatics deals with ontological matters. Another
way of saying this is to ask whether sentences like "God is" or
"Jesus is God's Son" say something about the *being* of God and
the *being* of Jesus. What does the word *is* signify when we use it
in theological talk? Do the *is*-statements in theology have the
same meaning that they have, let us say, in mathematics?[1]

All these questions belong within the province of dogmatics.
They confront us with genuine dogmatic issues in the authentic
sense of the word. The fact that hermeneutics is going to occupy
a good deal of our attention does not alter the dogmatic character
of our study. For dogmatics is deeply implicated in the question
of hermeneutics. Steiger is quite correct in insisting that hermeneutics is implicit in dogmatics.[2] Hermeneutical questions are
dogmatical kinds of questions, just as dogmatical questions have
a hermeneutical aspect. The job of hermeneutics is to set up rules
for reading the Bible; therefore, it also sets up rules for building
a dogmatics.

We must not go too deeply into the relationship between dogmatics and hermeneutics. But we ought to make at least two

---

[1] The following studies are of fundamental relevance to our present subject: H. Diem, *Theologie als kirchliche Wissenschaft*, II, *Dogmatik* (1955);
H. J. Iwand, *Nachgelassene Werke. Glauben und Wissen* (1962), pp. 17-
218; H. Gollwitzer, *Die Existenz Gottes im Bekenntnis des Glaubens*
(1963); H. G. Fritzsche, *Die Strukturtypen der Theologie. Eine kritische
Einführung in die Theologie* (1961).
[2] *Die Hermeneutik als dogmatisches Problem* (1961).

observations. First, hermeneutics is necessary for dogmatics to keep us from dogmatically preconceived interpretation of the Bible. The two disciplines are not the same. Their methods differ very distinctly. But they must not be separated from each other; they must be in constant touch, so that each can serve as a corrective of the other. Second, dogmatics and hermeneutics overlap one another materially. For this reason, one cannot talk for long about the one without getting into questions that also belong to the other. In fact, all hermeneutics has the flavor and tone of dogmatics and all dogmatics is conditioned by hermeneutics. I say this even though many scholars of hermeneutics today are likely to argue the point.

We have said enough here, I think, to show that our choice of the phrase *antimetaphysical trend* opens up a wide theological field, in which we can wander through several important theological issues of our time. We think that it will also help us get at the central question that lies behind them all.

From antimetaphysical theology to the essence of faith

The textbook example of antimetaphysical theology is Albrecht Ritschl. In his view, ontological judgments in traditional dogmatics are value judgments. Dogmatic statements are not meant to be descriptions of objective realities; they are personal expressions of faith. On one hand, Kant (as much the philosopher of Protestantism as was Thomas Aquinas of Roman Catholicism) demonstrated the impossibility of metaphysics with his devastating critique of the so-called proofs for the existence of God. If there is a God, which Kant did not deny, He cannot be known in any ordinary sense of knowing. On the other hand—and here Ritschl calls on Schleiermacher—faith is not in any case a belief of objective statements, but is an exercise in personal confession and action. For Ritschl, to choose an antimetaphysical theology is to choose a viable concept of faith.

Ritschl's two-pronged argument, which we have only hinted at here, has a familiar ring.[3] It is still being used to keep theology in

3 The antimetaphysical tendency in Ritschl's theology depends on a separation that he creates between the *Darstellung* (the task of historical research) and the *Interpretation* (the job of systematic theology) of the same biblical givens. Cf. Emanuel Hirsch, *Geschichte der neuern evangelischen Theologie,* V (1954), 558; also Gösta Hök, *Die ellyptische Theologie Albrecht Ritschls* (1942), esp. ch. 8.

its own province, and to preserve it from mythological language
and projections. The German existentialist theologian Friedrich
Gogarten describes the distinction between Bultmann's existentialist interpretation and orthodox Lutheran theology as a distinction
between "historical thinking" (Bultmann) and "metaphysical thinking" (Lutheran orthodoxy). Gogarten obviously equates the
word "metaphysical" with "obsolete"; at any rate, metaphysical
thinking is a mode of thought that has no contact at all with a
totally changed life-situation and a wholly changed feeling for
reality.[4]

The real world that men have to come to grips with today is
radically different from the world in which classical Lutheranism
and Reformed orthodoxy were at home.[5] How extensive and
profound these changes are we do not need to explore here. All of
us know something of how real the chasm is. For instance, the
question of the closed universe plagues us today even more profoundly than it did the people of Ritschl's time. God's fingers—to
put it in plastic terms—do not seem able to get through into our
affairs anymore. Natural science may prefer talking about statistics
to talking about causality in the strict sense, but in the world of
everyday experience the notion of causality controls almost every
account of natural happenings. One is mistaken if he suggests that
natural science has stressed statistics instead of natural causation
because regularity of cause and effect is no longer taken for
granted. Those who seize on this suggestion are not only ignoring
the assumptions of natural science, but are making illegitimate use
of natural science in the hope of showing that faith is able, after

---

[4] Gogarten consistently relies on this contrast. As an example, see *Die
Wirklichkeit des Glaubens. Zum Problem des Subjektivismus in der Theologie* (1957), pp. 21ff. Also instructive for this discussion are Wilhelm Kam-
lah, "Gilt es wirklich 'die Entscheidung zwischen geschichtlichem und meta-
physischem Denken'?", *Evangelische Theologie*, XIV (1954), 171ff.; H. W.
Bartsch, "The Still Unsettled Debate on Demythologizing: The Hermeneutic Problem in German-language Theology," *Religion in Life*, XXX (1961),
167-178. Bonhoeffer, too, puts "religious interpretation" on the same level
with "metaphysical reason"; cf. his *Widerstand und Ergebung* (1956),
p. 183.
[5] We must be cautious in using the phrase Reformed or Lutheran orthodoxy. Ratschow has rightly observed that we meet this so-called orthodoxy
mostly in the form of rigid compilations gathered from the time when
orthodoxy had already passed its creative peak (*Lutherische Dogmatik
zwischen Reformation und Aufklärung* [1964], pp. 11ff.).

all, to preserve some space for itself in the universe. Trying to make room for faith in this way is only to make faith a satellite of natural science, and this, theologically speaking, is bad strategy.[6]

The fear of making general statements that carry the pretensions of being *ontological* judgments is more prevalent today than it was in Ritschl's time. Ritschl knew this fear in theology; today it is equally present in philosophy and the general sciences. Functionalism and operationalism are the mode today. This is not merely to say that a great deal of stress is placed on function and practice. Functionalism is one aspect of a common skepticism about ontological statements that claim to have a basis in knowledge of objective being. Is there actually something like gravity, or is the word "gravity" at best a model, which provides us the most adequate approach to what really happens, and at worst only a working hypothesis?[7] Questions like this play an important role in theology today. If they do not arise from our practical awareness of modernity, they are provoked by theology's contacts with scientific development in the broad sense, a contact that theology cannot escape, and in fact must promote.

In the theology of existentialism, about which this book is chiefly concerned, theologians tend to distance themselves from almost everything that smacks of metaphysics while steering clear of the antimetaphysical assumptions of positivism and neo-positivism. They are trying to demonstrate that a third way exists between metaphysical theology, with its irrelevant abstractions, mythological conceptions, and unchecked projections, and positivism, with its habit of ignoring all the decisive questions that touch man in his personal existence.

One could raise the interesting question whether there may not be a closer affinity between existentialist theology and philosophical positivism than the existentialist theologians would have us suppose. It is a question, for example, whether the theology of

---

[6] Günther Howe does not wholly escape this objection in his essay "Parallelen zwischen der Theologie Karl Barths und der heutigen Physik," *Antwort. Festschrift zum 70. Geburtstag Karl Barths* (1956), pp. 409-422. A very promising grasp of the complex problems involved here is found in C. J. Dippel and J. M. de Jong, *Geloof en Natuurwetenschap*, I (1965).

[7] On the meaning of "model" in science and philosophy, see *Wijsgerig Perspectief 5* (1965), which is devoted almost wholly to this matter. An evaluation of functionalism and operationalism is found in A. L. Janse de Jonge, "Weten en geloven omtrent de mens," *Geloof en Wetenschap*, LXIII (1965), 105-108.

existence does not actually rest on the assumption that the posi-
tivist view of history is necessarily true. Would not the theology of
existence be badly and perhaps mortally wounded if the positivistic
view of history should prove to be very wrong?

We shall return to this question later. Meanwhile, in general
terms, we can say that the antimetaphysical slant of contemporary
existential theology links it with the neo-positivist-influenced
Anglo-Saxon theologies like those of Paul van Buren and John Wren-
Lewis. One can certainly assume that the functionalism of these
two men betrays an unmistakable point of contact with the theology of existence. It would be a mistake to confuse these two ways of
doing theology, but from the viewpoint of the subject we have
undertaken, it would be equally wrong to separate them.[8]

With this, we come back to the issue: the *is*-character of theological, or dogmatical, statements about God and His acts. Can we
hold to the *is*-character of theological statements without betraying
the *essence of the Christian faith* (as Ebeling entitles one of his
books)?

"Realitas fidei": objective and subjective genitives

We have spoken of an antimetaphysical *trend*. The word trend
suggests a movement or a change of position. We can perhaps get
a notion of what direction the movement is taking by using the
scholastic phrase *realitas fidei*—the reality of faith, or faith-reality.
The very ambiguity of this phrase can serve as a means of putting
the problem in focus.

To understand the phrase *realitas fidei*, we must deal with the
grammar of the genitive form *fidei*. In the terms of freshman
composition, is this an objective genitive or a subjective genitive?
Where is the reality to which faith directs us: does it exist outside
of faith or is it the reality of faith itself?

An illustration may help clarify the point. We have the same
dilemma—objective or subjective genitive—when we talk about
the love of God. When we say "love of God," are we talking about
God's love for us (subjective genitive) or our love for God (objective genitive)? Usually the context in which the phrase appears
determines which of these two meanings is intended. It makes a

---

[8] This question is discussed by P. R. Baelz, "Is God Real?", *Faith, Fact,
and Fantasy* (1964), pp. 47ff. We shall return to it later.

considerable difference whether, in this case, we mean our love for God or God's love for us; for example, Romans 5:5 speaks of the love of God, leaving it to the reader to decide which of the two is meant.

The similarity of this example to the interpretation of the phrase *realitas fidei* is apparent. The literal translation of the Latin is "reality of faith." But does this mean the reality on which faith focuses and to which it gives expression; in other words, does it mean that reality "out there" to which utterances of faith point (objective genitive)? Or does *realitas fidei* refer to the reality of the believing itself—of the unique, highly personal believing that is expressed in the utterances of faith (subjective genitive)?

The problem can be summarized by asking what is actually intended in expressions such as "God is" and "Jesus is risen." Do these words say something about God? Do they inform us of something that happened to Jesus of Nazareth? Or do these words only reveal something about the person speaking them? What is expressed in Christian confessions—the *foundation* of our faith or our *experience* of believing?

The antimetaphysical tendency in modern theology—historically considered—is a movement from an objective to a subjective genitive in the phrase "reality of faith." We shall consider this movement in the next chapter and give a sketch of its history, beginning with its impetus in the theology of Schleiermacher and following the line that binds his approach to the problem with the current hermeneutically oriented theology of existence. We hope to demonstrate that the theology of existence gives to hermeneutics the task of providing theological justification for its antimetaphysical tendency.

The last phase of this study is devoted to the question of whether there is a real dilemma between a reality "out there" to which faith witnesses and the reality of believing itself, or whether another route is open to us which is not only theologically meaningful, but theologically necessary if theology is to remain a science. We believe a third avenue is indeed open to us, and we hope to demonstrate that there is.

The practical side

Before concluding this survey of the field, we should perhaps

append an *apologia* for raising so many theological questions. All
these questions may give the impression that our concern is highly
theoretical and that we are dealing merely with formal and ab-
stract questions. Actually we are about to plunge into an extremely
practical affair. Our subject has direct and urgent implications for
the Christian community and the Christian individual, for we are
confronting the question of religious concepts and ideas. In a
nutshell, the practical theme is the *image-making of the Christian
faith*. This is an unusual way of putting it, but it is precisely what
we mean.

All human speech is a kind of image-making. The moment we
put concepts in words we have created an image. Even if we
should choose to classify them as special or higher forms of
images—as was popular in the nineteenth century—we would still
have to admit that they are images, no matter how refined we
make them. In practical terms, then, we are asking about the
meaning and value of our speech about God and His saving acts.
We are asking about the reality of the images that the believing
Christian community uses in its preaching and in theology. What is
the significance of Christian speech in terms of reality?

This brings us to the very heart of the question raised in our
own time. No Christian is so confident that he is wholly without
feeling for the insistent tone of the question. And he is aware that
the question does not only come from the outside world; he knows
that he experiences it within. Is God something more than the
image-ination created by our deepest longings? Are all the great
words of faith and theology empty once they are carried outside
the walls of the church or the pastor's study? Is an asphalt street
more real than God, forgiveness, redemption, guilt, and grace all
put together?

Naturally, there is a more direct and perhaps more authentic
approach to these questions than the theological one. No one ever
believes because he is impressed by theological arguments; nor
does a man become an atheist because of arguments against God's
existence. Theological reflection is not the ground of faith. Theology would be deceiving itself indeed were it to imagine itself to be a
basis for faith. The foundation of faith is none other and none less
than the speaking and acting God Himself, as He comes to us in
the living proclamation of the gospel and, further, as He liberates

and inspires us with His gospel and His command in real life.

But this is hardly to say that faith can get along quite well without theology. To say that theology is not the basis for faith is not to say that it is an expendable luxury. Faith does not exist without reflection and critical thought. No matter how minimal it is or in what form it appears—scientific or unscientific—faith leads to thought. If faith is human, it must also be reflective faith.

We are not trying to smuggle intellectualism back into faith. We are, however, trying to respect the unique way in which faith is effected. The lively proclamation of the gospel calls faith into existence; therefore faith is a response to words, and demands understanding of them. The living proclamation gets its message of salvation from the witness of the New Testament; that is, the gospel proclamation rests on what the writers of the Old and New Testaments put into specific words, concepts, and sentences to inform us of God and His saving acts.

This means first of all that we must know something if we are to be Christians. But that is not the whole story. The concepts, sentences, reports, and the like that the biblical writers give us stem from a time very different from ours, from a cultural epoch very far removed from our own. Consequently, the proclamation of the biblical message of salvation is possible only after reflection. Before one can preach from the Bible, he has to reflect on the meaning of biblical words and concepts and stories for *this* time, in which he, the preacher, lives. Since we have to know something in order to become Christians, faith is inescapably joined to thought.

Christians sometimes fail to appreciate this fact fully. They see the contents of the Christian faith as a simple starting point. They fail to see it as a climax of twenty centuries of more or less profound research, dialogue, and reflection. But the failure to recognize this cannot eradicate these twenty centuries of faith-reflection from even the simplest Christian confession. It does not require much experience to discern something of this history of reflection in any confession one might examine.[9]

Again, it is not as though reflection *creates* faith. But lack of

[9] This subject is developed further by C. H. Ratschow, "Das Christentum als denkende Religion," *Neue Zeitschrift für Theologie und Religion,* V (1963), 16-33. Ratschow's treatment of the transmission of the Christian message through tradition as typical of the unique character of the Christian faith is very useful.

reflection can create such confusion that faith seems hardly possible anymore. Does the Christian church talk about God and His
ways as they actually are, or do all its pious words hang in the air?
That is the practical dimension of this study.

Chapter One

THE ANTIMETAPHYSICAL TREND OF MODERN THEOLOGY

- What is metaphysics?
- The metaphysics of Protestant scholasticism
- Reactions: pietism, historicism, Lessing
- Kant and Schleiermacher
- Postmetaphysical attitudes in our time

THE ANTIMETAPHYSICAL TREND
OF MODERN THEOLOGY

Antimetaphysical theology was born; it was not implicit in Christian theology from the beginning.

The question of where this movement was born could lure us far beyond the boundaries of our subject; on the other hand, it is too interesting to pass by entirely. Ebeling would classify Martin Luther among antimetaphysical theologians;[1] indeed, long before Ebeling, Adolf Harnack pointed to Luther, and had his supporters in doing so.[2] If we can believe Harnack, the antimetaphysical movement began, in fact, with Augustine, the "first modern man."[3]

To call Luther and Augustine antimetaphysical theologians is not as bizarre as it may seem. Both of these men did the job of theology in a way that broke through the well-worn paths of their day, and they are almost unique in the whole history of theology. In this respect Augustine and Luther are sometimes called existential in their theological methods. And they were, indeed, if the adjective existential is intended to refer to a total and personal involvement in their theology.

But this does not actually tell us very much.[4] It might be

---

[1] *Wort und Glaube* (1960), esp. ch. 1, "Die Bedeutung der historisch-kritischen Methode für die protestantischen Theologie und Kirche." Ebeling's *Luther. Einführung in sein Denken* (1964) begins with a chapter entitled "Luther As Language-Event."

[2] Harnack, *Lehrbuch der Dogmengeschichte*, III (4th ed., 1910), 834. L. Feuerbach also traced his own critique of religion back to Luther (*Das Wesen des Glaubens im Sinne Luthers* [1844]). Also Gogarten appeals to Luther (*Entmythologisierung und Kirche* [1954], pp. 104ff.).

[3] *Op. cit.*, p. 106; whether Harnack invented this phrase is debatable.

[4] Though it says too little, it does provide some truth; notice Luther's pertinent rule: *Vivendo immo moriendo et damnando fit theologus, non intelligendo aut speculando* ("Theologians are made, not of intelligence, learning, or speculation, but in living—nay, rather in dying and damnation").

erroneously inferred from this that most other theologians have not been existential. Besides, to say that Augustine and Luther did their theologizing in an existential way does not get at the most significant dimensions of their theology. For these we have to dig somewhat deeper.

Augustine assumed, as did Luther, that theological statements that are meant as explications of the divine being of God are at the same time implicit definitions of the manhood of man. They were aware that statements about God carry this anthropological dimension.[5] Whether this justifies calling their theological method a new one is another question. What Hans Rückert says about Luther's theology holds for Augustine as well: their method of theologizing reveals certain facets that can be called preludes to the whole complex of modern thought. But, Rückert adds, to formalize these facets into a theological method would be saying too much, even as it would be saying too little if we ignored them.[6]

Rückert's observations are balanced, and recent historical studies confirm them, especially Heiko Oberman's study of late medieval nominalism. Oberman's picture of the situation gives new relevance to the question of whether later medieval theology—as seen in the work of Gabriel Biel—does not betray the clear influence of the Renaissance.[7] If it does, Luther was not the first theologian to respond to the this-worldly challenge of the worth of the human individual. Luther's was a second answer: the first (Biel's) came by way of underscoring the role of man in Christian faith, of demanding that man be recognized as a real factor in the event of salvation, that he be seen as a subordinate co-factor in salvation.

Luther's response was not to deny the great significance of man, nor his role in Christian faith, but to insist that to give man a

[5] For further remarks on the origin of modern theological methods, see Gerhard Gloege, "Der theologisches Personalismus als dogmatisches Problem," *Kirche und Dogma,* I (1955), 23-41.

[6] Hans Rückert, "Die Geistesgeschichtliche Einordnung der Reformation," *Zeitschrift für Theologie und Kirche,* LII (1955), 55. For a note on how reductionist the young Luther could be at times, see Axel Gyllenkrok, *Rechtfertigung und Heiligung in den frühen evangelischen Theologie Luthers* (1952).

[7] Oberman, *The Harvest of Medieval Theology* (2nd ed., 1967), pp. 20, 214, 260. Oberman says of late nominalism: "The dignity of man is as important a thing here as in its parallel movement, the early Italian Renaissance."

coordinate role in the event of salvation—by way of the doctrine of the two kingdoms—was a confusion of the law and gospel and, therefore, a perversion of the message of salvation.[8] Man's role is played in the *other* kingdom, the kingdom of this earth; here there is cooperation between man and God. But in the kingdom of heaven, grace reigns alone.[9]

We must, however, break this discussion off for now. As fascinating as the historical questions are, they do not really fit into our subject. The question of theological method will, however, be playing a big part in the discussion as it goes along.

What is metaphysics?

One can speak of an antimetaphysical trend only where there is a methodical resistance to a theology that is set up in the form of a metaphysics. This sort of resistance is first met at the end of Protestant scholasticism.

The word metaphysics is of course a complex and many-colored philosophical term. Anyone who has seriously asked the question "What is Metaphysics?" (the title of Heidegger's inaugural address in 1929) has discovered that he has to cut through several tight knots in order to get out of the tangle. We should thus add a word of warning about our own use of the words metaphysics and metaphysical. We shall not be talking about the so-called metaphysical bent of man, the basis of Schopenhauer's description of man as a metaphysical animal. Our meaning is something simpler and less pretentious: the conviction that we are not only part of a tangible world that lies before us, a world we can see and grasp, but that we are part of an invisible world, a world that lies in our background, the world of God as He exists in His own way. We are referring to the conviction that we can make universally valid statements about this invisible world just as we can make universally valid statements about the visible world. This conviction about the existence of another world and about our ability to talk common sense about it is the backbone of metaphysical theology.

This nontechnical description has the advantage of including

[8] For the terminology used here, see L. Schuurman, *Confusio Regnorum. Studie zu einem Thema aus Luthers Ethik* (1965).

[9] For a further exploration of the two-kingdom idea and for an effort to see its practical possibilities, see G. T. Rothuizen, *Primus Usus Legis* (1962).

the broad area of Lutheran and Reformed scholastic theology. Besides, it pinpoints precisely those elements in orthodoxy that the nineteenth-century theologians branded as odious pretensions.[10] With this somewhat peculiarly nineteenth-century description of metaphysical thought we focus on the question of the value of certain kinds of statements. For example, do dogmatic formulas and concepts about God and His essence, His works, and His words, answer to objective reality? Can we have any genuine knowledge of these things? To put the question without using the ambiguous term objective: are theological statements universally valid in the way that ordinary scientific statements are?

The entire issue eventually comes down to these questions. Supra-personal reality as such is not necessarily denied by anti-metaphysical theology. Divine Being is not necessarily denied by the nineteenth-century theologians, any more than by their twentieth-century kin. If the adjective metaphysical were applied to any theology (or philosophy, for that matter) that does not deny the existence of divine reality outside of man, then the theology of Ritschl would be every bit as metaphysical as the philosophy of the later Heidegger, the "philosophical faith" of Jaspers, or the philosophy of religion taught by Springer. [11] Remember the great respect with which the later Heidegger talked about Being, or the fluency of Jaspers about the Transcendent. One cannot get off the metaphysical wagon too easily. Antimetaphysical theology, at least that which we will be talking about, is not bent on denying divine reality. In fact, in order to qualify as antimetaphysical in most cases, theology is not even required to deny the possibility of our *talking* about divine reality.

The crux of the matter is rather whether we can formulate statements about God and His revelation that are universally valid. The antimetaphysical theologians—and philosophers like those we have just named—deny this possibility with one accord.

---

[10] For a broader view of Ritschl's antimetaphysical approach to theology, for example, see Gösta Hök, *Die elliptische Theologie Albrecht Ritschls;* also the lucid passage about Ritschl in H. Bavinck, *Gereformeerde Dogmatiek,* I (4th ed., 1928), 512ff.

[11] Springer's name is mentioned in view of his illuminating article, written in the spirit of antimetaphysical theology, entitled "Een godsdienstwijsgerige Beschouwing over het Openbaringsprobleem," *Nederlands theologisch tijdschrift,* XVI (1961-62), 378-394.

Being antimetaphysical means to reject as a pretension the belief that theology works with concepts, ideas, or notions that make sense not only for the believer who makes use of them for himself, but for all believers, indeed for all men everywhere.

The metaphysics of Protestant scholasticism

The dogmatic formulas of Lutheran and Reformed scholasticism were meant to be universally valid. The orthodoxy of the seventeenth and eighteenth centuries betrays no doubt at all that its statements describe objective reality. In fact, it was just the opposite: its whole enterprise was carried on in utmost confidence that it was as scientific—and therefore that its statements were as valid—as any other science and its established conclusions. The Bible was the sourcebook for these objective truths; the Bible gave theology the power and guarantee of divine revelation. Of course, it was granted that revelation was given in a form accommodated to man's limited ability to understand. As a correlative to this view of the Bible and revelation, faith gradually came to be understood as a matter of holding to be true the verities of revealed theology. And with this, theology gradually laid claim to being a scientific enterprise by which supernatural and natural verities were set out as logically as possible.

The use of the term supernatural helps illuminate the structural sketch we are giving. The term refers to the source of the verities; that is, as long as we are talking about truths of revelation, in distinction from natural truths, we may talk about supernatural truths. But there is no difference *in kind* between revealed and natural truths. Revealed truths are objective, universally valid, necessary in the sense that any rational being ought to agree with them; and therefore they are scientific. No less instructive is the phrase eternal verities. This phrase does not refer, as one might suspect, to the origin of these truths, but to their nature and their structure: they are eternal whether they are truths about nature or about supernature. All genuine truth is eternal truth. Truth is eternal because it is unbounded by time or place.

The theology of the seventeenth and eighteenth centuries also used the proofs for the existence of God as genuine and convincing arguments. An implicit trust in the possibility of demonstrating the necessary existence of God is a clear mark of the metaphysical structure of this theology.[12]

Such a close tie between Christian doctrine and a given metaphysical system is risky, as history shows all direct association between theology and a *specific* philosophy to be. Bavinck's remark is relevant to this: "Theology carries its own epistemology; it may be dependent on philosophy, but not on any specific philosophical thesis. . . . There is no particular philosophy that theology needs . . . , but it does need philosophical thought in general."[13] When a philosophical system comes on hard days, it tends to carry down with it the theological construction tied to it.

The relationship between theology and philosophy is full of practical consequences for the daily labors of the theologian. History has much to tell us on this score too. Considering the intimate relationship between orthodoxy and metaphysics, one can understand why anti-Aristotelian philosophers and theologians like Descartes and Petrus Ramus had such bitter experiences with orthodox theologians.[14] We would have to plunge deeper into the history of this matter if we were to get all our lines straight, but perhaps the brief summary above will be enough for our purpose. Even so, it is not so much for the whole of the story, but as a way of getting our hands on how, during a given past time, theologians tried to get a grasp of things.

Reactions: pietism, historicism, Lessing

There were, at the outset, two kinds of theological reaction to Protestant scholasticism: from pietism in one corner and from a rising historicism in another. Both of these antischolastic move-

---

[12] Among the many studies of the proofs for God's existence, see especially Dieter Henrich, *Der ontologische Gottesbeweiss. Sein Problem und seine Geschichte in der Neuzeit* (1960); and V. Brümmer, "Die Logika van Argumente vir die Bestaan van God," *Nederlands theologisch tijdschrift,* XVIII (1963-64), 193-206. Brümmer thinks they are useful as "evocative arguments."

[13] *Op. cit.,* pp. 468, 577.

[14] On the influence of Aristotelian philosophy on Reformed orthodoxy, see G. P. Hartvelt, "Over de Methode der Dogmatiek in de Eeuw der Reformatie," *Gereformeerde theologisch Tijdschrift,* LXII (1962), 97-149, esp. the section about Beza's argument with Petrus Ramus, 148f. Ernst Bizer details the controversy that Voetius waged with Descartes, "Die reformatorische Orthodoxie und der Cartesianismus," *Zeitschrift für Theologie und Kirche,* LV (1958), 306-372.

ments are alive today, and alongside of them a third, the rise of modern natural science.

Pietism merely dismissed the scientific system of dogmatics as useless for practical ends. Theoretically, at first, pietism left intact the whole structure that orthodoxy had built. But it added the demand that eternal truth be an experienced truth, and thus *concern* shifted. Pietism's interest in truth was in the subjective appropriation and experience of it. It did not deny the truth; it only asked that it be real *within* a man. Admittedly, orthodoxy had no real answer to pietism. Indeed, a tolerable kind of coexistence between pietism and orthodoxy is quite possible, as is illustrated by the peculiar mixture of the two in the Netherlands to this day.

Orthodoxy was and is much less able to cope with the rise of historicism. For in the case of historicism, the issue is not one of a fulfilment of the orthodox system, but of a question mark behind it, a question mark of such a fundamental nature that orthodoxy has yet to find an adequate answer to it.

Lessing put the problem raised by historicism succinctly in his famous rule: "Accidental truths of history can never be a proof of necessary truths of reason."[15] Lessing demanded that religious truth be reasonable truth, that its content appeal principally to man as a rational being and be assimilated by him in complete freedom. And a rational being can bow with good conscience only before "necessary truths."

But Lessing fiercely contended that nothing that comes to us by way of history is a necessary truth; in fact it cannot be necessary, because it is always accidental. Facts of history can never be part of a necessary insight; therefore they are not capable of being assimilated freely. They are accepted as true only because of the authority of tradition or religion, and thus they are accepted under compulsion.

History is unable to offer necessary truth in a twofold sense. On the one hand, as is obvious, to call something historical implies that it had a historical origin. And everything historical has something accidental about it; it always fails to be inherently necessary. Every historical fact could just as well not be a fact; everything could conceivably have happened differently than it did. On the

[15] For what follows Helmut Thielicke, *Offenbarung, Vernunft und Existenz. Studien zur Religionsphilosophie Lessings* (1957), pp. 156ff., is very helpful.

other hand, the adjective historical implies that historical facts came to us by way of history, riding the waves of tradition. They could not have been uncovered except by way of historical research, and we can have no more certainty about them than the certainty offered by historical science. Certainty about historical truth is thus only a relative certainty.

Both of these implications of the historical are decisive for Lessing.[16] Together, they make it clear that history is too relative a category to be an imperative foundation for religion. Religion for Lessing, we should add, includes the objective aspects (concepts and ideas) as well as the subjective (inner convictions and certitudes). For the objective truth as well as for our religious certainty, all that is historical is too accidental and too relative to be useful.

With this, Lessing laid the problem on the table in a sharp and unmistakable form. His problem did not get through to all the theologians of his own day. Perhaps it has not been until our own time that it has struck home. For Lessing posed what is today called the problem of the historicity of the truth; and he put it forth in a critical and radical way. Applied to the Christian religion and its truth, his "discovery" raises the question that has often been heard since then: what happens to Christianity if Christian truth is historical and therefore not absolute? Christianity is a religion that implies an association with the absolute. But do not the absolute and the historical exclude one another?

A desperate way out would be to declare that Christian truth is not historical. But this, according to Lessing, is not a viable option. He has only scorn for this sort of escapism, be it undertaken naively or by way of devious arguments. Anyone can see that Christian truths are historical, and that they are therefore not absolute. Moreover, he confronted the theologians of his day with the result of what was then recent historical research.[17] The enormous progress that historical sciences have made since Lessing's day has invested his question with even greater acuteness. Lessing's question has been shot deeply into Christian flesh by all

[16] Otto Weber holds that Lessing's point of view is relatively independent of his more or less skeptical view of history, and that his notion of religion is the main influence (*Grundlagen der Dogmatik,* II [1962], 10ff.).

[17] One should compare here the mild historical criticism found in Johann Salomo Semler. Gottfried Hornig has written a doctoral dissertation on Semler, *Die Anfänge der historisch-kritischen Theologie* (1961), in which he comes close to restoring him his due theological honor.

that historical sciences have done since he first flung his historicism into his own world.

We may wonder whether Lessing did his critical work with joy or with sorrow; but we shall have to let his own inner life alone. We need not even go into Lessing's own answer to his own question, even though much of the work of our own day was implied in it. For his answer one need only look closely at the title of his work: "On the Proof of the Spirit and the Power" (in which his "rule" quoted above appears).

We can let all this pass, because what concerns us here is clear: the discovery of the historicity of Christian truth—in both of the above senses of the word—meant for Lessing—and for the ortho-dox movement of his time—the bankruptcy of this truth. If Less-ing was right, the end of traditional Christian dogmatics had come. He and his opponents both believed that if Christian truth was historical in character, the pretensions of Christianity were over. This is why orthodoxy tried its best to prove that Christian truth was *not* historical.[18]

We are forced to suppose that both alike were convinced that religious truth cannot be historical, and that the background of this conviction they shared has to be seen in still another conviction that both had, namely, that religious truths are metaphysical truths. Since religious truth is metaphysical, religion and historicity are mutually exclusive.

In the light of what we have said about the metaphysical structuring of orthodox dogmatics, the above conclusion is self-evident. The heart of metaphysical conceptions of truth was the conviction that a divine being exists outside of our world, a being whom we can know and describe in conceptual forms. Knowledge of this divine being is the same kind of knowledge that we have of the visible world around us, and the concepts we form of this being are thus as intellectually valid as the concepts we form of things in the visible world. Only the way in which we acquire theological knowledge is different. We know the physical world through reason; we know the metaphysical world partly through reason (the so-called *articuli mixti*) and partly through revelation. But the sameness of structure that truths of the physical and truths of the supernatural world share is not affected by the differences in

[18] Walter von Loewenich, *Luther und Lessing* (1960), provides a critical summary of recent literature on Lessing.

the way we get at them. The theology of revelation works with concepts whose truth is assumed to exist in a timeless, undisturbed harmony between the thing known and the intellect that does the knowing.

But if these concepts were shown to be historical in origin, what would remain of their claim to be eternal and changeless truths? To put it another way, what is to be said about the *reality* of the dogmatic concepts that belong to Christian theology?

Christian theology has wrestled with the question of the reality of its concepts before. Consider the problem of the so-called anthropomorphisms that dot the pages of the Bible, the texts and stories found throughout the Scriptures in which God is portrayed in human form. The notion of analogy was helpful for a while. In view of the infinite gulf between the eternal God and finite man, it was said that the concepts derived from man and applied to God have only an analogical counterpart in God Himself.[19] But the notion of analogy offers no help when we face the claim that our concepts of God are all historically defined and originated.

Kant and Schleiermacher

Kant drew the obvious conclusion from Lessing's rule—that religion, at least a worthy religion, is not a belief in certain truths. And he ruined metaphysics for religion. Religion is not knowledge, he said. If it is to maintain a hold on the absolute and prevent its truth from sinking into historicity (or into anthropomorphism, as he typically called it),[20] it has to give up its pretension that its verities are universally valid, as though they represented objective reality. Religion must stop making believe that it is knowledge; only by letting go of knowledge can religion rescue faith. Kant himself says in the *Critique of Pure Reason*, "I must give up knowledge in order to make room for faith."

What drove Kant to this conclusion is well known. The abso-

---

[19] See H. M. Kuitert, *De Mensvormigheid Gods* (1962).

[20] For Kant "anthropomorphism" is the same as subjectivism, because it involves the use of concepts concerning which no one can determine whether they are mere projections or actually answers to objective reality. On Kant's notion of anthropomorphism see R. Eisler, *Wörterbuch der philosophischen Begriffe*, I (1927), 67ff. Feuerbach took the next step: for him there is no doubt that religious concepts correspond to no reality outside of man at all.

lutes of religion are the absolutes of the moral law within every man. To be religious means to honor the moral imperative as an obligation that is basic to one's very humanity.[21]

Schleiermacher drew another conclusion from Lessing's rule.[22] Instead of complaining about the rise of historicism or leaping to its embrace, he determined to turn the whole business to religion's advantage. Why could not the fact of being historical be the mark of truth? The historical character of truth is not a score against it, but a mark in its favor. Truth, just as the man who possesses it, is historical. Thus, it is changeable, it grows, and bears the stamp of every culture and civilization in which it lives and develops. This applies to biblical truth too—perhaps to it especially. When Schleiermacher called the Bible a "mausoleum of religion"[23] he was not being insulting. He was only drawing out the implications of his thesis that religion cannot exist in holding on to supernatural truths. Religion had its own province; it was the territory of feeling. Religious doctrines therefore are only embers bearing witness that a holy fire once burned there to refine precious gold, a fire that must be rekindled anew each day if it is to expose the precious metal again.

Schleiermacher remained loyal to this conception throughout his theological life. No matter how romantic his original addresses were, and no matter that he later developed his thought considerably beyond them, he held on to his basic thesis.[24] "Christian doctrines are accounts of the Christian religious affections set forth in speech."[25] The form that these doctrines take varies according to the cultural and historical situation from which they arise. We

[21] Kant's specific notion of religion carries—as do all notions of the nature of religion—an implicit hermeneutical program. Kant's question is whether the Bible has to be interpreted in terms of ethics. Kant has, as I see it, no place at all for a historical interpretation of the Bible. He was criticized by Gabler for wanting to return to an outmoded allegorical exegesis. Cf. Rudolf Smend, "Johann Philipp Gablers Begründigung der biblischen Theologie," *Evangelische Theologie*, XXII (1962), 345-357.

[22] See in this connection Hans-Joachim Birkner, "Natürliche Theologie und Offenbarungstheologie," *Neue Zeitschrift für Systematische Theologie*, III (1961), 279-295.

[23] *On Religion, Speeches to Its Cultured Despisers* (2nd speech).

[24] For an exhaustive study of Schleiermacher's concept of religion, see Hjalmar Lindroth, *Schleiermachers Religionsbegrepp, Förutsättningar och konsekvenser*, vols. I and II (1928, 1930); Richard R. Niebuhr, *Schleiermacher on Christ and Religion* (1964).

[25] Schleiermacher, *Der Christliche Glaube*, I, par. 15.

cannot measure the truth of "piety" or "religion" by them. The truth of religion has its roots in the "subsoil of the pious self-consciousness"—that is, in the experience of the eternal in the midst of the historical, the experience of the transcendent in the midst of the immanent. When this is our experience, we have gained true religion.[26]

We can almost say that the mark of an authentic religious statement, the test of an authentic dogmatic conception, is that it be a wholly individualistic expression of a wholly individualistic feeling. But, since Schleiermacher does not want to cut the individual loose, but insists that the individual is only an example of the generic man, this must be altered to read: in Christian faith-knowledge, or confession of truth, the wholly individual expression or wholly individual emotion is the deepest ground of personhood coming to the surface. An authentic confession of faith is therefore not a private confession. This is why dogmatics is still possible, in spite of everything said about subjectivity of faith-knowledge. Dogmatics—thus understood—could never be the same as the scholastics had made it. For Schleiermacher, dogmatics is "the science that systematizes the doctrine prevalent in a Christian church at a given time."[27] Given everything that has been said, this is about all that can be allowed to dogmatics.

Schleiermacher remained loyal to his understanding of dogmatic statements and concepts, from his basic idea of God (God "signifies for us simply that which is the co-determinant in this feeling and to which we trace our being in such a state")[28] right through to his concept of the Trinity (the Trinity is the combination of expressions that Christian self-consciousness provides for itself).[29]

In a formal sense, Schleiermacher managed to build a dam against the threat of a complete anthropomorphist theology. He did this by assigning three characteristics to dogmatic statements. They are (1) descriptions of human experiences of feeling; (2) concepts of divine attributes; and (3) diagnoses of the manner in which the world exists, "utterances regarding the constitution of the world." He lets all three stand, but he obviously prefers the first one. With it the essential character of dogmatic statements is

---

[26] *Ibid.*, p. 107.
[27] *Ibid.*, par. 19.
[28] *Ibid.*, p. 28.
[29] *Ibid.*, par. 170-172.

exposed. "Hence we must declare the description of human states of mind to be the fundamental dogmatic form; while propositions of the second and third forms are permissible only insofar as they can be developed out of propositions of the first form; for only on this condition can they be really authenticated as expressions of religious emotions."[30]

Thus, Schleiermacher (in which he was anticipated by Herder)[31] makes dogmatic statements a crystallization in language of the primitive religious experience.[32] We may demand that these statements conform to reality, but the reality to which they must conform is a subjective reality, not the objective reality orthodoxy thought they conformed to, which could be expressed in terms of "supernatural" or "natural" truths.

The experience that is formed in the words of theology must be real and authentic. There is a reality of faith. But the "of faith" has now become a subjective genitive, with no ambiguity. The word "reality" does not stand for the reality behind the religious concepts, but for the reality or authenticity of the believing, pious man's experience.

Postmetaphysical attitudes in our time

With this quick flight over a segment of theological history, we must be content. All we need to do now is underscore the tremendous theological discovery that we encounter in all this. Naturally, we could respond with practical rather than theological-scientific answers. Present-day Christians have learned this much—taught by Schleiermacher himself, among others.[33] But at the moment

[30] *Ibid.,* par. 30. His preference for the first characteristic comes out even more clearly in his argument with Lüche. For an account of this see Hans Joachim Birkner, "Beobachtungen zu Schleiermachers Program der Dogmatik," *Neue Zeitschrift für Theologie und Religion,* V (1963), 119-131.

[31] Klaus Scholder refers to this in his "Herder und die Anfänge der historisch-kritischen Theologie," *Evangelische Theologie,* XXII (1962), 425-440. The other component in his thinking—the development of mankind in general—joins Schleiermacher to the Enlightenment. Cf. Lessing's *Die Erziehung des Menschengeschlechts* (1780), about which Karl Aner's *Die Theologie der Lessingszeit* (1929), esp. pp. 343ff., is still much worth reading.

[32] On Schleiermacher and the problem of language, see his *Hermeneutik und Kritik;* on his hermeneutical program, cf. Joachim Wach, *Das Verstehen,* I (1926).

[33] Schleiermacher refused to identify piety with knowledge, he said, because to do so would imply that the smartest theologians are the best Christian men.

our job is to give theological answers to a theological question. What has been said so far can be summarized in the following. Orthodox truth was robbed of its metaphysical character in three ways:

(1) Pietism was more concerned with the subjective experience of the Christian person than with dogmatic propositions; (2) Kant, representing the critique given by verifying reason, did not deny that there is more involved in the world than what reason can grasp, but he did banish dogma from the house of reason; in this house science is king; and (3) historicism honored dogma only as religious experience set forth in words.

These three postmetaphysical attitudes control theological discussions in our time too. The third way, that of Herder and Schleiermacher, is the most positive. It is not content merely to say No to the old conviction that dogma is built on metaphysics; it has a positive thesis to offer as well. It knows not only how dogmatics must *not* be done; it knows—or at least thinks it knows—how it ought to be done.

The theological developments of our time attach themselves mostly to the third position. They also pay respect to the other two, and in fact have embraced them at times. It is even possible to classify the antimetaphysical movement of modern theology as an extreme form of pietism, which we now call functionalism. Or, it can be called an effort to reestablish the credit of Christianity with the "cultured among its despisers."[34] These are Schleiermacher's words, of course, and their intent is the same as what today is called "making the biblical message understandable for our times."

At this point we touch the sensitive matter of the motivation lying behind antimetaphysical theology. This will demand a longer look, but we must at least acknowledge it here. The motivation is not only respectable, but it is the same motive that drives every true theologian. Without it, there can be no real dogmatics at all. Moreover, the possibility of all theological conversation rests on our acceptance of this motivation and respect for it in the work of those theologians with whose dogmatics ours has little in common. The whole history of the church and its theology teaches

[34] Cf. such an effort by the author, "Verschraling of Verrijking? Over de vraag in welke richting de prediking zich sedert Barth ontwikkeld heeft," *Kerk en Theologie*, XVI (1965), 191-209.

this. Unless one respects the motivation behind another's theology, he cannot work in the awareness that his own theology must ever be reinterpreted or reformed in conversation. To preserve itself from sterility, dogmatics—no matter what its orientation—must keep a dialogue going between theologians of diverse confessions and convictions.

Of course, should theological dialogue ever be suspended because theologians do not have sufficient respect for one another's motivations,[35] we have recourse to a general dialogue between men as men. That is, when scientific dialogue breaks down, we can always try to understand one another as people and seek to discover what we share with one another as human beings. The breakdown of theological dialogue is tragic; but if it happens, we have to keep the human dialogue running for the sake of theology. Without dialogue there is no living theology. Much more is at stake in dialogue than merely a matter of games theologians play.

To respect the motives of the antimetaphysical theologians does not imply, of course, that we lay down our critical tools against them. In this book, we shall be trying to employ our critical instruments as seriously as we respect the background and motivations of the antimetaphysical movement.

[35] As Helmut Gollwitzer has shown, this is not a farfetched possibility. He raises the question of whether there is still a common horizon shared by him and, for example, Herbert Braun (*Die Existenz Gottes,* pp. 106ff.). Jürgen Fangmeier goes into this section of Gollwitzer's book in his own article on "Gott in der Theologie Gollwitzers," *Theologische Zeitschrift,* XIX (1963), 338-351.

Chapter Two

EXISTENTIALIST THEOLOGY AND THE PROBLEM OF HERMENEUTICS

- The science of theology
- Understanding understanding
- How can the New Testament speak to us?
- Myth and kerygma
- The need for the New Testament
- Historical criticism and the significance of Jesus
- The centrality of justification
- Existentialist pietism and the weakness of orthodoxy
- Bonhoeffer and existentialist theology
- Retrospect and prospect

EXISTENTIALIST THEOLOGY AND THE PROBLEM OF HERMENEUTICS

The question of hermeneutics dominates almost all of today's antimetaphysical theology.

That hermeneutics should occupy so important a place in theology is not surprising. A large part of today's theology seeks to validate its antimetaphysical character by means of hermeneutics. The validity it seeks is coupled to the question of motivation mentioned in chapter one. The large task given to modern hermeneutics is defining the boundaries within which faith must exist if it is to remain authentic faith and not revert to speculation, metaphysics, or projection.

In our exploration of the background and motivations that drive existentialist theology in the direction of hermeneutics, our aim is more than paying our respects to these motivations; we are also interested in protecting ourselves and others from the temptation of too hurriedly answering the challenge that this theology lays at the door of Protestant orthodoxy. Moreover, we have to let the existentialist theologian have his whole say, and not attack him before we learn from him. There are few theological fields that do not offer some measure of truth; theologies are always containers for truth as well as untruth. So, we start from the premise that we can indeed learn from existentialist theology.

The science of theology

To get the full picture of current hermeneutical efforts in focus, we should begin with a remark that will demand our attention again later on. It is this: existentialist theologians employ hermeneutics in a totally new effort to establish the scientific character of theology. Respect for theology as a science among sciences must be properly established in one way or another. The "distinctiveness of theological faculties"—to use a Kantian expression[1]—must not be pushed so far that theology can escape scientific criticism or avoid scientific responsibilities for its activities.

One may be tempted to wonder why theology should care so much about establishing its scientific character. Does not theology carry its own legitimacy? Does it not want to maintain the *special* nature of its task? Does theology have to answer to anyone for what it does? These are legitimate questions, and we do not wish to subtract any of their force. But when we ask about the scientific status of theology we are not trying to bolster theology with a respectability that it does not have in its own right. Nor are we trying to make it more attractive by borrowing someone else's prestige. What we are trying to do in asking about the scientific claims of theology is to penetrate to its final, deepest legitimacy as a vocation.

Theology moves between the poles of faith and revelation. That is, it moves within its proper field of action only insofar as a theologian lets himself become a prisoner of Jesus Christ.[2] Thus theology carries its own credentials, and does not have to subject itself to the norms of another science nor adapt itself to anyone's favorite notion of what is scientific.

But more must be said. True as it is, and self-evident as it may be for orthodox Protestantism, the fact that theology carries its own scientific credentials cannot be and never has been the last word on the subject. Reformed and Lutheran scholasticism never doubted the scientific nature of its theological work, even though it was conscious of the peculiar validity of theology as such. Nothing would have surprised the orthodox fathers more than to be told that their work was not scientific. The metaphysical structure of Reformed and Lutheran orthodoxy was, in fact, nothing less than an effort to do theology in tune with the spirit and fashion of its time. Theology demonstrated its scientific character by adapting itself to the larger metaphysical system into which philosophers caught the whole of reality.

The orthodox theologians did not look on this as a permissible

---

[1] *Der Streit der Fakultäten* (1798), *Gesammelte Schriften,* vol. VII (1907).
[2] R. Bultmann, *Theologie des Neuen Testaments* (4th ed., 1961). Bultmann paraphrases the words of II Cor. 10:5 quite rightly as, "the sacrifice of his former understanding of his self, the turning around of the former direction of his will" (p. 316).

luxury. They did it out of a sense of necessity. They saw that, if theology lacked this scientific character, it could not be in touch with the times, its culture, the world. They were convinced that theology's chance for dialogue with the world rested on its claim to be scientific. When they kept insisting on the scientific credentials of theology—and, with that, its legitimate place in the curriculum of the university—they were really claiming that a dialogue between theology and culture was possible and fruitful.

Of course, dialogue never comes easy at any time, nor is it as potentially fruitful during some periods as others.[3] But the theologian is never permitted to walk away from any discussion table too quickly. What we are told today about the fall of the *corpus Christianum,* the estrangement between Christendom and culture, is not imaginary. There is an undeniable development in this direction. But this is no reason for theology to give up on dialogue. The Christian church ought not to resign itself to the secularization of culture, even when secularization becomes institutionalized. It should be even less willing to sacrifice such a traditional institution as the presence of a theological faculty at the university. It ought to think long and carefully of what it is doing before it consents to any way of cutting off dialogue at all. True, the church should not be motivated by self-respect or self-preservation; but there is another motive in retaining the theological faculty, namely, that the bond and mutual understanding between church and culture be not wholly lost. This is for the good, no matter how tenuous the existence of the Christian faith into the contemporary world may appear to be. The abandonment of the metaphysical structure of theology requires of theology a new scientific basis. Since the metaphysical framework is no longer recognized by contemporary culture as necessary or legitimate in its quest for meaning, what general category can theology find to provide itself with scientific respectability? Into what scientific category can theology fit without cutting itself down to someone else's dimensions and losing its own soul?

Existentialist theology—our primary interest at this point—gives

[3] Ernst Hermann Hänssler, *Theologie. Ein Fremdkörper in der Universität der Gegenwart* (1960). Hänssler defends the title of his book by the following theses: Theology's dependence on revelation (1) disqualifies it as a science, (2) sets it in opposition to the accepted notion of truth in university circles, (3) implies a hegemony of the whole scientific world, and (4) declares philosophy to be impossible.

hermeneutics the job of answering these questions. Hermeneutics defines and establishes theology as a science. Hence, we must now ask: what is hermeneutics?

Understanding understanding

Hermeneutics has always meant the principle (*ars*) of understanding, the mastery of the knack or art of understanding a text. It is thus an auxiliary science for the exegete. Better, it is a "technique," which assumes only a technical problem of understanding.[4] In other words, it deals with the rules for interpreting a text whose central meaning one presumes already to have grasped before he even comes to it with the rules.[5]

For Bultmann, the originator of modern hermeneutical theology, hermeneutics has a much broader definition. It becomes a theory of understanding in general; it asks what it means to understand anything, and what understanding itself is. Further, it inquires into the sort of situations in which it makes sense to speak of understanding.[6] Here too hermeneutics has to do with "giving rules for understanding," but the rule-giving is determined by what Bultmann means by understanding. One provides rules for the function of a thing only after he has understood the thing; so hermeneutics, the rule-giving for understanding, presupposes an understanding of the nature of understanding.[7]

Since the rise of historicism, understanding has been recognized to be far more complex than had been realized. For instance, how can a piece of historical information or a text out of history have a meaning for me, in the sense of being significant to my own life? This is in brief the central question of the understanding insofar as it is involved in the interpretation of historical documents that

---

[4] This somewhat guileless definition is found in F. W. Grosheide, *Hermeneutiek* (1929); and in S. Greijdanus, *Schriftbeginselen ter schriftverklaring* (1946).

[5] Cf. G. Ebeling, *Wort und Glaube*, pp. 329ff., and H. W. Rossouw, *Klaarheid en interpretasie. Enkele probleemhistorise gesigspunte in verband met die leer van die duidelikheid van die heilige Skrif* (1963), pp. 140ff.

[6] For a digest of the new orientations in hermeneutics, see G. Ebeling, *Religion in Geschichte und Gegenwart*, III, 242-262; and Hans-Georg Gadamer, *Wahrheit und Methode* (1960), pp. 162ff.

[7] Bultmann's hermeneutic is scattered throughout *Glauben und Verstehen*, vols. I-IV. He provides a brief summary in *Jesus Christ and Mythology* (1964), and in *History and Eschatology* (1957).

contain historical facts. These historical documents reveal the great gulf between our present actuality and past history. They raise the question of how we can get across the gulf in such a way that the past becomes real to us.

The question of understanding in this context puts us before the "nasty big ditch" that Lessing talked about when he said that faith has nothing to do with "accidental truths of history." To bridge this gulf, we must—according to Bultmann—ask the question "What can I truly understand; what are the conditions for understanding?" Only after answering this question to our satisfaction can we begin to say what faith has to do with the text—the *historical* text—of the New Testament.

Bultmann's answer is that understanding is always characterized by what he calls a life-relationship. In this his view is close to that of Schleiermacher and Dilthey.[8] I can truly understand only that to which I stand in a life-relationship. A life-relationship is the necessary condition for authentic understanding.

The use of the phrase "life-relationship" implies that not all our relationships are living ones. A man may have business, technical, and scientific relationships that, though important in themselves, do not necessarily involve personal living. They do involve living in the sense of "earning a living" or even of consuming large segments of our lives. But a *life-relationship* is present only where the essential selfhood of a man is crucially at stake.

This is where Bultmann has gone further than any of his predecessors. He seeks to locate the life-relationship between the reader and the text; without it, there is no genuine understanding of the text. Schleiermacher and Dilthey established the relationship by noting that people are always people and that they can understand one another's language insofar as they can recognize their own concerns in the language of the other—language being, after all, the objectification of the human spirit. Bultmann finds this too limited. He insists that all men have one concern in common no matter how separated their times, namely, the concern for their own personal existence. A man *may* have deep concern for all

[8] On the shifting of hermeneutical orientation since Schleiermacher (*Hermeneutik und Kritik* [1838]), see H. G. Gadamer, *op. cit.*, pp. 172ff.; Heinz Kimmerle, "Hermeneutische Theorie oder ontologische Hermeneutik," *Zeitschrift für Theologie und Kirche*, LIX (1962), 114-130; and Bultmann, "Das Problem der Hermeneutik," in *Glauben und Verstehen*, II (1961), 211-235.

sorts of things and all kinds of people around him. But he *must* be concerned about himself and the way in which he exists as a person. To be concerned about one's own personal existence is implicit in being a human being. What binds the writer of a text in the past with a reader in the present is a common intense interest in the realization of one's own human existence, an interest that is *given* in their common humanity. This common concern is present no matter how great their differences of concern are in other respects. For this reason, hermeneutically speaking, we read the text with an eye to the "matter" and not to the person who is speaking—as Bultmann remarks by way of criticizing the romantic hermeneutic of Schleiermacher.

With this common concern a possibility of a life-relationship between the reader and his text is provided: insofar as the text touches the reader at the point of his very personhood, he can understand the text. Other facets of the text may be antiquated data or mere recital of questionable stories; these aspects belong to the text as a source of information. But in one sense man is always the same: in his speech and his actions a man of the past betrays his concern with his own existence as a person, which is none other than anyone else's own deepest personhood also. To obtain a genuine understanding of a text, we must first of all be spoken to in our concrete human-beingness.

Discussing the nature of understanding is necessary, because it is fundamental to Bultmann's existential interpretation of the New Testament. And the question we want the text to answer determines the scope and the objective of our interpretation.[9] People can have different objectives in going to the same text. An agricultural student, for example, may have a curiosity about what the New Testament says about ancient farming methods. A psychologist may be interested in the psychological insights of a given passage. The historian may be eager to trace the actual course of events described in the text.

The historian's interest is readily understandable as far as the New Testament is concerned. It is, after all, an ancient document that deals with ancient history. The historian is at home in the land of the New Testament. But his is surely not the only, nor even the final or deepest concern that one can bring to the New Testament.

---

[9] Bultmann, *op. cit.*, pp. 220ff., 227ff.

The more crucial question that one brings to the text is this: whether and how the New Testament reveals the authentic human-beingness of man. Only as the reader comes to the New Testament with this question can he expect to understand the text in its most significant sense. For here he enters the arena of shared human interest between the writer and the reader. If no other common concern between them were present, concern for the genuine humanness of man would remain.

To avoid misunderstanding it must be added that their shared concern for the genuine humanness of man does not mean that the writer and the reader share a common theory of man, although this could certainly be the case. Moreover, a common theory of man is not a condition for nor a feature of the so-called existentialist interpretation of the text. Bultmann is not the least bit eager to share Paul's or John's theory of man. What is common to the writer and the reader is the simple and formal fact that both are persons and both are burdened with a need to achieve their own personhood. The reader is able to discover this burden—along with many other matters—in the writings of the New Testament. And only along this narrow strip of formal commonness of person-hood, which is always present, is genuine understanding of the New Testament possible.

We are now in a better position to understand the sense of the phrase "existentialist interpretation." Bultmann means it to say that genuine understanding of the New Testament is possible only if we go to it with the question "What does the text mean to me in my actual existence as a person?" The goal that must guide us in putting our question to the New Testament is our understanding of human existence. That is, our goal is existential understanding.[10] "Existentialist interpretation" is not the same thing as "existential understanding" of the text.* The phrase "existentialist interpreta-tion" points to the *only* means of genuinely understanding the text. "Existential understanding" happens when the New Testament actually does get hold of me in my very existence as a person.

---

[10] *Ibid.*, p. 231. This has to do with the preunderstanding (*Vorverständ-nis*) of the "subject" of the text that is—implicitly or explicitly—necessary if the reader is truly to get at the text.

*Translator's note: I am using the word existentialist for the German *existentiale*—the hermeneutical principle, and the word existential for the German *existentiell*—the personal involvement in existence.

How can the New Testament speak to us?

What we have just said about "existential understanding" raises a
new question. When does the New Testament get hold of us in this
way? To answer this question we must plow another furlong in
Bultmann's theological field. His thesis—that understanding is actual understanding only as a biblical text strikes us in our personal
existence—sounds rather pietistic. It is a pietism, of course, that is
focused on the hermeneutical question.[11] We hope a little later to
demonstrate that existentialism does have a pietistic penchant. For
the time being we will simply call Bultmann a pietist, albeit a very
complicated one.

The groundwork for Bultmann's pietistic hermeneutic is provided
by the existentialist philosophy of the earlier Heidegger. He found
the same idea in Heidegger that he had already discovered for
himself—to be a human being is to exist. Humanness is existence.
This means in capsule that to be human is not to be a spectator of
the world, but to realize one's own personal existence in action.
Humanness is pure actuality; to be open to life, to be untied, to be
free from the fixed, closed world of things—this is to be a man.
According to his nature, man must—if he is not to waste his
authentic manhood—be on his toes, ever moving from decision to
decision. He is never established, but is always establishing himself
by continuously new decisions.[12]

What kind of decisions must a man make? What must he decide
to do in order to be a real person? At this point Bultmann bids
farewell to existentialist philosophy.[13] He uses philosophy only to
borrow its anthropological platform: from philosophy he sees that

[11] Bultmann's unmistakable pietistic leanings are discernible in one of his
earliest pieces, *Welchen Sinn hat es von Gott zu reden?*, which has been included in *Glauben und Verstehen*. We shall get back to this idea when we
talk about his program of action.

[12] Cf. especially Bultmann's "Die Geschichtlichkeit des Daseins und der
Glaube," in *Zeitschrift für Theologie und Kirche*, XI (1930), 339-364, along
with the abbreviated form of the same piece found in *History and Eschatology*, ch. 10; also the chapter "Wissenschaft und Existenz" in *Glauben
und Verstehen*, vol. III.

[13] That he actually does this is denied by Helmut Haug, rightly I think.
Cf. Haug, "Offenbarungstheologie und philosophische Daseinsanalyse bei
R. Bultmann," *Zeitschrift für Theologie und Kirche*, LV (1958), 201-254;
also Lothar Steiger, *Die Hermeneutik als dogmatisches Problem*, pp. 97ff.

human-beingness is to exist and that man must accomplish his own authentic being, step by step, in decisions to act or not to act.

This formal anthropological setup implies the right concept of understanding. We can now relate these two things: being human and achieving understanding. Since to be human is to exist, understanding of a text is achieved only when I am changed by it *as a person*. I understand a text when it grasps me and does something to me.[14] Put in a more sophisticated way, I understand a text whenever it opens me to a new act of self-realization, to a new decision in which I dare take responsibility for my existence.

Which decision? Which act? Philosophical analysis can provide no answer. The answer must come from another source. All that a philosophy can show us is that authentic understanding happens only when something affects us personally. It can only establish the condition *that,* to be understood, something has to happen in our understanding of ourselves *as* that understanding is actually achieved. But what it is that can strike us in this way philosophy is in no position to tell us. The answer must come to us at the decisive moment itself, and out of the life-situation itself. Or, to put it in religious terms, what the decision and act must be, becomes clear in the encounter.

We must not forget, meanwhile, how this discussion began. The question was: how can the New Testament, historical document that it is, speak to us in our time? We can now relate the answer Bultmann has really already given us to the understanding of the New Testament.

Bultmann gives this answer: since *men* are speaking in the New Testament, and since philosophical analysis has shown us that being human is "existence"—that is, that to be human is to be anxious about realizing one's own humanness in existence—there is only one possibility of leaping over the "nasty big ditch" (Lessing) between past history and present time. We must not be sidetracked by the conceptual world of the New Testament writers, nor by their penchant for giving out as history what we know now to have been apocryphal. In all that, the writers were children of their age. We must now try—guided by a new "objective in putting the question"—to pierce through to the real "subject" of the New Testament. We must ask what the basic human experience was

[14] We are translating Bultmann's term *Bedeutsamkeit*—more about which later.

that the New Testament writers explained and described in terms of what is now an antiquated conceptual apparatus. That is, we must look for the experience of man's encounter with God in His self-revelation. The New Testament is witness to this divine self-revelation, but it is that only in keeping with the basic rule that we can speak about God only in terms of what He does to us or of what He means to us in terms of an experience of our own genuine humanness.[15]

Following this ground rule, we shall have understood the New Testament only when (1) we see what this self-revelation of God meant for the human existence of the New Testament writers, and therefore reading their witness to revelation as a description of their *self-interpretation* evoked by God's *self-revelation*; and (2) when we ourselves are changed as the message of salvation actually takes hold and does something to us.

From this, once again, we can get at what "existentialist interpretation" of the New Testament is all about. It appears to have two faces. Its intention is to lead readers to an "existential understanding of themselves," so that the word of salvation is not an empty word, but one that actually speaks to our human condition. But it achieves this goal only as the biblical narratives and concepts are translated as a set of stories in which a new experience of authentic human existence is crystallized. That is, it is accomplished only by demythologizing the New Testament text. This means that the New Testament world must *first* be explained as "mythological,"[16] and the task of showing it to be so precedes the task of demythologizing.

Myth and kerygma

Now we have reached the actual subject that this book is about. We have been talking about the hermeneutics of modern theology in order to show that its hermeneutics is a justification of its antimetaphysical program. How then does existentialist interpretation of the Bible achieve its aim? What follows is a brief, summary answer to this question.

To begin with we can say how the New Testament should *not*

[15] *Glauben und Verstehen,* I, 36.
[16] Cf. Bultmann's article, "The New Testament and Mythology," in *Kerygma and Myth,* vol. I (ed. H. W. Bartsch, 1961).

be read, according to its existentialist interpreters. The general rule is that any interpretation of the New Testament concerned with anything other than the question of how I can be helped to gain my authentic existence as a person fails to convey the real meaning. Any concern other than my own existence—for example, a concern to get at the New Testament stories as stories—is merely a historical concern. Though this is not trivial, it is not existential. I am not changed by stories of what happened or may have happened in some other age. All that historical science can dig up by means of its critical methods is religiously insignificant, at least as long at it does not annul the fact of Jesus' existence and cross.[17] Faith does not need any more rootage in history than this.[18]

As far as the New Testament picture of the world is concerned, we must accept it as "mythological language." The writers of the New Testament expressed themselves as children of their times; they could not have done otherwise. But "mythological language" is an ambiguous notion in Bultmann.[19] On one hand, it amounts to a sort of "remnant," that which cannot be taken up into existentialist interpretation; or it is that part of the New Testament which existentialist interpretation recognizes as ballast as far as faith is concerned. But "mythological language" has a positive side, too, and existentialist interpretation is equipped to deal with it.

[17] What Bultmann considers to be known about the historical Jesus is found in his *Jesus* (1951; Eng. tr., *Jesus and the Word* [1958]) and in *Das Urchristentum im Rahmen der Antiken Religion* (1949; Eng. tr., *Primitive Christianity in Its Contemporary Setting* [1956]). His profound historical skepticism can enjoy free play, since the so-called historical Jesus, in the sense of mere datable history, has no significance for faith. This, he says, Paul in part and John wholly understood. Hence, he begins his *Theology of the New Testament* by saying: "The message of Jesus is a presupposition for the theology of the New Testament rather than a part of that theology itself," p. 3. Compare with this: "The message of Jesus belongs to Judaistic religion. Jesus was no 'Christ' but a Jew," *Primitive Christianity,* p. 78.

[18] The question of how salvation is rooted in history—the so-called salvation events—has evoked a huge body of literature. We mention here only the interesting contribution by J. Sperna Weiland, "Geloof en Geschiedenis," *Vox Theologica,* XXII (1952), 161-172. The writer pleads for a "theology of salvation facts" as a *sine qua non* if revelation is to be understood as something that really reveals.

[19] Bultmann's attention has frequently been called to the ambiguity in his concept of myth. Cf., for example, R. Prenter, in *Kerygma and Myth,* vol. II.

This becomes clear as we hear Bultmann tell us why we must dissociate ourselves from the world view of the New Testament. There are three reasons for this. First, he says, God is the "wholly other" who cannot be described in the this-worldly terms used by New Testament writers. Second, the world we know is governed by natural causes; modern men cannot honestly accept the possibility of supernatural intervention. Third, above all, a man is not helped to achieve authentic personhood by accepting as true this or that statement about metaphysical matters. Man is not a speculative being, but a decision-making being.[20]

The church cannot honestly ask its people or modern pagans to accept all the stories the New Testament tells about Jesus as true. Even if everything happened as the Bible says it did, this would not be our concern. To hold as true whatever story or doctrine the New Testament offers is not the same thing as entering a life-relationship with what the New Testament is actually about, that is, with the actual "subject" of the New Testament. A life-relationship, as we have seen, is the precondition for true understanding. As long as the false notion is kept alive that Christian faith is holding something to be true, real understanding of the Bible has no chance. And, since right understanding is the precondition for faith, there can be no true faith without a genuine and honest understanding.[21]

Now then, for existentialist interpretation, "mythological language" is not merely a remnant of an antiquated world that is certainly not to be accepted today, but it is also the way in which the first believers expressed their own totally new and unique interpretation of themselves, as they gained it under the power of the divine revelation in Jesus Christ.

To use what is probably the most familiar example, the story of Jesus' resurrection is *not* a report of what actually happened to Jesus; it is the story of the disciples' discovery of the unique meaning of Jesus' death for their own discovery of themselves as

[20] On these arguments, see J. M. de Jong, *Kerygma* (1958), pp. 281ff., and the author's *De Mensvormigheid Gods*, pp. 182ff.

[21] "Faith and unbelief are never blind, arbitrary decisions. They offer us the alternative between accepting or rejecting that which alone can illuminate our understanding of ourselves," *Kerygma and Myth*, I, 41.

authentic persons.[22] Jesus grasped them in a way that radically changed them into truly existing persons. The resurrection—along with all other christological matters—interprets the powerful meaning of Jesus *for us.*

Bultmann's use of the word "significance" (*Bedeutsamkeit*) is indicated by his discussion of the title "Son of God." How is this title to be understood? Bultmann puts it this way: "Does He help me because He is the Son of God, or is He the Son of God because He helps me?" He chooses the second alternative. To speak first about a divine nature of Jesus is to be guilty of metaphysics; it is not to speak about faith.[23] Faith is not an agreement with statements that do not affect us.

To get back to the mainline of our discussion: only as we let existentialist interpretation of the New Testament preserve us from all forms of belief as holding something to be true, and only as we let it keep the New Testament before us as an account of human experience of God in our own existence, can we truly preach in a way that opens a man up in the depths of his existence for God's salvation. Preaching Christ must do something to a man here and now. This is what revelation is all about.

We have now introduced the matter of proclamation: the point on which Bultmann's intentions are concentrated. The proclamation, or kerygma, is the occasion for man in his own existence to experience the speaking God.[24] If this profoundly authentic experience is to occur, we must remove everything that stands in the way of the speaking God, and we must scrap everything that could be confused with His speaking. The Word of God is not dogma, nor the Bible, nor the sermon. The Word itself must sound. And the only organ on which it can play is human existence, the

---

22 The offense of the cross is overcome in the faith that Jesus arose. Faith in the risen Jesus cannot rest on a historical fact, as Paul wrongly suggests in I Cor. 15. Faith in the risen Jesus involves a recognition that "what does take place is that an historical person and his fate are raised to the rank of an eschatological event," *Theology of the New Testament,* pp. 33f.

23 In this context Bultmann's critique of the doctrinal basis of the World Council of Churches is interesting. The basis is criticized as a threat to the above thesis ("Das Christologische Bekenntnis des Oekumenischen Rates," in *Glauben und Verstehen,* II, 246-261).

24 A salvation event is an "eschatological event" that "is present only in the challenging, demanding, and promising Word; a recollected history, a proclamation of a past event, cannot make an 'eschatological event' visible," *Theology of the New Testament,* pp. 301ff.

concrete living person who is changed by its sounding. The conceptions that the authentic experience subsequently may evoke
must never, at any price, be turned into "truths of faith" that we
are duty-bound to accept.

We need not argue long to show how amazingly empty of
content the kerygma becomes when Bultmann's conditions are
taken seriously. Bultmann himself has reservations about this. He
does give the kerygma some content taken from the gospel; he
wants to give the cross and forgiveness a real role to play. But this
qualification is present in spite of, more than because of, his
premises.

Bultmann makes it clear, moreover, that no preacher has it in
his power to bring about a confrontation between God and man.
That preaching ever comes to this is God's secret and God's
freedom. Men can do no more than provide a kind of handbook as
to how the New Testament can be preached in a way that meets
all human conditions to provide the *occasion* of a real encounter
between God and man. This handbook is entitled "Existentialist
Interpretation."

Understanding the New Testament is not a matter of getting
hold of the past and the things that happened (or did not happen)
then; it is a matter of what happens today. Herein lies the motivation, spurred by his analysis of human existence, for Bultmann's
existentialist understanding of preaching. Does Christ speak to me
today? Does He forgive me here and now? Does He do something
to me? These are what the matter is all about. This is why the
kerygma has to be geared to how God speaks to me now, and this
is why it is not geared to the so-called historical Jesus of yes-
teryear.[25]

The need for the New Testament

We have been talking about Bultmann's theological motivations. It
was very necessary for us to do this. But meanwhile, if we look at
the matter as a whole, a curious situation is apparent. The New
Testament, the basic document of Christianity, is a historical text

---

[25] The Christ proclaimed, not the Jesus of history, is Lord, according to
Bultmann in *Glauben und Verstehen,* I, 208. He supports this notion in
Das Verhältnis der urchristlichen Christusbotschaft zum historischen Jesus
(1961).

in the double sense of the word—its text comes to us out of the past, and it informs us of events that happened in the past. Yet, Bultmann is not really interested in the past. Faith has nothing to do with the past. Bultmann waves aside any suggestion that would anchor faith to the past. And he does this in order to preserve the genuineness of faith.

But, if preaching and faith get along without the past, how is Bultmann able to convince anyone that the New Testament, as a document of history, is still needed for the proclamation of the Christian message?

At this point, Fuchs and Ebeling take up where Bultmann stops, but they stay, it seems to me, on the same path.[26] According to them, hermeneutics must not be thought of as a theory by which we arrive at a right understanding of a text. Hermeneutics does not aim at understanding a piece of language; its aim is to bring *us* to understanding *by means of* language. An event must happen that is itself hermeneutical in nature—an event in which a man is brought to a new understanding of himself, thanks to a word that is brought to him. We do not illuminate reality with words. Rather, reality shines as a light in and through words. Fuchs and Ebeling call this event a word-event. Our words are not objects that we must understand; they are the *subjects* of the event of understanding. Words are agents of understanding.[27]

This is the purpose of words, of spoken words in particular, but this must be achieved hermeneutically. That is, understanding as a "word-event" can be aborted, and when this happens, understanding is not born.

The task of hermeneutics is not merely to understand the "word-event" in general; it is concerned with the practical prevention of obstructions and disturbances that can abort the event. This task can be done only by the use of new and different words. In short, hermeneutics is working with words, and theological hermeneutics is working with the Word (with a capital letter). The latter is preoccupied with the relation between the Word and our words.

One can be busy with hermeneutics with several different interests in mind. The same hermeneutical differentiation is at work in

---

[26] For what follows the reader should consult G. Ebeling, "Wort Gottes und Hermeneutik," in *Wort und Glaube,* pp. 319-348; E. Fuchs, *Hermeneutik* (1963).

[27] Ebeling, *op. cit.,* pp. 334ff.

Fuchs and Ebeling as is found in Bultmann's comment that people can read the Bible with many different interests.

Thus, to begin with, language frustrations can occur that are relieved only partially with philological skill. Consider the grasp of a foreign language. Much more is involved in this than mastery of grammatical and philological details. The problem increases in dealing with an ancient language, as one must when studying an ancient historical document. Even a historical grasp of this piece of language demands more than philological skill. But is our interest in a historical document satisfied with a historical understanding of it?

Thus the central question of understanding confronts us again. For Ebeling and Fuchs, as for Bultmann, this is the question of how a text from the past can have meaning for us today in another, deeper sense than our intellectual grasp of the past. Is there a common personal horizon that binds me with the past reported in the text?[28]

In studying the New Testament the importance of this question is obvious. Can the New Testament have a more than merely historical significance for the present? For Bultmann, as we have seen, the New Testament is understood only when it does something to us that changes us. The existentialist interpretation is meant to lead us to this kind of authentic understanding of the New Testament. Fuchs and Ebeling are no less committed to the existentialist interpretation than is Bultmann. That is, they want to set the question of understanding within the bigger question of what is essential and necessary for man if he is to realize his own existential selfhood.[29]

But for Fuchs and Ebeling existence is something more than a continuous decision-making. For this reason understanding is also

[28] The word *Einverständnis* (Fuchs, *Hermeneutik,* pp. 134f.) is a problem for translators. It intends to set the notion of "meaning" and "communication" in combination as a fundamental aspect of language. Speaking and sharing understanding must go together if language is fulfilled. A word may have the kind of meaning reflected in the dictionary definition. But the word does not have fulfilled meaning until its meaning is communicated to the reader or hearer. *Einverständnis* tries to get at the notion of fulfilled meaning in this sense.

[29] This is the way Fuchs puts it. What he says stands in a context where he is summarizing Bultmann's hermeneutics. But it fits his own as well. Existentialist interpretation, he says, asks how anyone, in encountering the text, decides the issues of his own life (*op. cit.,* pp. 143, 155).

a larger event than the experience of an authentic encounter that here and now does something to me. This shift in the concept of man is related to the fact that Fuchs and Ebeling are more indebted to the later than to the earlier Heidegger for their philosophical, "fundamental-ontological" analysis of human existence. Authentic humanity, for Fuchs and Ebeling, is achieved not first of all in *decision*-making, but in "*word*-making" or "*language*-making."[30] The translation of all reality into words is what makes us most characteristically human. Man, uniquely, is the place (*der Ort*) where everything comes to verbal expression. This separates him from the rest of nature. Only man makes words.[31]

Naturally, we have to think of words and language in a sense more profound than their use to convey factual information. Words do indeed communicate facts. But this is a more superficial use of language; it is only the skeletal part of language. In its depths, language is a far more mysterious event; when language is used, it is as though revelation takes place. Language brings reality light; the word gives reality sense, makes it speak, and, in turn, answers it.[32] The ultimate reality—God, as the deepest ground of human existence—comes to light through words.

This last thing does not happen merely by spelling the word G-o-d. What can modern man do with a mere name? In any case, modern man does not hear the same thing in this name that men of another time did. But if modern man hears something other in the name God than what men of other days did, the name is not doing the same job anymore. Religious language of the past no

[30] The philosophical shifting is discussed by S. U. Zuidema, *Van Bultmann naar Fuchs* (n.d.).

[31] Heidegger's later anthropological views have been the most influential here. J. M. Robinson's "Heilsgeschichte und Lichtungsgeschichte," *Evangelische Theologie*, XXII (1962), 113-141, is written wholly in the spirit of Heidegger. H. G. Gadamer, *Wahrheit und Methode,* seeks to apply Heidegger's notion of language to hermeneutics universally. Klaus Rosenthal, "Das Wesen der Sprache in Denken des späteren Heideggers," *Kirche und Dogma,* pp. 284-290, makes it undeniably clear that Heidegger sees language as a medium of revelation, though a revelation not of Israel's God.

[32] The hermeneutical question is a question of meaning; meaning is a matter of sense and association, and thus language is a medium of meaning. This is not as true of Bultmann's definition of "understanding." Ebeling remarks in this vein that hermeneutics is closely bound up with the Greek idea of *logos* (*op. cit.,* pp. 335, 339). Cf. also Gadamer, "Martin Heidegger und die Marburger Theologie," in *Zeit und Geschichte. Dankesgabe R. Bultmann zum 80. Geburtstag* (1964), pp. 479-490.

longer speaks. It is therefore more of a hindrance to understanding than an agent of understanding. How can we bring to speech now what men of other times understood when they heard the word God?

Again, we are back to a question we asked before: how can a piece of language from the past, burdened with antiquated and worn-out concepts, be an agent of self-understanding today? How can we escape the net of historicity? This is Fuchs' and Ebeling's problem, just as it was Bultmann's. And, as Bultmann did, they think they have found their way out by means of hermeneutics.

Ebeling and Fuchs—and this separates them from Bultmann— go at the problem by leading the question of understanding back to the question of "what speaks to me." As Bultmann demanded that a text *do* something to me, Fuchs and Ebeling demand that a text *say* something to me. By using "speaks" instead of "does," we are trying to suggest the side of the language-event that brings about a disclosure of meaning. It certainly contains the idea that we communicate with Jesus via the medium of language, and should thus not be taken altogether figuratively.[33] The problem of understanding, which is really a given of the historicity of human existence, is soluble only when a common inner-understanding (*Einverständnis*) between the past (others) and the present (myself) occurs. This does occur, in fact, whenever we come to see that words and language always *signify* the bringing of oneself into real existence through his answer. (To be able to *answer* is to be *response*-able.) Man has always been and always will be really human only in this sense. Understanding of the past (the other) is achieved, then, when there is an inner-understanding between ourselves and the real "subject" of the historical text. That is, we understand the text when that which the text really does (i.e., when it brings a person into expression of his real self) also truly happens to us (i.e., when it makes us answer as persons).[34]

In this we see the task of theological hermeneutics. It is the same job that all theology has.[35] Of course, it does not have the job of getting people to understand in the genuine sense; this is

[33] Cf. Fuchs, *Hermeneutik,* p. 262.

[34] That is, only as I try to explain further what the text is about. *Ibid.,* p. 176; also his "Das hermeneutische Problem," in *Zeit und Geschichte,* pp. 357-366.

[35] Ebeling, *Wort und Glaube,* p. 23; cf. Fuchs, *Hermeneutik,* pp. 265ff.

God's doing, this is the Word-event. But the Word is never understandable without words. Hermeneutics can pinpoint the real "subject," and it can provide the preunderstanding that we must heed
if we are to get understanding itself. The understanding we seek is
that of man in his language.

If understanding of the New Testament requires an inner-
understanding in common with the men who wrote the New
Testament, we must grasp the way in which human existence, as
believing human existence, comes to word-revelation in the language of the New Testament. Fuchs thinks that human existence is
experienced concretely in the quest for meaning and being; Ebeling in the quest for certainty and ground.[36] Faithful to their
concepts of concrete human existence, they insist that hermeneutics must go to the language of the New Testament to ask how the
writers gave verbal form to their meaning and certainty, *how* their
discovery of meaning and certainty was expressed in their words.

We must pause here to reflect on the intransitive use of the word
"understand." Existentialist theologians tend to talk about understanding without using an object, without reference to what is
understood. Why does everything turn on understanding by itself?
What we have been saying makes clear, I think, what is behind this
way of talking about understanding. To understand one thing (in
this case, the New Testament) always involves the understanding
of something else (in this case, ourselves, in our effort to realize
our true existence). For this reason, "understanding" is an end in
itself. We are not trying to understand a thing; we are trying to
"get understanding." At the end of this chapter, we will try to
show what is actually afoot in this matter.

Historical criticism and the significance of Jesus

Our discussion to this point has focused on the hermeneutics of
the New Testament. That the New Testament is a historical document that reports information concerning Jesus of Nazareth is
obvious, and raises no insurmountable problem for the understanding. At least its historicity is no problem, as long as we
understand the New Testament's witness to Jesus Christ in terms
of its real "subject," of human existence as the quest for ground or
meaning. We shall then see that *the answer* to this basic question

[36] *Theologie und Verkündigung* (1963), pp. 85ff.

of human existence came to expression—was given words—in Jesus. When this happened, it happened in such a powerfully unique way that the early church rightly invested a decisive significance in Jesus.[37]

The first believers expressed this significance in the language of their time. This is why hermeneutics, for Fuchs and Ebeling, is—in the most literal sense—the "linguistics of faith" (the comment with which Fuchs begins his *Hermeneutik*), or linguistics in the service of preaching. Hermeneutics teaches the preacher anew to speak of God, not in the fashion of Paul or John, but in the style of today's man. Salvation must be translated. In terms of language it must be transferred from one form to another. The theologian must help the preacher get at the syntax of the language of faith. Hermeneutics is the "methodology of translating the biblical word-event."[38]

Gogarten urged this years before. Theology, he insisted, had to discover a *new* language—not a slightly refurbished one. His demand seems to be getting through to Fuchs and Ebeling. If we are to speak of God today in a genuine sense, we can no longer speak the language of a strange and antiquated reality; we have to talk in the language of the reality for which we are now in the most personal sense responsible.[39] This, then, is the mandate for the new hermeneutics: make straight the highway for a new word-event. What becomes, then, of the "antiquated" stories and concept-world of the New Testament? The question that prompts this book is deeply concerned with what Fuchs and Ebeling have to say of this. On this point, they walk with Bultmann part of the way; but at a certain juncture they veer a bit to the right. They leave Bultmann at the point where he tries to find a basis for preaching

[37] For Ebeling's Christology, see "Die Frage nach dem historischen Jesus und das Problem der Christologie," in *Wort und Glaube*, pp. 300-318. Also his *Theologie und Verkündigung*, pp. 19ff., 83ff.

[38] J. M. Robinson, "Heilsgeschichte und Lichtungsgeschichte," *Evangelische Theologie*, XXII (1962), 113-141. Inasmuch as the New Testament teaches us the "language of faith" it is itself a textbook of hermeneutics. So says Fuchs in "Das Neue Testament und das hermeneutische Problem," in Robinson-Cobb, *Neuland in der Theologie, II, Die neue Hermeneutik*, 147-186.

[39] Gogarten was asking for a new language already in 1948 when his *Verkündigung Jesu Christi. Grundlagen und Aufgabe* appeared. We find him later saying that the importance of Jesus for Christology must be discussed only after the unique nature of faith is explained (*Die Wirklichkeit des Glaubens*, pp. 18, 20ff.).

without the historical Jesus. For Fuchs and Ebeling, this is pure futility. Christian faith is deeply involved with the history of Jesus of Nazareth; indeed, its interest in Him provokes its interest in the entire New Testament. We have to know what it was that came to expression in Jesus; moreover, we must know whether the apostles' and evangelists' reports (i.e., the church's proclamation) of Him correspond to what really came to expression in Him. Did these writers listen well? Did they really grasp what it was that came alive (through words) in Him? And did they translate it accurately?

Hermeneutics, we see, is a critical discipline; it looks hard at the text of the New Testament. It has to indicate what the New Testament confession of Jesus of Nazareth is really about and what it is not about. It must keep faith within its own sphere. For though faith has a positive stance in regard to the historical Jesus, faith's interest is not in the miraculous adventures of Jesus, nor in metaphysical concepts, nor in supernatural or divine invasions into human history. All this—and it takes in a good share of the New Testament—is at the disposal of historical criticism, which exposes the mythological proportions of the New Testament, and indeed must expose them, in order to preserve the true arena of faith for faith alone.

Thus, historical criticism is given a double function, as it was by Bultmann. This must not escape us. For so far as we understand this, we will grasp why the historical-critical method takes on such dogmatic dimensions in this theology.[40] In the first place, historical criticism stands guard at the house of faith. It protects faith from foreign intruders, and at the same time lets faith be itself. Ironically, however, it sheds faith of security; it will not let faith go outside its own arena to seek certainty. For only as faith gives up certainty can it be real faith.[41]

---

[40] Concerning the dogmatical presuppositions of the historical criticism, see Götz Harbsmeier, "Der Dienst der historisch-kritischen Exegese an der Predigt," *Evangelische Theologie,* XXIII (1963), 42-55. Cf. also the harsh judgment of Bultmann's form-critical studies by J. M. de Jong, *Kerygma,* p. 190.

[41] I have discussed the relation between "uncertainty" and "offense" in existentialist theology in "Heilsbodschap, skandalon en geschiedenis," *Vox Theologica,* XXXV (1965), 41-54. See also P. Althaus, "Zur Kritik der heutigen kerygmatischen Theologie," in Ristow-Matthiae, *Der historische Jesus und der kerygmatische Christus,* pp. 236-265. Althaus denies that the so-called "uncertainty" is the same as what Luther meant by *sola fide.*

Second, historical criticism provides the link connecting modern understanding of our world and our own selves to the historical documents of the New Testament. Its fundamental thesis—from which exegetes of the Bible may not waver—is this: what actually happened in the New Testament may not be determined with any other criterion than that with which the facts of all other history, indeed all reality, are determined. On this basis, historical-critical research is not able to reach any other solution than that the New Testament stories about Jesus of Nazareth are, for the most part, mythological. That is, they are stories that cannot answer to historical reality.

The second function establishes the first: in this way, historical criticism helps to keep faith true to itself. We cannot seek a basis for faith in the past, for there is no basis to be found there. Indeed, we may not seek it there, for to do so is to distort fatally the very nature of faith. Were the Christian church to bind people to the acceptance of so-called facts of salvation, it would be reversing faith and turning it into a new law. And this would be the surest proof that the church was doing wrong.[42]

We saw that, in spite of all this, Fuchs and Ebeling, in contrast to Bultmann, want to invest significance in the life of Jesus. But this "life" is not the historical event; *this* "life" is rather that which came to expression in His history. Our task is to bring the same thing into new verbal expression for today.[43] When Christian faith sets itself to this job, it is really doing the very same thing the first

---

[42] Cf. F. Gogarten, *Was ist Christentum?* (1956), p. 35. Gogarten says that a holding to be true is a "law" rather than gospel. In the same vein Fuchs (*Hermeneutik*, p. 121) brands commitment to "objective facts of redemption" a kind of "legalistic thinking." He remarks (p. 123) that to talk about the "content of faith" is to devalue faith to a "teachable human work." G. Ebeling characterizes a similar notion of faith as a Catholic rather than an evangelical idea (cf. *Wort und Glaube*, pp. 203ff.). The trouble with these criticisms is that, while they are true enough, they do not indicate that existentialist theology points us to a better way. The thought that faith should not be given a specific obligatory content if it is to be preserved from a new kind of law comes to expression over and over again. Wilhelm Herrmann introduced this thought forcefully, and Ebeling and Fuchs both orient themselves to his writing. Cf. Jürgen Fangmeier, *Ernst Fuchs. Versuch einer Orientierung* (1964), p. 17.

[43] "Encounter with Jesus means encounter with what came to expression in him," says Ebeling (*Theologie und Verkündigung*, p. 81). Fuchs writes: "The history of Jesus is the history of Jesus' speech" (*Hermeneutik*, p. 138).

Christians did in their own way and in their conceptual world when they created the mythological stories of the Gospel record. In these myths of incarnation, ascension into heaven, resurrection, and physical return, the early believers were giving expression to what they heard *in* Jesus; that is, they "put into words" what "came to expression" in Jesus. The stories were the offspring of faith. First came faith, then the resurrection; not the other way around.

Existentialist theologians echo something of Wilhelm Herrmann, whose influence on them is considerable. The resurrection of Jesus, Herrmann could say,[44] must be seen as a product of Christian faith; it is a way of saying that we dare to call Jesus of Nazareth the risen Lord. In confessing the resurrection, we are expressing our limitless trust in that which came to light in Jesus. Herrmann calls that which came to light in Him "the inner life of Jesus," a phrase roughly like Ebeling's "that which came to expression in Jesus." In both cases, we have a clear attempt to capture for faith an area that cannot be attacked by historical-critical method. Christian faith is liberated from bondage to historical "factuality."[45]

The comparison between Herrmann and the existentialist theologians can be drawn further.[46] Ebeling too says that faith risks Jesus Christ; it dares to say that Jesus is the Christ, the risen and

[44] *Der Verkehr des Christen mit Gott, in Anschluss an Luther dargestellt* (1908), p. 333. The line that binds together Schleiermacher, Ritschl, Herrmann, and the existentialist theologians can scarcely be drawn too clearly; for a good examination of it, see Albrecht Peters, "Betrachtungen zum sittlich-personal geprägten Gottes- und Christusbild des 19. Jahrhunderts," *Kirche und Dogma*, IX (1963), 122-166. As to the more specific relationship between Herrmann and Bultmann, see Otto Schnübbe, *Der Existenzbegriff in der Theologie Rudolf Bultmanns* (1959).

[45] For a discussion of Herrmann's removal of the word "fact" from the arena of history (in the sense of the facts of redemptive history) and placing it in the arena of personal experience (the irrefutable fact that I have had a "Jesus-experience"), see Hayo Gerdes, "Die durch M. Kählers Kampf gegen den 'historischen Jesus' ausgelöste Krise," *Neue Zeitschrift für systematische Theologie*, III (1961), 175-202. For an analysis of the reciprocal relationship of faith and revelation in Herrmann's thought, see G. C. Berkouwer, *Geloof en Openbaring in de nieuwere Duitse theologie* (1932), pp. 24ff.

[46] We shall note a little later how the word "ground" is used by Herrmann as well as by Ebeling in a way that shows how the experience of certainty— as it is commonly thought of in pietistically oriented theology—is very central. Ebeling reveals how important the experience of certainty is in his *Theologie und Verkündigung*, pp. 83ff.

glorified one.[47] It dares to say this, not because Jesus did rise in any historical sense, or was glorified in any literal sense, but because He has taken a permanent and irreplaceable hold on our lives in view of what came to expression in Him. To confess the resurrection is not to assert a historical fact, as though what happened to Him at one time could be of help to us now; it is rather to make a value judgment,[48] to put into words what not everyone dares to say. There is, thus, a "factual" side to Christian faith. But it is a factuality about faith itself. A confession that Jesus is the risen one is an expression in words of our personal experience of certainty, as we have gained it from Jesus—the witness of faith.[49]

This phrase—"Jesus the witness of faith"—offers a useful epitome of the significance of the historical Jesus, as we see it in Fuchs and Ebeling.[50] If all the kerygmatic and mythological stories were sliced off the New Testament, what would remain would not be a historically insignificant figure (apart from his

[47] *Das Wesen des christlichen Glaubens* (1959), ch. 5. Here Ebeling discusses the resurrection accounts as the creative origin of the early church in the sense that they are votes of confidence in Jesus as the "author and finisher of our faith." The certainty that one had about Jesus in the common faith was given expression in language in the form of the resurrection stories. The early Christians "dared" to believe in the face of Jesus' public death; they expressed their daring by writing the resurrection accounts (cf. *Theologie und Verkündigung*, p. 91). Fuchs also speaks about "daring" in his "Zum hermeneutischen Problem in der Theologie," *Gesammelte Aufsätze*, I (1959), 347ff. Bultmann talked about the "daring of the Easter faith," *Kerygma und Mythos*, I, 51.

[48] Althaus sees a parallel with Ritschl here; Ritschl understood the christological message as "value judgments," judgments that demonstrated the "redeeming value of Christ for us" rather than as pointers to the historical figure of Jesus (cf. his *Zur Kritik der heutigen Kerygmatheologie*, p. 262). It is interesting that G. C. van Niftrik refers to Paul van Buren's Christology as a construction based on an *a posteriori* value judgment, and says that it is a Ritschlian revival ("Paul van Buren's The Secular Meaning," *Kerk en Theologie*, XVI [1965], 1-19).

[49] Ebeling wants to build a bridge between the so-called historical Jesus and the (risen) Christ of faith; this is why he refers to Jesus as a "witness." The phrase is meant to explain how the church came to talk of Jesus as the risen one even though, in terms of historicism, He was in fact not risen. This was mentioned already in *Wort und Glaube*, pp. 311ff.

[50] See E. Fuchs, "Jesus und der Glaube," *Zeitschrift für Theologie und Kirche*, LV (1958), 170-185 (this article was later printed in *Gesammelte Aufsätze*, II, 238-257, under the title, "Zur Frage nach dem historischen Jesus"). What Fuchs says goes also for Ebeling: "to believe in Jesus means to believe as Jesus believed. . . ," *ibid.*, p. 185.

crucifixion), which we could do without, but the Jesus who witnesses to faith and whom we would still find inexpendable. Indeed, He would still be necessary in the conversion of men to faith. For His own "certainty-inspiring certainty" brings us to certainty today.[51]

Now, this last dimension is brought to expression in the christological preaching as well as in the mythological Christ-stories of the New Testament. We must understand biblical christological preaching in the final sense as explications, further unfoldings, of the homology: *I believe* in Jesus.[52] In a sense, they express what refers to Jesus. His "certainty-inspiring certainty" is inexpendable for our certainty. To this measure Fuchs and Ebeling still speak of faith in Jesus Christ. But this does not mean that the believer makes Jesus the content of his faith. Jesus' "certainty-inspiring certainty" is the "ground" or the "footing" for faith; but He is never the "content" of faith.[53]

Christological preaching really expresses that there is someone here who really does believe, someone who believes as Jesus believed, who has come under the unique spell of Jesus' "certainty-inspiring certainty," and has discovered Jesus' certainty as his own, who therefore dares to express his share in Jesus' certainty by saying "Jesus is the risen one." Genuine faith comes to light in this daring confession. To believe in Jesus as the risen one is to have authentic faith. It has nothing to do with holding certain historical events to have really happened. Such historical trifling is only to undermine and disturb true faith.[54]

A similar line of thought comes out succinctly and pointedly in the theology of Herbert Braun.[55] One ought to avoid setting Braun in the same circle as Ebeling, Fuchs, Robinson, and others;

[51] Cf. *Theologie und Verkündigung*, p. 90.

[52] *Ibid.*, pp. 83ff.

[53] On "support" (*Anhalt*), see *Wort und Glaube*, p. 311 and *Theologie und Verkündigung*, p. 81.

[54] In "Jesus und der Glaube" Fuchs agrees completely with Ebeling, even to the point of similar terminology. For example, Fuchs says that one can give value to the historical Jesus for our faith only by calling Him the risen one (*ibid.*, p. 172; *Zur Frage*, p. 241).

[55] *Gesammelte Studien zum Neuen Testament und seine Umwelt* (1962). In this collection, especially significant are "Der Sinn der neutestamentlichen Christologie" (pp. 243-282); "Die Heilstatsachen im Neuen Testament" (pp. 299-309); and "Die Problematik einer Theologie des Neuen Testaments" (pp. 325-341).

Braun himself would warn against such oversimplified line-ups.[56]
Still, both Bultmann and Hans Conzelmann have endorsed Braun's
radical stance, and Ebeling has not made an effort to dissociate
himself from it.[57]

Whether Braun represents a radical but logical development of
Bultmann's thought is problematic. It would be just as reasonable
to say that Braun is able to put existential theology in a simpler
(which is to say, less German) style than his predecessors did.
Braun is convinced that the historical character of the New Testament demands the historical-critical approach to it and excludes
all others. This implies that we have to work with the New
Testament as we would with any other historical document. If we
do set to work at it in this way, we are forced to conclude that the
only objective historical fact about the Gospels is this: there was
once a community that confessed Jesus as the Christ. The rest of
the events that are described as though they actually happened,
including the christological utterances ascribed to Jesus of Nazareth, are all mythological constructions scooped out of the Hellenis-
tic religious world of that time (*Gesammelte Studien,* p. 302). Anyone who holds on to them as "facts" simply destroys the possibilities
for human knowledge; to assert the Gospel stories as facts is, in
effect, to assert that $2+2=5$ as truly as $2+2=4$ (p. 303). The
so-called redemptive history is not real history; but it does have a
history (p. 302).

This fact does not make the Gospels worthless. On the contrary,
once we are liberated from the forced demand that everything
really happened the way the evangelists wrote it, we are open to
the true significance of the confusing conglomerate of Christologies
in the New Testament. We can learn to read them as a series of
renewed signs of faith interpreting itself (p. 252), that is, of the way
in which "men understand themselves before God" (p. 281). New
Testament Christology is a way of expressing one's anthropology
(p. 272). In Jesus Christ, the early community of faith signifies how

---

[56] *Ibid.,* p. 302.

[57] Bultmann says that Braun has understood him very well (cf. *Das Verhältnis der urchristlichen Christusbotschaft,* p. 21). Conzelmann, "Rand-
bemerkungen zur Lage im 'Neuen Testament,'" *Evangelische Theologie,*
XXII (1962), 232n. In *Theologie und Verkündigung,* p. 64, Ebeling admits
a certain constancy in the self-understanding of faith; but his reason for
it is that the name Jesus is a constant element in Christology. The latter
remark is so self-evident that not even Braun can overlook it.

God's Yes makes a man an authentic human being; Jesus stands for what authentic humanity is. The early church wanted to do nothing more with its Christologies than to confess its faith—not *in* Jesus, but through a recollection of the event that occurred in Jesus and occurs and must occur in us and our humanity. To confess Jesus as "Lord" or Jesus as "Son of Man" or Jesus as "Christ" means to believe that what happened in Jesus must happen again and again (p. 282).

The christological message is, in other words, a value judgment. Or to use Braun's words, Christology must be seen as a means by which the disciples of Jesus expressed how significant Jesus was for their faith (p. 305).

One must admit that this is all understandable. But is this much different from Ebeling's idea that the christological messages must not be exiled to the status of "historical curiosities," but must be experienced as a new faith—which is to say, a new self-interpretation?[58] Is it much different from Fuchs' notion that the christological passages of the New Testament are "language events" of new interpretations of the self that were inspired by Jesus?[59]

We should not try to level out the variations—which holds true for the differences of emphasis between Fuchs and Ebeling too—but we must conclude that Braun's interpretation fits within the intentions of Fuchs and Ebeling. A common theological pattern is visible here. The fact that not only Fuchs and Ebeling recognize a common approach between them, but that all existentialist theologians feel a common bond at this point, says something about their common point of view.

The centrality of justification

Existentialist theologians all tend to center their interest on justification by faith, and thus we can speak of a theological pattern in the movement. To be sure, it is a formal pattern, but it is signifi-

[58] *Theologie und Verkündigung,* pp. 46ff. See also *Wort und Glaube,* p. 317, where he speaks of the "erroneous setting for and propagating of the resurrection of Jesus as an objective fact." To confess the resurrection means, according to Ebeling, to come to faith (*ibid.,* p. 315).

[59] Fuchs, *Hermeneutik,* p. 155. He adds that this must not be falsified by making it a pointer to a so-called objective fact (*ibid.,* p. 145).

cant: existentialist theologians model—and limit—their theology
structurally as a theology of justification.

This is not to say that they reduce theology to this model,
although one sometimes senses a trend here. There is much more
to theology than the justification of the individual sinner:[60]
creation, providence, and eschatology are just a few of the important matters that existentialist theology is concerned about. But the
next chapter will provide us the opportunity to speak about these.
What concerns us here is the place of justification in traditional
dogmatics.

Justification falls within the application of salvation to individual people. But theology is also concerned with the implications of
this: the unique *structure* of justification as the liberating Word of
God to the sinner, the Word in its immediate and personal character. These two aspects of the traditional doctrine of justification
form pillars on which existentialist theology rests, which accounts
for its frequent appeals to Luther.[61]

Clarification for this can be found in examining Herbert Braun's
rather curious terminology. Braun speaks of Jesus as occurring
over and over again. Jesus is the name for an "event" that occurs
within my own existence. It is the event by which my existence is
made a believing existence. This event is definable further in the
personal relationships between man and fellow man. In contact
with my fellow man I experience, in concrete encounters, my
unconditional duty and my enormous privilege to be a man in the
sense of "being with others." This experience, says Braun, is an
experience of God.[62]

The presuppositions lurking behind this thesis are too complex

[60] We must see studies like Wilhelm Dantine, *Die Gerechtmachung des
Gottlosen* (1959) and Peter Stuhlmacher, *Gottes Gerechtigkeit bei Paulus*
(1965), as warnings against making the truth of justification by faith a
formal, theological structure.

[61] Bultmann calls justification—observe the functionalistic note—Paul's
genuine Christology (*Glauben und Verstehen,* I, 162). He appeals to Me-
lanchthon's famous words *Hoc est Christum cognoscere beneficia eius cognoscere* ("To know Christ is to know His benefits for us"). See also Hans-
Joachim Iwand, "Vom Primat der Christologie," *Antwort,* pp. 172-189, who
argues that there *are* no benefits—not even justification—if the New Testament Christology is reduced to mythology. In the same spirit is Hermann
Diem, "Christologie und Rechtfertigung bei Karl Barth," *Evangelische
Theologie,* XXIII (1963), 197-213.

[62] Cf. here especially "Die Problematik einer Theologie des Neuen
Testaments."

for us to go into at length. But a word should be said about them. According to Braun, we must dare to talk about God in language that traditional forms can no longer give us. The classic Christian vocabulary has become impossible for modern men to understand. The Word of God does not speak to man unless we are able to set it within the real-life situation of today. The reality of today's situation is that of the relationship between man and his fellow man. Like Gogarten, who maintained ahead of his time that the only arena in which we can understand God is the arena in which men encounter fellow men,[63] Braun seeks to place our encounter with God in the sphere of fellow-humanity. God is, so to speak, a "certain kind of fellow-man-ness."[64]

Braun does not want to identify God with fellow-humanity in any simple sense. God is, rather, another name—a very special name—for a very special event that takes place in our experience of fellow-humanity. Here, in this situation, we encounter the reality of what the words "I may" and "I must" mean; they reveal that which makes us truly human. God is that which makes us men in community.[65]

The heavy moralizing of Christian faith (shades of Kant) is striking.[66] No less obvious is the line between Braun and Bishop John A. T. Robinson and his associates.[67] The same consequences for Christian faith are involved in both. But what is of special concern to us here is the note of eventfulness in divine revelation. God's self-revelation is an "event," "a moment," something that happens.

[63] "Man has no other reality besides his being addressed by others" (Gogarten, *Ich glaube an den dreieinigen Gott* [1926(!)], p. 114).

[64] *Op. cit.,* p. 341.

[65] In his reply to Gollwitzer, "Gottes Existenz und meine Geschichtlichkeit im Neuen Testament," *Zeit und Geschichte,* pp. 399-421.

[66] See Helmut Gollwitzer, *Die Existenz Gottes,* pp. 63ff. We could add that there are in this connection more extreme notions than this that pass for interpretations of the Christian faith. Cf. Manfred Punge, "The Challenge of God's Goodness—Ethics in the New Testament," *Student World,* LVII, no. 3 (1964), 228-236. Punge explains Jesus as an example of freedom that was, unfortunately, strait-jacketed by a church that was not able to enter his heritage of liberty.

[67] This applies to the thesis that God is revealed as the "unconditional" in the relationship between man and fellow man. Cf. J. A. T. Robinson, *Honest to God* (1963), pp. 50-57. Cf. also Manfred Mezger, "Redliche Predigt," *Zeit und Geschichte,* pp. 423-39. Mezger's argumentation is, in my judgment, evidence of how little the Bultmann school has to say in criticism of the theology of Bishop Robinson.

Braun gives an excessively moralistic slant to this "at-the-moment" character of God in His revelation. God *is not* as a matter of course the event that occurs between man and his fellow man; but He can *become* that event. Or, rather, man can experience Him in the moment in which he discovers himself to be engaged by an unconditional duty to be a fellow man. Bultmann does not lay things out in such a moralistic fashion; but the pattern has become a stereotype. What we experience, here and now, is not merely a mysterious "Thou shalt" that rises from our community with fellow men. What we experience is in fact forgiveness. The message of salvation is the message of the justification of the ungodly. But this message seeks to be experienced here and now as the message of the forgiving God. God does not merely exist as a being out there: He demonstrates Himself here and now in the actual experience I have of being liberated for new action.

The same thing is true for Fuchs and Ebeling. The difference between them and Bultmann lies in what is seen as the content of our experience. Forgiveness is not the central thing; for Fuchs and Ebeling justification by faith is not the be-all and end-all,[68] as it is with Bultmann and, in a measure, with Gogarten. Faith to them is more of a "faith in general" without the specific content of forgiveness. And what Bultmann still calls kerygma, Fuchs and Ebeling call a "language event."[69]

Still, the pattern remains. God reveals Himself in language as the ground of humanness, as the meaning or "last horizon" of humanity. God is not language; the Word is not words. But God, the deepest reality, comes to expression "in language" at the moment when I feel myself being grounded anew in humanity through preaching.

This existential character of God's revelation is demanded by the concept of man implied here. To be man is to exist, to fulfil oneself step by step. When the concept of revelation is combined with this notion of man, it makes for a revelation that springs on

[68] Wilhelm Dantine is correct in calling attention to this, "Die Rechtfertigungslehre in der gegenwärtigen systematischen Arbeit der evangelischen Theologie," *Evangelische Theologie,* XXIII (1963), 245-265. This is also associated with Ebeling's predilection for the logos-character of language. See above, note 32.

[69] A critical summary of Ebeling's concept of faith is found in Friedrich Dünsing's "Fragen zu Ebelings Glaubens- und Gottesbegriff," *Evangelische Theologie,* XXIV (1964), 34-45.

us moment by moment, one that has no continuity and can never be given continuity. We should not forget, of course, that for Fuchs "present" means Christ's presence. If revelation were somehow constant, existence would be drowned in past history, or would become a tangible something, a dogma; and in any case it would lose its existential quality. More about this later.

We are concerned here with the motivation and intention of existentialist theology. The actualistic construction of this theological line follows from the notion of justification as a personal act of God by which man—today, actually—is forgiven. The real motivation for centering everything on justification by faith is a desire to bring man's experience and divine revelation into correspondence. Should it turn out that human experience in the long run controls and overwhelms revelation, we must not overlook the motive that governs the way the model is set up. God must speak for Himself—only then can revelation be real. And He speaks when He is actually experienced in our experience of forgiveness (Bultmann). Or, He speaks when we experience a firm ground of being for life (Ebeling). Or, He speaks when we experience our fellow men in a truly human engagement (Braun).[70]

The correspondence between revelation and existence does not occur as a matter of course. The basic problem was, as we have seen, the problem of historicity. How can the Gospel, a document out of the ancient past laden with concepts and images of a time no longer familiar to us, still have significance for our existence in the here and now? How does theology manage to emerge from the morass of historicity? That is, how can it do justice to the historicity of the New Testament and, on the other hand, show that the New Testament is still revelation to us at this moment?

The solution offered by existentialist theology is that history, in the sense of ordinary, chronicled events (*Historie*),[71] is not the arena in which God reveals Himself. Revelation takes place in the arena of human existence, in the history (*Geschichte*) of our own personhood as it is achieved in actual life. It is in this dimension of the person that categories like "Word," "Faith," "Speech," and "Understanding" are at home. Here alone authentic revelation is

---

[70] Mezger's article is not less radical than Braun's: he says that God "occurs" whenever I am addressed by my fellow man (*op. cit.,* pp. 491ff.).

[71] Again, illustrative of Mezger's article is this: "In this arena [history] my salvation can never be decided" (*ibid.,* p. 491).

possible, for here alone we can talk about the unique manhood of man in the experience of revelation. To borrow a phrase from Lessing: Revelation is that which demonstrates itself in terms of Spirit and Power for the realization of my own special humanness.

In a practical sense, this means that existentialist theology tries to leap over the problem of historicity and take a whole new route. It avoids the question of history in the ordinary sense by concentrating on history as that which registers in the isolated cell of human decision and experience. Revelation is that which we experience here and now in a uniquely personal sense; it is what becomes true in our action as personal.

Existentialist pietism and the weakness of orthodoxy

We have hinted above at the pietistic, or functionalistic penchant of existentialist theology. We must now push into this idea a bit further to see whether it can help us get a still better hold of the matter.

That truth must be practiced, experienced, and made incarnate in life is not hard to understand. Has anyone within Christian tradition ever suggested that it must not? The Bible surely wants us to know that truth is a practical and not a theoretical matter. The language of both the Old and New Testaments never lets us forget that we have to be *doers* of the truth.[72]

But the full extent of the existentialist's practical accent cannot be grasped until we probe into the function that practicing the truth is given in his theology. Let us here, anticipating the next chapter, draw a rough sketch of what will occupy us in more detail there.

The axiom that truth must be practiced or experienced functions in a way that forces us to state the axiom this way: only what is done or experienced can be called true. In other words, only what we make true by experience is truth. Truth, in the religious sense, is defined by action, experience, or the subjective or personal life; this is what gives truth its authenticity.

The axiom, then, is restrictive, for it limits the significance of

---

[72] For a discussion of the word "truth" in the Bible, see my article "Een immes bakje koffie. Een profane titel voor een serieus onderwerp: het waarheidsbegrip van het Oude Testament," *Bezinning*, XV (1960), 204-225. Fuchs offers this pregnant remark: "Truth is always unmediated." That is, truth is not a theoretical matter, but it is a reality that comes to expression (*Hermeneutik*, p. 109).

the traditional church dogmas and faith concepts. Its restrictive character gives the hermeneutics of existentialist theology a unique tone and tenor. Hermeneutics becomes a kind of search into the possibilities for translating the traditional truths of the Bible and dogma into life. It has its eye, above all, on the application of the truth.[73] Here, for the first time, the restrictive character of its point of view is seen in its true depth. In fact, it means this: insofar as the New Testament is applicable to life here and now, it is true. Or, in Fuchs' words: insofar as the New Testament is applicable here and now, it becomes a genuine text rather than a historical document.[74] By way of analogy, Ebeling makes a distinction between "interpretation" and "realization" of the text. In the former, we have an ordinary historical concern that does not touch us genuinely, since it does not affect our human existence; in the latter we are involved with the text personally.[75] This can only mean that the truth of the text of the New Testament hinges on the possibility of its personal application.[76] In existentialist theology,

[73] For a discussion of the stress on application of the text in his hermeneutics, see Emilio Betti, *Die Hermeneutik als allgemeine Methodik der Geisteswissenschaften* (1962). Betti, addressing himself especially to Gadamer, insists that interpretation is something other than merely making something useful today. Heinz Kimmerle, "Metahermeneutik, Applikation, hermeneutische Sprachbildung," *Zeitschrift für Theologie und Kirche*, LXI (1964), 221-235, directs a criticism against both Gadamer and Ebeling. Barth, in his address to Bultmann, has also responded to excessive applicatory demands as a criterion in hermeneutics (cf. his *Rudolph Bultmann. Ein Versuch ihn zu verstehen* [1952], pp. 46ff.). The excessive stress on application of salvation is learned, according to existentialist theology, from Luther. Ebeling says that application hermeneutics is in the genius of the Reformation (cf. *Wort und Glaube*, p. 22).

[74] According to Fuchs, "text" is present wherever we find ourselves again as "people of the future who are aroused to speech by God's call" (*Hermeneutik*, p. 61). He says this in a discussion of Bultmann, but he clearly means to express his own view too. See, for example, his "Das hermeneutische Problem," in *Zeit und Geschichte*, p. 365; he distinguishes there between the text as "mere source for research" and as the "text of proclamation." Further, see his *Zur Frage nach dem historischen Jesus*, pp. 281ff., where he distinguishes methodologically between "exegesis" and "interpretation," the former being a question of philological significance and of the text, and the latter being a concern for the "subject-matter" or "truth" of the text.

[75] *Wort und Glaube*, p. 347. Ebeling makes the same distinction between the philological concern and the concern for the matter of the text.

[76] Compare with this the much cruder formulation by J. A. T. Robinson in his *Honest to God*. Robinson lets the truth of the New Testament hang on what modern men find "credible." But meanwhile existentialist theology, too, insists that truth depends on the possibilities of applying it, possibilities that in turn hang on a specific view of man.

this means that past history, about which the text reports, is sacrificed to its actual significance for the present time.[77]

It will be beneficial for us to linger here a little while, for at this point we are close to the heart of all theological difficulties. The solution discovered by existentialist theology is to scrap history as a fundamental category of divine self-revelation and to limit that revelation instead to the sphere of actual, here-and-now human existence. This way out of the problem exposes both the weakness and strength of existentialist theology. It helps explain why this theology has won to its side very considerable sections of the Western theological world, and influenced much of both Reformed and Roman Catholic theology.[78]

The conquests of existentialist theology can be explained by its demands for the application of the biblical text. Anyone who puts the application of the Holy Scriptures in the *center* has taken the route of pietism; and this route, we must remember, has been followed by the most orthodox of people. There is apparently a structural weakness in traditional Reformation orthodoxy. For orthodoxy has almost always left pietistic reactions in its train.[79]

We mention the structural weakness of orthodoxy only to get an insight into the vigor of existential theology. The source of this vigor is its concentration on the application of divine redemption to man in his human existence here and now. With this concern, existentialist theology fills a vacuum created by a theological structure that allowed no significant place within its walls for human

---

[77] Betti (*op. cit.,* p. 49) makes the same comment.

[78] In view of the association that existentialist theologians make themselves, it is understandable that A. Hulsbosch speaks of the reformational character of demythologizing ("Het reformatorisch karakter van de 'Entmythologisierung,'" *Tijdschrift voor theologie,* IV [1964], 1-34). He means in fact existentialist theology in general. Still, it is doubtful whether he is correct. First, it remains to be demonstrated that existentialist theology is in any sense reformational. Hulsbosch's own criterion is dubious; he rests his case on the notion that reformational theology was always "relational." It is also interesting that a Roman Catholic Bultmann disciple like Gotthold Hasenhüttl thinks otherwise (*Der Glaubensvollzug. Eine Begegnung mit R. Bultmann* [1963]; cf. also *Der unbekannte Gott?* [1964]).

[79] To support our characterization of existentialist theology as a form of pietism, we should make three remarks: (1) subjectivism is too philosophically tinted a term to use for this religious motif; (2) the existentialist theology operates in that theological sector of dogmatics called "application of redemption" and seeks to bring all of theology under that locus; and (3) we prefer the word pietistic to reformational because we are sure that Reformation theology was not one-sidedly concerned with application.

existence. For the same reason, it gains entree into, and oblique support from, the nontheological, but pietistically slanted orthodox communities. One may suspect that existentialist theology is a victim of its own one-sidedness, but he must admit that it fills a vacuum created by orthodox one-sidedness. Its questions and its answers speak to many ordinary members of the conservative Christian community.

We have not said anything decisive as to our judgment of the theological validity of these questions and answers. But we have seen that we cannot explain existentialist theology away with a stroke of an orthodox brush. It has a powerful attraction for many Christians of our day, especially when it is presented in popular form. And this is true, no matter how infected it may actually be with a philosophical virus that infects its entire theological body. Countless ordinary Christians demand an answer to the same question that existentialist theology asks: what does the Word say and do to me today? Theologians ought to rejoice to see this day. But whether theologians rejoice or not, no one can persuade ordinary Christians that the practical question is not the important one.

There are more people than orthodox leaders would like to admit who are tempted to accept the gambit of existentialist theology: Jesus is really Jesus when He becomes Jesus for us. He is Saviour when He is experienced in a concrete encounter with Him. Faith is something far more real than a belief that Jesus in fact was raised from the dead once upon a time. In any case, a past event called "resurrection" is not yet a concrete event for us. Christmas is real when it is Christmas in my heart; Christ, as the old verse had it, may be born in Bethlehem a thousand times, but it does not touch me unless He is finally born in my heart. What is important is not who Jesus *was,* but what He *is* today; this is what has to be brought to expression in theology. Or, what matters is not what God *is,* but what He *does to us.* "We can only talk of God when we talk of what He does to us."

We met that last sentence before.[80] Bultmann recalled it in Wilhelm Herrmann, who in 1914 wrote a little book called *De Wirklichkeit Gottes* (*The Reality of God*). The book breathes the same pathos that moves all of existentialist theology: what causes a Christian to be a Christian is authentic experience. Whether Jesus

[80] Cf. *Glauben und Verstehen,* I, 36.

in fact talked and acted and saved in the past is not the important question. Even less important is whether one repeats the same dogmas that were precious to his fathers of yesterday. Does Jesus speak to me today? This is the only thing that matters.

We allowed the subject of the last couple of paragraphs be unclear on purpose. Who says these things? The existentialist theologians or the ordinary church members of today?[81] My purpose is to stress that today we cannot theologize in a vacuum any more than we ever could; we work in a climate of thought that pushes theology toward the application and functioning of divine redemption in the here and now.

The enormous risks in this way of thinking lie close at hand. If the real question is not what previous generations said about God, but whether I encounter Him in my experience, the implications for theology are great; theology becomes a critical description of what "experience" is. We would then have a theology that not only has an anthropological accent, but in fact *is* anthropology. Bultmann, in fact, has assured us that his theology is anthropology by intention.[82] Of course, he said more than he really ought to have said. He is more of a theologian than he wants to be. Consistent anthropological theology is achieved only by Herbert Braun's conviction that theology can be done without the Word of God.[83] If we can speak of God only insofar as we experience Him, we can also analyze that experience without the help of the

[81] Fangmeier (*Ernst Fuchs,* p. 13) recalls that Fuchs, as a genuine pietist, tells his students, just prior to Christmas, that he hopes that Christmas will take place anew for them. Fuchs, in another instance, calls pietism a "new Protestant source of power." Again, in connection with Phil. 2:5-11, he remarks that before we can understand the meaning of doubt and death, we must taste them ourselves (*Hermeneutik,* p. 108). In the same vein, Ebeling insists that to be justified is a wholly different thing from accepting a doctrine of justification (*Wort und Glaube,* p. 206). This corresponds to Fuchs' statement that revelation is quite another thing than the church doctrine of revelation (*Hermeneutik,* p. 123). These remarks remind one of Lessing's words about the difference between the story of a miracle and the miracle itself.

[82] This is seen in Bultmann's rule that "speech about God" is possible only as "speech about us" (*Glauben und Verstehen,* I, 28). Fuchs offers the same thought (we can speak about God only in terms of what is explicated in human existence) in his *Hermeneutik* (pp. 10ff.). As hermeneutics, theology is necessarily anthropology, since it is an interpretation of language that comes from past time (cf. *Zum hermeneutischen Problem,* p. 220).

[83] *Gesammelte Studien,* p. 297.

Word of God. The best theology is then the theology that brings this off successfully.[84]

Existentialist theology, thus, has a close affinity with the kind of pietism practiced in the Christian community. It also makes contact with the unhistorical, uprooted man of our time. It seeks this contact, for it has a feeling for the problem of how a generation that feels little tie with the past, that thinks of past history as one passé thing after another, and that is reared only in terms of the moment, can be reached by the gospel of Jesus Christ.

Existentialist theology has drawn a bead on today's post-traditional man. It did not set out to break with the traditional confessions of the church. Anyone who thinks of it merely as a theological revolution against the faith of the church has not begun to gauge its true motives.[85] It seeks a new language, a new way to talk that is "with it," that speaks to men of *this* and not a former day, that can address this generation as Luther talked to his. This is the task that existentialist theology calls its own, and gives it its right to speak.

It would not be fair to demand that critics of existentialist theology have a better alternative ready. But it is fair to ask that anyone who takes it on himself to attack this theology have wrestled through the same questions that existentialist theology is trying to answer. Unless, that is, he is willing to solve these problems by denying their existence; but turning one's back on the question is seldom a successful way to solve it.

These remarks are relevant to the dynamic of existentialist theology. What we have said does not remove its weak points; it only serves to underscore them. We have already hinted at the weaknesses. They lie in the restrictive character of its concentration on the application of revelation. It is restrictive because it cuts faith here and now off from the historical past.

---

[84] See Gollwitzer's *Die Existenz Gottes,* pp. 63-76, for a general critique of Braun. We shall return to this subject later.

[85] We find the same thought in E. Schweizer, "Die historisch-kritische Bibelwissenschaft und die Verkündigungsaufgabe der Kirche," *Evangelische Theologie,* XXIII (1963), 31-42. But Schweizer remarks that the language of the existentialist theologians sounds far more foreign to the average modern man than does the language of Luther's translation of the Bible. Walter Kreck, "Die Frage nach dem historischen Jesus als dogmatisches Problem," *ibid.,* XXII (1962), 460-478, remarks that the drive behind Ebeling and Fuchs can be appreciated only against the background of the sterility of much pulpit language.

The restrictions are present even where they are less dominant than is the case in Herbert Braun. They are implied in the thesis that religious or revealed truth *is* what is *personally* real *to me*. This thesis is, I suggest, the point of departure for existentialist theology.

With all due respect for the extraordinary seriousness that drives existentialist theologians to this thesis[86] (and we must go back to Kierkegaard to discover a like seriousness) and with an awareness that there is a sort of orthodoxy that creates a vacuum by splitting up action and confession as though the former were a matter of practice and only the latter of truth—a vacuum filled by the excesses of existentialist theology, we must still conclude that existentialist theology exiles itself from a necessary area of theological truth by restricting truth to personal experience.

Bonhoeffer and existentialist theology

We could hardly leave this subject without reference to Dietrich Bonhoeffer. On this point there is a clear conjunction between him and the existentialist theologians. But there is also a tangible difference.

First, the point of agreement; one can hardly escape it. Throughout Bonhoeffer's theological work there runs a strong current of concern for the functional. Faith is real faith only as it begins to function as faith. The accent on a "working faith" rises powerfully from the pages of *The Cost of Discipleship,* obviously; but it surges through his *Ethics* and his *Letters and Papers from Prison* as well. Christian talk about God has become a foreign language to this generation; neither the church nor its preaching manages to speak in today's tongue. How can preaching be done in a way that religionless man can understand the content of the redemptive message?[87] This is Bonhoeffer's question; it is his "concern for understanding," as Van Buren has said.

This is Bonhoeffer's share in the existentialist motive. But is there a material identity as well? This question is complex and requires a longer discussion than this one. Bonhoeffer deserves

---

[86] Ebeling speaks of "making the truth true" as a matter of "preserving oneself in the realization of his existence" (*Wort und Glaube,* p. 198).

[87] Cf. *Widerstand und Ergebung* (1956), esp. pp. 183ff.

more than a marginal treatment, especially in view of the literature already devoted to him,[88] but we cannot pass him by altogether. He is too great a man not to be listened to and dealt with in a deep measure of respect. So we offer here a digest of what we understand his message to have been.

In connection with the present discussion, we are especially interested in his nonreligious interpretation of the biblical message. This he saw as the program for the theology of the future.[89] Would this program be primarily hermeneutical, dogmatic, or perhaps pastoral-psychological? There are Bonhoeffer readers ready to emphasize each of these.[90] But it probably would not accomplish much even if we could decide this question. The very interrelatedness of these disciplines makes it clear that all three would have to be involved. If one says that Bonhoeffer's program would be pastoral in nature, he has already included dogmatics and hermeneutics with it. And if one claims that the nonreligious interpretation of the Bible is a dogmatic task, he need not and ought not exclude hermeneutics from involvement in the program.

Actually, all three notions help illuminate the vision that Bonhoeffer was striving to capture in his diary. There is just one limiting factor, and it should not be ignored. We are referring to the identification that existentialist theology makes of hermeneutics with the existentialist interpretation of the New Testament. Some people take this identification for granted, unfortunately; but it is in fact a usurpation of hermeneutics for a favorite cause. There are other hermeneutical objectives, and they ought not be neglected.

If we refuse to marry hermeneutics to existentialist interpretation, we can get a clearer picture of Bonhoeffer's intentions. We shall be able to recognize the nonreligious interpretation as the hermeneutical program it was really meant to be. Furthermore, we shall be able to grasp the undeniable fact that Bonhoeffer never had existentialist interpretation in his purview.

What we have just said is crucial in the question of whether

---

[88] See *Die mündige Welt,* I-V (1955ff.).

[89] For his sketch of it, see *Widerstand und Ergebung,* p. 257.

[90] Ebeling sees the implications of a hermeneutical program here, but G. Harbsmeier denies it ("Die nicht-religiöse Interpretation biblische Begriffe bei Bonhoeffer und die Entmythologisierung," *Die mündige Welt,* II, 74-91).

Bonhoeffer and Bultmann were actually saying the same thing.[91] As long as hermeneutics and existentialist interpretation were given the same meaning, the relationship between these two men was confused. For instance, it has been said that if Bonhoeffer had only gotten a clearer hold of his own intentions, he would have also made it clear that he was of one mind with Bultmann. Or, as it has also been said, had Bonhoeffer only understood Bultmann better, there would have been no disagreement between them at all. Or, again, had Bonhoeffer only given the same specific content to his ideas that Bultmann did, they would have been of a single mind.[92]

These conjectures do not ring true; that they do not is due to the existentialist penchant for identifying revelation with existence— man coming into his own as authentic personhood. It is as though the crisis in understanding could be resolved by making a kind of "religious adjustment," albeit a radical one. In short, existentialist interpretation is made a touchstone of all interpretation.

On one hand, this is too mild for Bonhoeffer. On the other, he insists that Bultmann's existentialist interpretation goes too far.[93] That he can say both of these things is understandable in the light of what we said before. It is too mild for Bonhoeffer because the crisis is too profound to be solved by a new touchstone for interpretation. The crisis is something to endure as an enormous burden; something of what Ebeling meant by his remark about "bearing up under the very reality of God."[94] Bonhoeffer's pressing question is: how does Jesus Christ act as Lord of the religionless man of our time? Bultmann's hermeneutics only bypasses this question. The existentialist touchstone is not big enough to be applied to the great issue. This is why Bonhoeffer recognizes that Bultmann *did not go far enough.* But he also goes too far. Bonhoeffer discerns in existentialist interpretation—following its meaning to the letter—a typical "liberal reductionism."[95] As he sees it, the demand for application of the kerygma has led to an adjust-

[91] Cf. the summary of this discussion by Gerhard Krause, "Dietrich Bonhoeffer und Rudolph Bultmann," in *Zeit und Geschichte,* pp. 439-460.

[92] The sharp tone that Krause uses against Barth is rather striking. Cf. Krause, *op. cit.,* pp. 459ff.

[93] Not far enough: *Widerstand und Ergebung,* p. 183; too far: *ibid.,* p. 220.

[94] *Wort und Glaube,* p. 159 (*Die mündige Welt,* II, 73).

[95] *Loc. cit.*

ment of revelation to existence; revelation is trimmed to the shape of authentic manhood.

Bonhoeffer saw through the fact that the hermeneutical problem had to be set within the dogmatic-theological circle of his question: in what sense is Jesus Christ Lord of religionless man? He was convinced that if the hermeneutical question were not kept in this context, his own question would be sidestepped.[96]

Bonhoeffer's *Letters and Papers from Prison* confirms our judgment. Traces of his personal life and thought as they come through his prison writings can illustrate this. A number of little things crop up that simply cannot be fit into the existentialist style. For instance, notice how this remarkable man finds strength in prison from reading his pietistically oriented *Tageslösungen*, how he is constantly praying, and how large the Old Testament looms as he begins setting up his theological program.[97] Put all these together, and you do not have the typical existentialist style.[98]

The question of how to understand Bonhoeffer can rest here. We merely wished to note that Bonhoeffer's profound practical concern does not make an existentialist theologian out of him. Bonhoeffer does not erase the boundary between revelation and existence; he does not let the truth of Christian confessions become the handiwork of the truth-creating person.

When theology looks away from truth that is independent of the receptive and creative person who lives the truth, when it ignores the fact that truth is tied to a reality at work outside man's actual experience of it, then that theology is on the verge of becoming an interesting sideline of anthropology.

[96] This point is made, properly, by Benkt-Erik Benktson, "Kristus och den myndiga världen," *Svensk teologisk kvartalskrift,* XL (1964), pp. 105ff.

[97] See *Widerstand und Ergebung,* pp. 112ff. (to accept the New Testament too quickly is not yet to be a Christian), pp. 182ff. (the resurrection of Jesus, along with the entire New Testament, must be read against the background of the Old Testament), and p. 225 (Jesus Christ becomes a mythological figure if He is set loose from the Old Testament).

[98] Hannelis Schulte concludes that the God of the Old Testament could pass for the commander of Auschwitz; in any case, the God whose Word is Jesus Christ is another than the Old Testament God ("Rudolph Bultmanns Stellung zum Alten Testament," in *Zeit und Geschichte,* pp. 720ff.). This terribly Marcionist notion can, with some justification, be defended from Bultmann's point of view. Bultmann says that in view of the gospel, the law is unbearable; but he also says that in the concrete Old Testament the law is not really necessary. With this the principial necessity of the Old Testament falls away. Cf. Bultmann, "Die Bedeutung des Alten Testaments für den christlichen Glauben," in *Glauben und Verstehen,* I, 313-336.

Since existentialist theology attempts to provide a new scientific basis for theology, we must make a few remarks in this area. Amid all the scientific concerns of a university faculty, theologians talk about God (once again I am stating the matter vaguely on purpose). Whether God can be an "object" of scientific study is debatable. But the simple fact remains that theology has to do with God. There is, therefore, no justification for the existence of a theological faculty if theology concludes that its talk about God is only oblique talk about human existence. If theology's task is to talk about man, then anthropology, philosophy, or the historical sciences can do its job as well if not better. When theology tries to establish its scientific character by becoming anthropology, it has surrendered the theological field and turned in its credentials as a legitimate science.

Retrospect and prospect

We have come to the point in this chapter where a summary of our discussion may be helpful. Let us try to set the current hermeneutical situation in some perspective, and thus try to give it its due.

Hermeneutics has been used by Bultmann—as it has by Fuchs, Ebeling, and other existentialist theologians—as a defense of the antimetaphysical glasses through which the New Testament and church dogma are read. Understanding is limited to what grasps me, speaks to me, and does something to me here and now; thus, understanding is made a critical and subjective moment as over against the text itself. This must be so, according to existentialist theology. We may not ask of a man more than he can himself grasp. Nor may we seek in the New Testament message more than we can be grasped by.[99]

The central religious motif that forms the background for this reductive approach to revelation is a pietistic concentration on man's experience or application of revelation. Whether we think of God in terms of the liberator (Bultmann), or as the "meaning" and "ground" (Fuchs and Ebeling), or as "interpersonal event" (Braun), the focus on experience is the same. In all these instances—and in many others which we shall meet—the substructure for pietistic concern is built from material provided by an existentialist analysis of the human situation. The notion of what it

[99] Cf. Fuchs, *Hermeneutik*, p. 61.

means to be human is sketched beforehand by existentialists as *the possibility for personhood*. Bultmann adds to this that the real man is the morally free person. Fuchs and Ebeling add that man is *homo interpretator*, a "language being." Man is the "place" where personal "response" is put into language. Since man's true being comes to reality in language, he is the locale of revelation.

This concept of man, even though it is a formal one, is decisive for the unique kind of reductionism that existentialist theology applies to the New Testament text. Since man is this kind of being, faith can have no other structure than that defined by "existence" or "language." Everything that the text tells us about God and His acts, over and above what is captured within our existence, is metaphysics. Everything that does not fit into the structure of "faith as decision" or "faith as experience" is "mythological language" or a projection.

This consequence betrays something significant. It shows why the terminology of existentialist theology is rather shifty. Terms like metaphysics, projection or "mythological language," remnant, ballast of faith—all these signify what is *not* at stake in faith: truth "out there."

Something else comes to light in this. The pietistic or functionalistic hermeneutics of experience has to do with the event as the text sets it in motion; the text itself is of interest only as it can be interpreted within the structures of events that may possibly be set loose by it. This brings us to a third observation, which can be put as the question whether the text itself sets the event in motion. It was on this point that Fuchs and Ebeling criticized Bultmann: no text was really needed in Bultmann's theology. But is it for Fuchs and Ebeling?

We could go a long way in arguing that the "hermeneutical events" that both men speak of assume the presence of a text that can be interpreted in a way that can be applied to a specific experience. But it can also be argued that this event does not take place *because* of the text.

Take, for example, the texts that report the resurrection of Jesus of Nazareth. The hermeneutical procedure is to ask what the texts (i.e., the reports of the resurrection) accomplish. What they do accomplish is a link between a faith-experience and the historical Jesus; the faith-experience is a Jesus-experience minus the mythological story of the New Testament.

The hermeneutical function of the text, then, is not to provide a catalyst for an event of faith; the text only gives a name to an event that does not actually need the text in order to take place. So, what Fuchs and Ebeling find lacking in Bultmann is not necessary to their own hermeneutics. Again, this is reminiscent of pietism in its historical forms, which likewise cut itself loose from Scripture as a necessary creative source of faith. The pietistic formula of this hermeneutics likewise has the real matter of the text in hand before it even approaches the text itself.[100]

Our final observation is that existentialist interpretation needs a received tradition in the form of a text. It deals with the text as a vehicle of the subject-matter which it already knows prior to approaching the text. The subject-matter is our divine- or ground-experience. It interprets this subject-matter according to the canon implicit in the subject-matter. *Pre*-understanding of the Scripture is in fact *the* understanding of Scripture.

One can, to be sure, legitimately read the Holy Scripture as a vehicle of another person's experience—as long as the nature of that experience has not been dogmatically defined ahead of time. The Old and New Testaments lend themselves to an existential interpretation in this sense, just as any other text can. This is true as long as we understand existential interpretation in this way: to encounter in the text the humanness of a fellow man, and in this manner to enter into communion with a fellow man—a man out of the distant past, for all that—is not only a legitimate hermeneutical expectation, but an event that is indeed profitable for a man of the present. For in this way our humanness truly does come into expression.

A good many orthodox sermons attempt precisely this. The preacher uses the text as a reminder of what the congregation already knows, or he reads the text as the vehicle for an experience he hopes the congregation will have. Indeed, we may ask whether this is not an inexpendable ingredient in preaching. But then we must also ask why the existentially interpreted New Testament should be so significant for our humanness at this precise time? What gives Holy Scripture unique significance for our humanness

---

100 Cf. Betti's assertion that the text can never bring any surprises to the reader when one approaches it with a preunderstanding of its concern, in Bultmann's sense (*op. cit.*, p. 35). Gollwitzer makes the same point in *Die Existenz Gottes,* pp. 24ff.

when, in fact, all texts—as long as they are existentially inter-preted—can be important to our humanness?

Existentialist theology is unable to give a satisfying answer to this question; it is prevented by its own premises from giving the answer we need.[101] It leaves us with the question of whether it can really aid preaching, in spite of its constant concern with the kerygma. Must not existentialist proclamation be limited to an analysis of our humanness, an analysis that happens to be aided by the language of a given text? No matter how interesting and instructive such sermonizing may be, it is hardly what the Re-formation understood by preaching.

With this we bring to a close our first excursion through the workshop of modern hermeneutical theology. We would be the last to argue that there is no real tension between past and present. On the contrary, we will need ample room to find our own way through the woods that the problematics of historicity have grown. But that the way out follows the trail blazed by the existentializing of established tradition is even at this point dubious.

---

[101] For this question see further H. W. Wolff, "Das Alte Testament und das Problem der existentialen Interpretation," *Evangelische Theologie,* vol. XXIII (1963).

Chapter Three

THE REALITY OF SALVATION

Existentialist Theology and Its Concept of Freedom
  • Free expression: the mark of personhood
  • Revelation and existence
  • Christian faith: the foundation of freedom
  • The character of reality
  • Hermeneutics and the reality of faith
Existentialist Theology and Natural Science
  • Eschaton, resurrection, and reality
  • Reality and language

THE REALITY OF SALVATION

We have been trying to get at the religious motivations at work in existentialist theology. To do this successfully would be the fairest approach to the subject. Surely there is more to be said than that we are dealing with a pietistically tinted theology.

We hope in this chapter to talk about what more must be said. It would not have been fair to begin by concentrating on negative criticism, for we have no right to make it easier for ourselves than the subject permits. One could simply write off existentialist theology as being founded on a philosophical-anthropological basis, in other words, as having a nonbiblical foundation. But that would be to use a double standard. One can catch orthodox Reformed tradition in its dependence on Aristotle as confidently as he can trap existentialist theology in a Heidegger snare. If we do not want orthodoxy to be hanged with a metaphysical rope, we should not then use that same rope on existentialist theology. If orthodoxy does not stand or fall with the metaphysics it has employed, why should existentialist theology be made to stand or fall with its ontological (anthropological) association?

For this reason we began with an effort to get at the religious drive within existentialist theology. Only now are we prepared to dig deeper into the material concepts with which existentialist theology tries to provide the superstructure for its religious concerns. Here at the beginning we wish only to raise the question of whether what appears to be the superstructure is actually the foundation, or whether the superstructure is passed off as the actual shelter that was meant to be built around it.

EXISTENTIALIST THEOLOGY AND ITS CONCEPT OF FREEDOM

Free expression: the mark of personhood

We concluded the previous chapter with the remark that the pietistic reduction of God's self-revelation—or simply, revelation, as existentialist theology usually says—was the effect of a certain notion of "understanding." "Understanding" itself was given a hermeneutic function: only what a man can understand should be sought for in the New Testament. We saw that the possibility of understanding is based entirely on a specific view of man, which can be put in the one word "existence." In our judgment, the telling point of existentialist theology is focused on this word existence. One could go along with the pietistic concern that drives existentialist theology, including its centering on hermeneutical method, were it not for the way it works with a concept of existence or "person" given to it by existentialist philosophy. Put another way, there is not a single objection—including anything that could arise from the hermeneutical problem—to asking what the gospel message does (or what it says or what use it has) out of a concern for the human existence of man. To see this one need merely remind himself of the sort of questions found in the Heidelberg Catechism. Nonetheless, we must define the humanness of man differently from the way in which existentialist theology does in its effort to make its concept of existence the only valid one.

We shall have to postpone discussion of our own idea of how to approach Scripture from the point of view of man's humanness. We shall confine ourselves here to an effort to demonstrate that the peculiar concept of man that existentialist theology uses to give power and validity to its pietistic objectives is very inadequate. Having seen *that* and *how* this concept of man takes a key position in hermeneutics (as every concept of man does), we hope to show in this chapter *why* this concept of man forms the kind of key that it does: in deciding for the concept of man the decision is already made as to what is reality and what is not. Thus, our concern here is with a concept of reality that flows from the existentialist concept of humanness as existence or as person.

The concept of person or existence has become a fantastically complicated one because these words have such a large variety of associations. Existentialist theologians mean something simpler by existence or person than many philosophical elucidations may lead us to suppose. We shall not analyze these two terms in a philosophical-anthropological sense. We merely want to observe how existentialist theologians use their concept of man, and the theological consequences of it.

Bultmann furnishes us a point of departure with an illuminating rule of thumb, which gives the conditions to which concrete understanding is bound, and which provides the arena in which concrete understanding must be attained if it is to be a genuine and true understanding. His rule is: "Only in action, as the free expression of a person, rather, only as a person exists totally as a person, can a person enter into relationship with a person."[1] This means that what makes a person a person is his act, his concrete action as "free expression." A genuine relationship in which genuine encounter occurs is possible only between such "persons."

We shall not be off base if we elaborate in this vein. We must accept "free expression" as the typical mark of personhood—or of existence, as Bultmann puts it—when we try to provide a theological interpretation of faith. Whatever else faith is, it sacrifices its authenticity if it is not a free expression of the person. The phrase "free expression" implies action. A man is a man in his *doing*. This has to do with one variation within man's basic structure: man can function in freedom in ways other than "doing."

A principle taken from Fuchs' *Hermeneutik* will serve as an illustration. Explaining how understanding actually operates, he uses the example of a cat. We are not able, he says, to explain *what* genuine understanding is; we can, however, recognize the conditions necessary for achieving it.[2] In order to know what makes a cat a cat, put a mouse in front of one. "One will then see the cat itself demonstrate what a cat is."[3] The cat acts in complete freedom as an authentic cat when it responds to the mouse. The example illustrates a hermeneutical principle, a principle that is inlaid in the nature of man. What is manhood and when can a concrete man claim to be a genuine man? The cat-and-mouse story

[1] Cf. *Glauben und Verstehen*, I, 36.
[2] Cf. pp. 103ff. This is written completely in the spirit of Schleiermacher's new hermeneutical approach: hermeneutics defines the conditions for understanding. Cf. the previous chapter, and also Ebeling, *Wort und Glaube*, p. 331.
[3] *Hermeneutik*, p. 109.

tells us: we know what manhood is when we see a man in a situation in which he responds as freely and authentically as the cat did when it saw the mouse.

In other words, the situation of free *response*-ability is the situation in which man demonstrates what manhood is. "He who seeks to understand manhood must be able to allow him freedom." Does this mean that to understand man is to allow him freedom? Fuchs says yes, freedom is constitutive for genuine manhood.[4] Bultmann defines this freedom as "free expression" in action; Fuchs and Ebeling characterize it further as freedom to use words. Wherever a man is free, wherever he expresses himself in full responsibility or puts what he understands into words, there understanding is true understanding; for there man is genuine man, a true person. Freedom in language is what makes man man.

We have mentioned the words responsibility and freedom in the same breath. These two words explicate each other and can be interchanged, for they both provide the clue to what constitutes man as truly human. Seen from this angle, understanding is the same as expressing oneself in free responsibility. For Bultmann this occurs in each new acceptance of one's humanity in an ethical decision. Fuchs and Ebeling see it as taking place in each acceptance of one's humanity in the act of expressing it in words.

All this might be clarified by introducing the phrase "authentic history" (*Geschichte*), which the existentialist theologians distinguish from ordinary history (*Historie*). To describe the humanness of persons with words like freedom and responsibility is to say that the authentic history of men is not the ordinary horizontal course of time. So far this is saying nothing. A wheel can turn and a corpse rot in the ordinary flow of time; but nothing has really happened here. History as eventfulness is present only when human beings are on stage, acting and talking in a way for which they accept full responsibility.

---

[4] *Ibid.,* pp. 110, 143; cf. *Zeit und Geschichte,* under the title "Das hermeneutische *Problem*," p. 365. In practice, the hermeneutical principle comes down to the "ethical seriousness of the interpreter himself." This is what Ebeling means by "conscience" as a hermeneutical principle (cf. *Wort und Glaube,* p. 348). By this he means the way in which a decision is made as to whether a person is really in the truth. Conscience is called a "place." This does not mean that conscience is a place within man, but it is the place *of men*; the place where man becomes a real man (*Wort und Glaube,* p. 404).

While metaphysics was predominant in theology, this facet of man was not given its due. Existentialist theology considers it the good fortune of our time to have learned to think of man historically, as a creature who reveals his true manhood when he accepts responsibility in freedom for himself and his own world. The authentic or real man is the man who interprets himself in a time-bound way. Or, to put it another way, his "historicity" is his reality.[5]

Let us pause here for a moment. What we have just said should make clear that behind the terms "freedom," "historicity," "person," and "existence," lies something more than a formal philosophical concept that is out of place in the realm of theology. The vocabulary of the New Testament reminds us that these are theologically weighted words. Freedom is a keynote in the New Testament. Recall, for a moment, what freedom means to Paul. Freedom from the law is identified with the "elements of the world" (Gal. 4:9), that is, with the "ordinances" under which human existence is carried on.[6]

With this in mind, we can sense that the existentialist theologians are on the track of biblical-theological prey. When the biblical writers speak of guilt, they betray a strong consciousness that man—*coram Deo*—is and remains responsible for what he has made of his own existence and his own world. The consciousness of personal guilt may have been frozen deep within a misused doctrine of original sin, but it remains senseless to speak of guilt when we fail to realize the full responsibility that man has for his own existence. But responsibility is unthinkable without freedom from coercion.

To this we must add that no matter how badly man's responsibility has been underplayed in a doctrinal community where total depravity—the doctrine of the "bondage of the will"—is given top billing, nothing can wash away human responsibility. No one can ever make sense of talking about guilt if one is a sinner because fate has made him one. In the context of guilt, we live in a man-made world. Ordinary and decent Christians sometimes tend to look fatalistically on the human situation in its frustration and

---

[5] Cf. Gogarten, *Die Wirklichkeit des Glaubens*, pp. 20ff., which is manifestly written in this spirit.

[6] On the "elements" in Gal. 4:9, see G. Delling in *Theologische Wörterbuch zum Neuen Testament*, VII, 684ff.

guilt, as if it were a kind of necessary consequence of an original sin. When people look at their human situation in this way, they have sacrificed the very ground for human responsibility and guilt. I mention this here as a reminder that we must not attack the existentialist stress on human decision too quickly.

The words "freedom" and "responsibility" are not the flies in the existentialist ointment. These are good words, and they belong in Reformed dogmatics. Only a shortsighted person would surrender them to the existentialists. But we must persist in our efforts to discover how these words function in existentialist theology, and what bearing they have on the idea that to be human is to exist. At this point, we shall have an opportunity to deploy and to illuminate the conclusion of the previous chapter. We saw that faith is real only when revelation does something or says something to me. That is, faith is real when I give myself a new interpretation in acts or words. We came across this idea of faith in connection with the search for authentic, genuine, irrefutable experience of faith as a fact that cannot be argued away. No one ought to be able to be talked out of this kind of faith; for if faith is once reduced to experience, then the question of certainty must be resolved in terms of experience. We saw how the experientially tinted word "ground" has, since the time of Herrmann, gradually shoved the word "content" out of the area of faith; faith must not be encumbered with the problem of its content. We were inclined to call this drift away from content to experience a pietistic movement.[7]

Revelation and existence

Now we must try to get a sharper focus on the nature of the humanness that demands that revelation must "do" or "say" something existentially if it is to create faith. The way man functions as a kind of organ of revelation reveals a special trait of pietism. In this respect, existentialist theology is a modern-day experiential theology: it is modern and therefore a new type because it introduces a new type of man into the experience, a kind of man other than the classical orthodox and pietistic theologies had in mind. This will become clear if we follow the line of thought a bit

---

[7] For the philosophical background of Herrmann's experiential theology, see T. Mahlmann, "Das Axiom des Erlebnisses bei Wilhelm Herrmann," *Neue Zeitschrift für systematische Theologie,* IV (1962), 11-88.

further. Authentic humanity reveals itself in its self-expression in free acts or words (recall Fuchs' cat-and-mouse illustration); since this is true, everything must be brushed aside as irrelevant that does not impinge on this personhood, that does not push man into genuine personhood.

We said that what does not touch authentic personhood *must* be disregarded. In the previous chapter, we understood this in the sense of "alas, it must be so; it cannot be otherwise." Looking back now, we see that this could be misunderstood. The restrictive character of revelation as being that which touches only on person-hood in its authentic historical character is not a regrettable neces-sity. Rather, it is only if this is so that we can have a genuine act of faith. Hence, existentialist theology insists that the involvement of the person in revelation has to be a conscious, purposeful decision. The discounting of the metaphysical is, on one hand, the implication of the historical character of man. Man is authentic man only as he accepts his own existence in free responsibility. Since this is true, metaphysics can only be a bad temptation for man to replace the restless, time-conditioned manner of human existence with the "eternal rest" of a timeless, static ideology.

We have used the word "temptation,"[8] suggesting that anything that takes the edge off my "historical character" is far more than a mere "look at the other side of the picture." It is a threat. The first mandate of faith is that it must burn its bridges behind it and, like Abraham, get moving to territories unknown.[9] The fire must sweep the bridges of history, too, in the sense of stories of past events. Neither metaphysics, nor history in the linear sense, includ-ing so-called revelation-history, can establish our humanness. Such stories cannot possibly be revelation. This is simply an irrefutable fact for existentialist theology. Such stories simply do not touch our human existence here and now. If it is true that we can speak of God in His revelation only insofar as it involves our human existence, and if it is also true that our humanness consists in "decision history" and not in "reason" or anything similar, then a fundamental ontological analysis of man demands that revelation must be anything but linear history. To put it graphically, revela-tion is not a historical, horizontal line, as Bultmann speaks of it. It is, at least virtually, a series of discrete vertical lines, as many of

---

8 Fuchs uses the same word in this connection (*Hermeneutik*, p. 156).
9 *Ibid.*, p. 147.

them as there are decision moments. Hence, revelation does not look like

(a) —————————————→

but like

(b) ↓ ↓ ↓↓ ↓↓ ↓↓ ↓↓ ↓

In Fuchs' words, if man is "time"—in the sense of *geschicht-lich,* as in the vertical lines—then revelation (after the historic church doctrine of accommodation) is not only "time," but is the act of God, in its redemptive sense, by which He establishes or grounds human existence as "time." That is, it is God's act by which He makes man "historical" or "timely," and thus brings him into essential and authentic self-expression by means of words or acts.[10] If man is "time," then eternity, revelation, and truth must be part of time if they are to reach man.[11] To insist stubbornly on the notion of revealed truth as a set of teachable propositions that must then be believed is to maintain a notion of faith that is born in an anxiety of losing oneself.[12] This anxiety, says Fuchs, is sin, and it only undermines authentic selfhood. The very reality of man's manhood is decided by whether he is willing to be complete-ly of time or whether he retreats into the timeless truths or "salvation facts" of past time.[13]

Revelation does not dehumanize man by making him timeless; on the contrary, it comes as "grace-time" to be the ground of man as Christian man. Stronger, the reformational insight that man is not man in order to become Christian, but that man is Christian in order to become man means, in our context, that man becomes Christian in order to become authentically time-bound. Revelation is that which "grounds existence," and existence is the place or time—place and moment converge—where revelation comes to "expression." To give the name revelation to anything other than that which makes me, today, a "man in process of realization" is a denial of true faith.

What is the real significance of this correlation between revela-tion and existence? Or, better, how does it work? To get this

10 *Ibid.,* p. 156. "Grace seeks to be the ground of concrete existence. This is why grace-time must be truly temporal."

11 Cf. *ibid.,* p. 142: "Our existence is temporal; it comes and goes. There-fore, truth is also temporal." This means that truth is always an expression of the immediacy (or authenticity) of our experience.

12 *Ibid.,* p. 123.

13 *Ibid.,* p. 156.

clearly in view, we must remember that the connection between being human and having revelation is not in itself a unique one. Theology is always carried on this way. Nor is the notion of God's self-revelation as a ground of human existence a novelty in the history of theology. Certainly it is not novel in the church's preaching. Neither Augustine nor Calvin would have had it any other way. What is important here is how we understand the humanness of man that is grounded by revelation.[14] It is here that we encounter the peculiarity of existentialist theology.

When revelation is looked to as the ground of existence, we are faced with a number of presuppositions that have considerable significance, especially in view of the understanding of existence involved here. We saw this when we looked at existentialist hermeneutics. Existence appeared to function as a standard of interpretation that brought about a pietistic transformation of how the meaning of a text is to be gauged: a text had to be understood in terms of what it could do for the realization of authentic manhood. The theological defense for this canon of interpretation was based on the notion that the text was an accommodation to human needs. If man is "time," eternity had to be accommodated to time; eternity actually had to *become* time. All this is in line with the doctrine of accommodation in the classical view of revelation: revelation accommodates itself to man for the purpose of making itself understandable to him. Hence, the doctrine of accommodation became the theological *apologia* for making man in his temporal humanity the canon for all interpretation.

The structure of revelation is modeled after its human subject. Classical theology viewed man as essentially reason; so revelation was viewed as essentially rational in structure and therefore the ground for man's existence as rational existence.[15] The theology of existence views man as "time"; man is authentic man as he decides to act, and only then. Revelation also has a "time" character. For this reason it can be the ground of man as "decision history." But the fact that it sees revelation as accommodated to its human subject does not distinguish existentialist theology. Its pe-

[14] Hence, the concept of correlation gets a very diverse content. One need only compare the use of the concept in G. C. Berkouwer and Karl Barth, and then a use very different from both as found in Paul Tillich. What lies at the bottom of the difference in use is a difference in the concepts of man that are employed in it.

[15] Cf. the author's *De Mensvormigheid Gods*, pp. 88-121.

culiar view of man does. Man as "decision history" forms the
specific hermeneutic key to the Scriptures, and, furthermore, the
key that unlocks the nature of reality. Indeed he is the former only
because he is the latter. For what is man as "time"—that is, as
self-fulfilling history? In their own meaning and scope these words
point to man in his principal distinction from anything that can be
measured, counted, or manipulated in the world of tangible things.
What makes man man is that which cannot be measured, that
which is free, creative, surprising; what makes him man is that
which we encounter in him as a person and which escapes everything that can be called nature or history—or world. Only man is
existence; only man resists classification among things.

No matter what is added to this characterization of man, a great
deal has already been said. To depict man thus is to associate
oneself with the Kantian scheme, which sets man as free over
against nature as necessity, and to accept a duality that goes back
to Greek philosophy and has since dominated European philosophy, the duality of man against the world that circumscribes him.
How can man maintain himself in this special place? This is the
question that has pressed hard on us since the dominance of
natural sciences in modern times. Where can we find a guarantee
that man himself has not become an object, a thing among things?
How can man maintain himself in his uniqueness as a deciding
subject, a uniqueness that Descartes carved out for him so confidently and so radically?

Christian faith: the foundation of freedom

The spirit of European thought hovers about the question of the
grounding of man as acting subject. Every apparent success at
answering it has in its turn been brought into doubt and has been
rendered untenable. Since the time of Kant European philosophy
has sought the answer in personal freedom—in the humanity of
man as a *possibility* rooted in personal freedom. To threaten
human personal freedom threatens the essence of man, for in his
"free expression" (Bultmann's term) lies his authentic personhood.
Since Kant the penchant for digging in at the point of personal
freedom as the last-ditch chance to find the essence of man has
taken on a distinct soteriological slant. How can we find assurance
that man will not *lose* his freedom, that he will not be crushed by

the technological and scientific steam roller, that he will not be turned into a mere product of his fateful past? These are the haunting questions of an age that has seen the techniques of natural sciences grow to gigantic proportions, and which has grown up under modern technology. They help explain the redemptive overtones of present-day philosophy. For modern philosophy, with the help of its own analysis of human existence, seeks to provide a saving answer to the threat that the times pose for human freedom. One could note the soteriological dimensions of late Greek philosophy as a striking parallel.

Modern philosophy's soteriological interest notwithstanding, the question of man is still looked at as part of the broad issue of man against nature. In this sense, the question is part of the picture as European culture has painted it since the time of the Greeks. The problematic is basically the same: in his center, man is *atopos* (without a fixed place).[16] This was nonnegotiable for Aristotle; it is for modern philosophy as well. In his personhood, man is not manipulable; one cannot "get hold" of him. If the authenticity of man is situated at this point, there is only one way to preserve his humanity: he must keep this freedom at any price if he is to be a genuine man. Existentialist philosophy is settled on this as its program—to maintain man's personal freedom as the core of his authentic selfhood.

Existentialist theology, on the other hand, is an effort to translate Christian faith in terms of this program. Materially this means to interpret Christian faith as the true foundation for man's freedom and thus to preserve—or restore—the authenticity of man as person. This is the context in which we must understand the notion of revelation as the "ground of existence." Man first understands revelation, the speech of God, and so forth, only as he is in fact awakened to his authentic selfhood. But it means more than this: it means that God's revelation, or God in His self-revelation, creates man as freedom and maintains man as free in opposition to the "powers" of nature and history that constantly threaten him, just as the gods of the nations constantly threatened to bring Israel into subjection to them. The huge role that the word "freedom" plays in modern theology speaks volumes in this respect. It is the point of concentration for existentialist theology, including almost everyone from Gogarten to Fuchs. We have already touched on

16 On this see H. Van Oyen, *Theologische Erkenntnislehre* (1955), p. 156.

the lines that bind this concern for freedom to the New Testament
and its cultural background.

There is a striking parallel between our own day and the
beginning of our Christian era. Both betray man's feeling of being
threatened by nature and history—or, in the language of the
ancient world, by death and *ananke*. It is no wonder that the New
Testament provides a relevant response to the question of personhood as it is defined these days, the question that arises out of
man's insecurity over against the world around him. The gospel of
Christ appears to speak directly to this question. One need recall
only such passages as Philippians 2:5-11; Galatians 4; Colossians
1; Ephesians 1; and Hebrews 1 and 2.[17] There *is* a threat of
bondage to the "powers" of the world and history; they do threat-
en to put man's neck into their yoke; and the New Testament
witnesses powerfully to that danger. Hence, one is saying far too
much if he claims that existentialist theology is only a kind of
theological Kantianism. There is more here than a simple dialectic
of freedom versus nature. On the other hand, everything that these
theologians say about freedom, responsibility, and personhood is
heavily tinted with the hypothesis of this dialectic. The concept of
freedom used by existentialist theology is not the same as the
New Testament concept of freedom.[18]

The character of reality

What we have just said calls for more elaboration than we are able
to give here. But I think we can clarify it sufficiently even in the
brief compass of this chapter. The genesis of the concept of
freedom used in existentialist theology has had a decisive influence
on the concept itself. Our criticism will be concentrated on this.
We have already noted that the origin of the freedom concept is
the history of man seeking to maintain his identity as the genuine
subject of his acts and thus maintain his genuine humanity. Man
as subject in existentialist theology is still burdened with the problem of freedom. Illustrative of this is the thesis that recurs in

---

[17] For a compelling interpretation of the Philippians passage, see Ernst
Käsemann, *Exegetische Versuch und Besinnungen*, I, 51-95.

[18] There is a discussion of freedom in G. C. Berkouwer, *Faith and
Sanctification* (1952), pp. 163ff., and *Man, the Image of God* (1962), pp.
310ff.

theologians from Bultmann to Fuchs that the heart of genuine humanity is man holding on to himself as subject.[19] This thesis is implied by the thesis that man is freedom. To demonstrate this, we recall the notion of guilt Fuchs uses to clarify his point. Consciousness of guilt shows that the heart of humanness exists in man's relationship to himself, a relationship that is, in fact, the condition for the rise of guilt consciousness. I would have no sense of personal guilt if the axle around which the wheel of my existence turned were not my own relationship to myself.[20] The presence of man's sense of guilt was introduced into the discussion of his freedom and responsibility; there can be no real sense of guilt unless man also senses himself as free and responsible. The conclusion is inescapably clear: existentialist theology's concept of freedom is surely related to the New Testament understanding of freedom, especially in the cases where the New Testament talks of freedom as liberation from the cosmic "powers." But the crucial point is that the existentialist concept of freedom is *grounded* elsewhere than freedom in the New Testament is.

Freedom in existentialist theology—as the heart of personhood —is the converse of man's holding on to himself as subject, which is the primal anthropological datum for existentialism. With this, however, existentialist theology accepts a concept of freedom— along with the set of problematics that goes with it—that rescues man in his authentic humanity by establishing him as a monad. Existentialist theology is unable to rise above this monadic existence of man. It may reshape it according to the dialectic that we have discussed, but it does not escape it.

The theological structure of existentialist theology demonstrates clearly where and how it is caught in this dialectic.[21] We shall now try to clarify this from three points of view.

[19] See especially Bultmann's *Theology of the New Testament,* where he claims to find this thesis, which is fundamental for existentialist theology, in Paul's concept of body (pp. 192ff.).

[20] Fuchs, *op. cit.,* pp. 117ff.

[21] Existentialist theology is unable to be precise as to whether the "faith commitment" completely overlaps the "existential commitment" or whether "faith commitment" is a special form of the "existential commitment," the special form that turns existence into Christian existence. Bultmann chooses the latter; Schubert M. Ogden the former (cf. his *Christ Without Myth* [1961]). Ogden is criticized for this by Paul van Buren, *The Secular Meaning of the Gospel* (1963), who says that Ogden threatens the central place that the man Jesus of Nazareth has in the Christian faith (p. 79). Ogden in turn says that Van Buren is a victim of the tragic antithesis between tradi-

(1) The correlation between revelation and existence means that
man is not only understood as existence—the only way to preserve
his authentic personhood—but also that revelation sets and holds
him in his position as authentic person. Even stronger, that which
divine revelation accomplishes in the last analysis is this: it establishes this structure of humanness by allowing man to transcend
the factuality of nature and history in free and actual self-
expression and thus to be a genuine self. Wherever this free
act—this free "speech"—occurs, revelation occurs; and at that
moment man becomes his true self.

This means, moreover, that existentialist theology puts God's
revelation in the service of man's freedom. But this freedom is
freedom as defined by the struggle against nature and history
(herewith the old concept of freedom intrudes itself into the picture
again). God is the guarantor of humanness in opposition to the
world that hems man in. To say this is to shrink the meaning of
revelation. We shall come back to this later; we want to call
attention to it here simply because it shows how the existentialist
concept of revelation is coupled to the nature-freedom dialectic,
and how the entire church tradition is bound to be meshed into the
same perspective if it is going to have a meaningful place in the
theological sun.[22] This means materially that while the message of
salvation is indeed a message of redemption, redemption is going
to be defined in a new way. It becomes redemption from the fist of
fate, from existential despair, from unauthenticity, from mean-
inglessness, from the surrender of true manhood to natural causation, and so on.

There is some truth in this setup. The existentialist structure
helps us enrich our understanding of the breadth of redemption.
But redemption of man from nature and fate still is a one-sided
selection from the many components that form the whole story of
redemption. The great drama in this picture is the drama between
man and his world; the conflict is between man and nature. The
problem to which this redemption is an answer is no longer
Luther's "How do I find a gracious God?" but instead, "How can I

tional theism and nontheistic extremism. Some Catholic theologians com-
bine existential commitment and faith commitment in the manner of the
traditional nature and grace combination, and are thus able to maintain
the former (they overlap) as well as the latter (they are distinct).

[22] The point is made by Helmut Gollwitzer, *Die Existenz Gottes,* pp. 24ff.

escape domination by the dehumanizing and destructive powers of nature?"[23] The basic question of religion is turned into "How can I master life?"[24]

It is clear that the concept of redemption given us by existentialist theology is relevant only as it functions within the nature-freedom dialectic. In the drama played out between man and nature God stands on man's side—witness His revelation in Christ—maintains man's true selfhood as personal selfhood, as freedom over against fate, and establishes man as a person in the midst of the anonymous world of thingness. Undeniably, some evangelical truth is brought to light here. But it is just as true that, due to the selectiveness involved, a revision of the gospel of redemption has occurred.[25]

The New Testament tells us much more than this about redemption. This is why it also sometimes speaks the same language existentialist theology does; but it speaks it differently.[26] There is a drama between God and man unfolding in the New Testament, and existentialist theology turns its eyes away from *this* drama. Having done so it leaves begging the question whether man has not first decided on his role as man and afterward called on God to help him play his part.

(2) To establish and undergird human existence, divine revelation creates a paradoxical situation. Instead of binding to Himself man in existence as a covenant partner, God in His revelation supports man in his own self-declared independence. In one instance—as one keeps talking about God the personal "over-against"—this tends to make of God and man two independent agents, each with his own interest; that is, two competitive enterprisers. This picture does in fact loom in the background of existentialist concepts of revelation. True, the personal concept of

[23] I am not using the literal form in which this question is ascribed to Luther; but it does serve to introduce the central answer of salvation (*einen gnädigen Gott*).

[24] Cf. Albert H. van den Heuvel, *These Rebellious Powers* (1965), pp. 23ff.

[25] This does not mean, of course, that another selection is to be preferred to it.

[26] The conclusion of Bultmann's *History and Eschatology* exemplifies this. The tensions between flesh and spirit, between being of the world and in the world, and between being both sinner and justified are interpreted wholly within the perspective of the tension between nature-history and freedom.

God is considered to be an antiquated mythological form; but the "myth" takes this form because of the view of man as freedom. If one wants to hold on to this view at any price (but why would he?), he will finally arrive at Sartre's "God is Emptiness." The whole complex notion of God as "emptiness" is conceived in the womb from which definitions are born that speak of man as freedom and of God as our transcendent selfhood. But this finally comes down to saying that God has sunk beneath the horizon. He is the Absentee. He cannot get on stage anymore.

As existentialist theology developed its theology of revelation as "event" or "the moment," it tended to make the same mistake as the old church theology made: it did not build its concept of man on the God who was allowed to sink beneath the horizon. To demonstrate this, the theology of negation *(theologia negativa)* played as fundamental a role in church orthodoxy as it does in existentialist theology. That we cannot say what God is forms a programmed rule for every theology of negation,[27] and it has its roots in a specific concept of man. In existentialist theology, man is thought to be pure freedom. In this concept man is a monad, and the relationship of self to itself is the basic anthropological premise. Considered either from a biblical-theological or an anthropological point of view, *this* notion of man is the prime mistake of existentialist theology.[28] Given this notion of man, we can still talk about a relationship between God and man, but it is a relationship in which man as freedom stands over against God as "custodian of freedom."

Indeed, according to this viewpoint, man and God are involved in an unbreakable relationship, but we must in no sense understand this relationship as a personal matter, no matter how often the adjective personal is used in existentialist discussions. The word personal has sense only if it implies a situation in which there are two who say "You" or "Thou" to one another. To seek for man in the terms of a "possibility," and therefore to see his humanity as

[27] For Bultmann also. We will come back to the role of negative theology in Paul van Buren. The subject itself is discussed in the author's *De Mensvormigheid Gods*, pp. 122-163.

[28] This is very clear in Fritz Neuegebauer, "Die hermeneutischen Voraussetzungen Rudolph Bultmanns in ihrem Verhältnis zur Paulinischen Theologie," *Kirche und Dogma*, V (1959), 289-305. He shows that Paul cannot be read as defining human-*being* in terms of existence in the sense which Bultmann gives to existence.

defined primarily by his freedom, is to lose the chance to arrive at
the true personality of man or God, a chance that is offered in the
biblical story of God and man in covenantal fellowship.

(3) What has just been said carries through to the concept of
reality, our chief concern here, which goes hand in glove with the
existentialist view of man that led to the reduction of the redemptive message that we talked about in the previous chapter.[29] The
dialectic of nature and freedom in which existentialist theology
moves is the structure in which the enormous concern for human
freedom, for man as a free subject, is inlaid. It is consistently so,
for man is authentic man in the state of freedom alone.

This way of stating the matter carries with it the idea that
revelation—God in His godhead—is the guarantor and maintainer
of man's freedom over against the hostile world of nature. But it
goes deeper than this. It means that man in this sense of freedom
must be kept free from bondage to divine revelation itself. Revelation, therefore, cannot be accepted as revelation as long as it is
part of nature and history. As long as we are human beings in the
authentic sense of our "free expression" of ourselves, revelation
cannot compete with man's "free act" or "free language-forming."
After all, revelation cannot frustrate man in his authentic selfhood
as freedom; it must create larger room for man to express his
authentic selfhood.

We should try to get a clearer focus on this if we can. We have
not merely said that, according to existentialist theology, God's
revelation does not frustrate man's achievement of authentic selfhood. No one in the Christian tradition would argue with this,
even though he would not have gotten to the heart of redemptive
revelation by saying it. But when we situate this authenticity of
personal selfhood in the area of "free expression" and then con-
tend that only that which I in my "free expression" can accept as
revelation is indeed divine revelation, we have quite another bird
in our cage. For this means simply that revelation is by definition
limited to what I in freedom recognize as revelation. It means that
the reality of divine revelation is determined by nothing greater

---

[29] The concept of reality as very commonly used today is a most ill-
defined concept. We wish to discuss some of the problematics that it introduces into theology. For more profound consideration of it, we must defer
to professional philosophers, for example, Wilhelm Weischedel, *Wirklichkeit
und Wirklichkeiten* (1960); C. A. van Peursen, *Feiten, Waarden, Gebeur-
tenissen. Een deiktische Ontologie* (1965).

than myself. If this is untrue, then the whole structure of existentialist theology falls, for it is a theology built on the premise that "free expression" is the essence of authentic personal existence.

As an illustrative example, we can point to the clear treatment that Fuchs gives us of faith and reality.[30] Strictly speaking, that which *is* is reality. For our worlds of house, garden, and kitchen, reality consists of those things that we measure, count, and control. That is to put it uncritically—in these cases "being" means that reality exists in the form of *things*. People can be numbered among these realities of the natural-science type of world, at least insofar as they belong to the past and can be the objects of scientific research. In a word, we ordinarily hold to be real those things that can be studied and examined as objects.

Paul tends for a little while to make the reality of the Lord's resurrection this kind of reality in I Corinthians 15.[31] But he knows better. One can talk about reality as something that does not touch our own selves; that is, we can deal with reality in a way that leaves our "free expression" unaffected. This is the controllable reality that we deal with in natural science. But as soon as we ask about ourselves, we are asking about another kind of reality; we are no longer working with reality "as it stands before our eyes." We are talking about something that, although not "out there" in front of us, is still very real. Indeed, this is *really* real. I can run away from all the reality that stands tangibly "before my eyes" without undoing my own humanity; I can simply close my eyes to what stares at them. This is why the tangible, controllable, datable, and measurable reality is not the *really* real. Genuine reality is recognizable by the way that "I relate to it as reality."[32] That is, the first condition for the genuinely or really real is that I experience it as the unavoidable "present." Reality exists at the point where "present" meets "present." In less academic terms: wherever I as a man who realizes himself in free, actual response ("present") come to grips with something that establishes and liberates my responsiveness ("present"), there I have encountered reality.

But what is the "present"? We have seen that for Fuchs "free

---

[30] *Hermeneutik,* pp. 126ff.; we could as well refer to Ebeling, *Wort und Glaube,* pp. 192ff. and 393ff.

[31] Fuchs, *op. cit.,* p. 127. One simply cannot discuss I Cor. 15 with Bultmann.

[32] *Ibid.,* p. 130.

expression" is present when I give meaning to reality in language
or words. Where "freedom to give expression in words"—words
that create meaning—exists, there man is authentically man. This
is why reality must not only be "present" to me, but it must be
"able to be brought into expression in the present."[33] Reality,
then, is not that which stands before my eyes; it is that which I, in
"free speech," without compulsion from any other, can recognize
and express as meaningful for my human existence. Only what in
my own judgment touches me directly (that is, is meaningful to
me) can be called reality.

This is *not* to say that man creates his own reality; he does not
provide the possibility that lies at the bottom of all reality. But it
does mean that reality can be ascribed only to that in which
meaning that expresses man is involved. "There is no reality
without language."[34] Language means that which is articulated in
speech. Thus, we must say that there is no other reality than what
I experience as relevant for my free interpretation of myself and
can therefore articulate to others. Having said this, we have said
that reality is defined—though not created—by man. Reality can
be talked about only by the meaning that expresses man, for
reality exists only where man is present, acting or interpreting,
within the world around him (this is why reality presupposes a
relationship). The world has to be put into words. It must reveal
by language its relevance and importance for our human existence.
This is the point of the rule: "Where language is made, there reality
is."[35]

When we engage in free translation, when we are busy giving
significance to things via language, we have come to grips with
reality, and not before. When language is created, we have a whole
new situation; for by it the world around us is translated into the
reality of the world.

The character of reality is ascribed, then, only to that which has
significance. This is actually a sloppy way of putting it. Reality is
that in which *I experience a significance for my genuine existence
as man*, and to which I can in full freedom *ascribe* such significance. If I do not discover a significance for my authentic personhood, I have not encountered reality. Again, less academically,

[33] *Ibid.*
[34] *Ibid.*, p. 131.
[35] *Ibid.*, p. 128.

applying this to the propositions of theology, we can accept these
propositions and pass them on to others only as we can live into
them as something meaningful for our human existence. We have
both the right and the duty to make this demand if we are to
remain honest and authentic persons.

Hermeneutics and the reality of faith

It is very clear by now, upon examination of its concept of reality,
that existentialist theology is not about to desert the philosophical
outlook of the time.[36] Indeed, it tries to the bitter end to fit the
Christian message into terms that are borrowed from the conceptual apparatus of modern philosophy.[37] For this reason, we must
take still another look at hermeneutics. What, precisely, is legitimate under the terms of existentialist hermeneutics?

We noted in the previous chapter that hermeneutics was employed to defend a reduction of the salvation message to that
which "does something for" or "speaks to" man's condition. And
we also noted how the word "man" was given a most precarious
place in this portrait. As long as the word was not filled with a
specific concept of what man is, the pendulum could swing in
either direction.

We have been occupied in this chapter with the view of man
entertained by existentialist theologians, and we have seen that
they have introduced a fairly clear theory of reality into their
concept of man. Understandably, then, Ebeling insists that hermeneutics, as he understands it, has a good deal to do with modern
concepts of reality.[38] Hermeneutics, as we have seen, is an effort
to connect a text with man in his personal existence. We can also

[36] This demonstrates that philosophical systems are not merely neutral, in
spite of the denial of that fact by existentialist theologians.

[37] Even if one insists—with some reason—that the intention of Fuchs,
Ebeling, *et al.*, is *not* to limit all reality to speech or words, but rather to
understand reality as the product of God's eschatological word of creativity,
it is nonetheless true that the concepts in which this is discussed betray more
than a mere terminological dependence on the later Heidegger. Cf. Fuchs,
Hermeneutik, pp. 70-72.

[38] Ebeling says specifically that the change within the concept of reality
is the connection in which the hermeneutical problem must be discussed.
See *Wort und Glaube,* pp. 403ff., and his article, "Hermeneutik," in *Religion
in Geschichte und Gegenwart,* III, 257. All this is part of an effort, which
must be respected, to guide faith through the spiritual rapids that run from
the Enlightenment.

say that hermeneutics, in view of the existentialist view of man, tries to make a connection between the text and the notion of reality that has been current since Kant. In fact, existentialist hermeneutics is an effort to support the legitimacy of this view of reality as a framework for understanding within which the text of the New Testament really is able to do something to or speak to men of today.[39] In this sense, hermeneutics is indeed, as existentialist theologians hasten to agree, a form of anthropology; moreover, since theology as a whole is hermeneutics—"linguistics"—it too is a form of anthropology. As linguistics, hermeneutics leads faith to express itself in new forms, to express itself in words that are not descriptive of a reality "lying before our eyes," but in words that *reveal* reality as that which is relevant for one's own humanity as it exists in free acceptance, in free decision, or in free "expression." The variation in the formulations need not hold us up here. They stand clustered under one umbrella, the conviction that faith may not claim as reality anything that it cannot express as a living present.

Careful note should be taken of the terminology being used here. Existentialist theology is concerned with the question of how faith acts or speaks in terms of genuine reality. We shall have to sidestep the fact that one can also question the real reality of reality itself.[40] The preoccupation with faith in the existentialist enterprise is part of the stress it lays on the application of revelation. The question of the nature of reality can be resolved with the help of concepts gained from modern philosophy, but this should not close our eyes to the fact that in the question of what reality actually is we are involved with the question of the reality of God in His redemptive revelation. The whole discussion turns on this religious context, the philosophical jargon notwithstanding. When is God in His revelation a reality? It is to this question that existentialist theology tries to give its own compelling answer.

We may compare the existentialist answer to the traditional answer of the church, so that we can grasp it in its religious

[39] Hans Schmidt, "Das Verhältnis von neuzeitlichem Wirklichkeitsverständnis und christlichem Glauben in der Theologie Gerhard Ebelings," *Kirche und Dogma,* IX (1963), 71-101, concludes that Ebeling has capitulated to the newer concepts of reality.

[40] We are referring here to Tillich's theology. It would require an entire book to discuss what binds him to and what separates him from existentialist theology. There is more that associates him than separates him.

context as well as its philosophical. There is a parallel and also a distinct contrast between existentialist theology and classical orthodoxy at this point. Classical theology interpreted religious reality to be of a metaphysical sort. To put it rather prejudicially: religious reality was seen as that which was relevant to man's metaphysical appetites. This is why classical orthodoxy had more images of reality than it could answer for.[41] Its metaphysical thirst could hardly be slaked. This is why it attributed reality to more things than were involved in God's redemptive revelation in Jesus Christ. Its thirst was—theologically, at least—more metaphysical than soteriological. Revelation was as much a disclosure of supernatural truths as a redemptive act; salvation tended to be identified with metaphysical knowledge; and faith—at least partly—became a matter of assenting to metaphysical facts on the basis of another person's (or institution's) authority.

Pietism was, to follow another parallel, oriented more toward soteriology than toward metaphysics. Religious reality for pietism was that which is directly useful to man. And what is useful in this sense? Pietism answers—that which satisfies the actual inner needs of man. Hence, pietism needed fewer dogmatic formulations; indeed, all dogmatic formulations lost some of their importance. Revelation had to be real redemptive revelation; of this pietism was very sure. But salvation tended to be aimed at the provision of one pressing need, hence the experiential character of faith for pietism. Faith is the experience that one's inner need is truly met, that salvation is verily accomplished. Pietism signals a shift away from orthodoxy in its concept of reality. Salvation is a reality only as it is *applied* reality.

Existentialist theology defines reality no less practically than did pietism: revelation is a revelation of salvation, and salvation is that which meets man's need to be an authentic person. But personhood, or human existence, has already been so sharply defined that salvation can be understood only within the categories of a self-realization that occurs in a free decision of faith. Pietism's need for an experience affected the question of when salvation was a reality. Existentialist theology has the same experiential de-

---

[41] To give a few sketchy examples: what sort of picture can we make of *limbus patrum*? or *limbus infantium*? Does the phrase *radix fidei* have a correspondence in reality? Is there a topography of the other world?

mands. But its view of man inserts a restriction into the question of salvation's reality; it restricts the possibilities of what real salvation can be. Its answer is consistent: salvation is identical with the authentic act of faith itself.[42] Given the categories of its view of man, salvation reality can be no other.

To summarize the three approaches to the problem: (1) Traditional metaphysical theology sees the reality of God and His redemptive revelation as a reality outside of and above faith. Its conception of reality—oriented to metaphysics—implies that God's reality is timeless, eternally the same. The validity does not go any further than the proposition that this God really exists. Metaphysical truth is thin.

(2) Pietism goes halfway into a new era. It too speaks of God's reality; His redemptive revelation is a universally valid truth. But it goes on to ask the question: *when* is redemption a reality? It senses that the application of redemption to man is part of redemptive revelation. What it does not do is hazard a definition of man; this leaves one wide open for many alternatives.

(3) Existentialist theology does define man, and does so in a way that decides beforehand *what* salvation is. If one determines beforehand what man is, he has set limits on what saved man can be. Therefore, the reality of God's redemptive revelation is not made of universally valid truths, nor of specifically defined religious experiences; it is a reality only as "realized faith" itself comes to expression.[43] The reality of faith is faith itself; when faith is authentic, it has come into the only reality it knows.

No elaborate argument is needed here to demonstrate that this means a considerable reduction of religious reality. After the act of faith, or the experience of faith, is made the center, which in turn has been determined by a prior decision as to what reality is, a whole dimension of "the real" is bound to be cut away. The concept of reality used by existentialist theology functions as a potent ferment within the concepts and stories out of which the Christian church has built its message to the world. Indeed, it reshapes the whole message. The pietistic focus on truth as being truth only as it is experienced as a genuine experience of our own

---

[42] Cf. Ebeling, *Wort und Glaube*, p. 252: "Faith is in the end saving faith; indeed, it is salvation itself."

[43] Fuchs, *Hermeneutik*, p. 139, speaks of faith as one's coming to himself.

human existence, signals a distinct paring down of the church tradition.

Existentialist theology achieves a twofold reduction, the second part being as much a revision as it is a reduction. God, revelation, truth—in fact the whole of redemption as the tradition of faith witnesses to it—have to be translated in terms of what is relevant to or expressive of human "existence in realization." That is, all this must be confined to terms created by translating "nature" and "history" into terms of genuine reality, terms that have "significance" for human nature as existence.[44] In a word, the reality of faith is "faith," insofar as faith expresses our actual, here-and-now, realized humanity.

Can a man, after all, digest more than he can understand? In general the answer is obvious. But it seemed to us that "understanding" implied for existentialist theology a whole theory of man. And this theory is an implication of its concept of reality. The peculiar idea of "understanding" concealed a prejudice that determined its notion of what is real in faith. And this in turn explains why its hermeneutics turns out the way it does. If it had introduced a larger or another kind of reality than it allowed for at the beginning of its hermeneutical programming, it could not have come out where it did. And this was, of course, the intention of introducing its concept of understanding into the picture. For only in so doing could it keep its hermeneutical method under control. Interpretation is done rightly—one has control of interpretation—only if it is able to achieve in the end what is put into the text at the beginning.[45] Meanwhile, we prefer to say that existentialist theology keeps control of its hermeneutical method by using a concept of reality that is predefined as realized personhood.

We can go a step further and say that the reality of faith is subjected to the criterion that one uses for the reality studied by natural science. It must be universally available and verifiable if it is to deserve the predicate "real," in distinction from fictional or visionary. We touch this possibility in present-day neo-positivism as it protrudes through certain Anglo-Saxon theology. The next sec-

[44] Cf. *ibid.*, p. 104: "All translation involves self-renunciation."
[45] The circle must remain a circle. The hermeneutical circle, however, is not made legitimate simply because it is a circle.

tion will deal with the question of how much the Anglo-Saxon and existentialist theologies have in common.

EXISTENTIALIST THEOLOGY AND NATURAL SCIENCE

Eschaton, resurrection, and reality

In this section, we shall take a look at a side of existentialist theology's view of reality that has been kept in the dark until now. Existentialist theology has not been victimized by reductionist or transformationist tendencies; it has consciously and purposely followed this route. Is existentialist theology so sure of the theological advantage that its position offers that it gladly accepts the reduction in the wages of reality that it requires?

The answer to this question, besides what we pointed to in the previous section of this chapter, brings us to the matter of the relationship of existentialist theology to the natural sciences. We must begin by taking a sounding of the way in which redemptive revelation is transformed into genuine experience of existence, or eternity into the "here and now."[46] We can do this by the use of some typical terminology that offers a rather good general perspective on existentialist theology in general.

The characteristic vocabulary involves the words "eschatology" and "eschatological." (We can speak of it as being characteristic in spite of the nuances that prevail throughout the whole of existentialist theology.) The interpretation of eschatology in existentialist theology betrays the influence of its view of reality on its concept of the Christian faith. Traditionally, eschatology has to do with the end of history, the end of the historical sequence of events. To append the adjective "eschatological" to an event signifies that that event points to the future end of the linear process of time (in which the present is included). The way that traditional dogmatics worked out its eschatology is not our concern here; nor are we concerned with the valid criticism of it that biblical theology is able to make.[47] What does interest us is the linear pattern of

---

[46] The Dutch title of Bultmann's *History and Eschatology—Eeuwigheid hier en nu* ("Eternity here and now")—is inspired; it says volumes about Bultmann's intent.

[47] For this see G. C. Berkouwer, *De Wederkomst van Christus,* II (1963), particularly the chapters on the "signs of the times," the Antichrist, the millennium, and Israel.

history that traditional orthodoxy assumes and of which the eschaton is the historical end.[48]

Nothing could be more foreign to existentialist theology than this understanding of eschatology. For Bultmann, no less than for Karl Barth or Oscar Cullmann, the eschaton is the "final (that is, decisive) revelation" of God. But the description of humanness as existential involves—one could even say, prescribes—that definitive revelation must have a "here and now" character if it is to accomplish something "for me." For the sake of "decision history"—a man in his free responsibility—ordinary linear history loses all real relevance for the humanness of man. That is, history in the traditional sense as a continual succession of events cannot serve, any more than can nature, as an organ through which revelation comes. Quite the contrary. The notion that God would reveal Himself in either nature or history is one of the mistakes of natural theology. In the vocabulary of existentialist theology, natural theology is any pretension to knowledge of God that does not come to reality in actual, authentic, existential encounter with God, for example, any theology that depends on nature or history. Natural theology is metaphysics. This, by the way, shows how many definitions phrases like natural theology are heir to.[49] In fact, since Ritschl the phrase natural theology seems to have become a synonym for all "bad" theologies.

For existentialist theology any theology is bad that pretends to discover revelation of God in nature or history. Christian faith liberates us from this error. It knows no other reality of God than His reality that is "present" in the here and now. To have faith is to turn away from history and to seek no foundation for faith in any event that occurs in ordinary, linear history. Only as faith turns away from any such foundation can it be genuine faith. This is to say that faith is genuine faith only as it lets itself be founded by God Himself in the here and now; faith fails whenever it looks

---

[48] N. A. Dahl, "Eschatologie und Geschichte im Lichte der Qumrantexte," in *Zeit und Geschichte,* pp. 3-18, defends this linear-historical pattern, correctly in our judgment. On the currently popular distinction that exegetes make between eschatology and apocalyptic, see Ernst Käsemann, "Zum Thema der urchristlichen Apokalyptik," in *Exegetische Versuche und Besinnungen,* II (1964), 105-131.

[49] See further Hans-Joachim Birkner, "Natürliche Theologie und Offenbarungstheologie. Eine theologiegeschichtliche Ueberblick," *Neue Zeitschrift für systematische Theologie,* III (1961), 279-295.

to what someone else in the past has said about God. "Today, if ye hear his voice" (Heb. 4:7) is the basic text for existentialist theology's effort to connect revelation and the existential.

This puts us in a rather awkward situation. The same word that sets linear history in the service of revelation for Oscar Cullmann and his theology of salvation history is used by existentialist theology to make linear history wholly irrelevant to revelation.[50] The eschaton makes the linear kind of history obsolete; it cannot be used at all in divine revelation.[51] To do away with linear history does not, of course, mean that it is not important as such, but merely that it is unusable as an organ of God's act of self-revelation.

The adjective eschatological, then, carries the implication that an event so modified cannot be one belonging to ordinary history; an eschatological event is liberated from the confines of history. For this reason, the term "eschatological" fits neatly with the word faith. Faith as an eschatological possibility means that the significance of ordinary history for faith has been nullified. That is, faith has risen above history in new freedom. To use Bultmann's words, faith brings man into a state of "unworldliness"; it "de-worlds" him and so makes of him a man who is in but not of the world.[52] To eschatologize revelation does not, strictly speaking, mean a demythologizing of Christian faith; but it does dehistoricize it. Faith is dehistoricized both from the front (the future) and the back (the past). Everything must be set within the here and now in deference to the correlation between revelation and existence.[53]

The linear future, the expected historical reality, has always been a firm ingredient of Christian faith. Existentialist theology may put a heavy accent on faith "here and now" (Bultmann), or faith that works out tangibly in love to fellow man (Braun); but

[50] For a summary of Cullmann's theological point of view, see his *Heil als Geschichte. Heilsgeschichtliche Existenz im Neuen Testament* (1965).

[51] Cf. Bultmann: "Eschatology in its genuine Christian sense is not the future end of history; rather, history is interlaced with eschatology," "Geschichte und Eschatologie im Neuen Testament," in *Glauben und Verstehen*, III, 91-106.

[52] Bultmann regularly appeals to John 17 to support his understanding of eschatology; but so does Gogarten.

[53] The new "today" is introduced by Jesus. Jesus creates a new turn in history. This is stressed more by Ebeling and Fuchs than by Bultmann. Fuchs writes: "In the events surrounding Jesus Christ the history of human self-interpretation takes a new turn. . ." (*Hermeneutik*, p. 155). This suggests something of a remnant of saving fact in Fuchs' thought.

can it get away with a faith empty of futurist expectation? Can faith ever exist without hope? One is inclined to wonder whether any concept of faith that holds no future perspective can bear a genuine similarity to the faith held out by the New Testament. For if anything is clear in the New Testament, it is faith's marriage to a hopeful perspective of the future. What are the consequences for the structure of the Christian faith of the concept of reality held by existentialist theology? It takes away the past as the decisive time of God's self-revelation; it takes away the future as the decisive orientation of Christian expectation.

Kant was perhaps one of the first dehistoricizers, and without him existentialist theology is unthinkable.[54] Strictly speaking, in all honesty we shall have to admit that Reformed and Lutheran orthodoxy has never been able to do much more with eschatology than make it an appendix of dogmatics (besides using it practically as a warning of the future judgment). Traditional orthodoxy hardly knew what to make of the final judgment and its subsequent events other than to give it a purely chronological relation to the present time. Another sort of future, one that reveals the meaning of things, was recognized by orthodoxy only in general terms, and then in a separate locus of dogmatics.[55] Orthodoxy tended to dehistoricize faith, albeit wholly unintentionally. But in existentialist theology the dehistoricizing was intentional and methodological; it took place in its conviction that a new concept of reality would have many advantages and no disadvantages for theology.

What we are inclined to think of as a reduction is, of course, looked at very differently by its defenders, who see it as the rescue of faith from the cause and effect nexus of history and nature. In this connection, the subject of our present section is the reverse side of that which we discussed in the previous one. Keeping the dialectic of nature and freedom in mind, we can distinguish two movements in it. On one hand, freedom, man in "self-realization," pushes nature and history to the fringes of reality; nature and history tend to move centrifugally. But, on the other hand, nature and history gradually push human freedom towards a central

---

[54] Kant's negative reaction to the notion of a linear-historical eschatology is illuminated by H. A. Salmony, *Kants Schrift Das Ende aller Dinge* (1962).

[55] James P. Martin demonstrates this in his book *The Last Judgment in Protestant Theology from Orthodoxy to Ritschl* (1963).

position in reality—the point of the needle on which the medieval angels danced, swinging unhindered (or undetermined) by nature or history. The impulse of freedom is to keep that point for itself; it must be the genuine centripetal force.

This centripetal movement is a very instructive aspect of existentialist theology. It reveals its apologetic motive. For it seeks to open a new way for faith by means of the view of reality that was demanded by its concept of man as "existence." To put this a little less guardedly, but somewhat more clearly: it wants to develop a new space for faith to operate in, a "storm-free area" that it lacked ever since Kant chased faith out of the arena of nature and history.

What existentialist theology means with this "third way" and how it wants to deploy it apologetically can be seen by looking at the New Testament witness of the resurrection of Jesus Christ. No other point of Christian confession touches the problem of reality at so sensitive a spot. Moreover, no facet of the Christian confession makes it clearer to us how important it is for theology to keep its concept of reality open-ended.[56]

If Jesus of Nazareth actually lived this history, was dead and did rise again, and if the stories of the resurrection do undeniably inform us that the resurrection did occur as "something that happened in history," then no one can prevent the historian from subjecting these events to his own kind of scrutiny with his own methods of historical research. In saying this, of course, we must keep in mind that the historical method operates with a number of presuppositions that play their own demonstrable role, varying with the particular standpoint of the individual historian. But even where the presuppositions have a minimum of influence, the results of pure historical research remain fairly modest. The historian does not get far with the means at his disposal. And what are his means? One of them that interests us here is the concept of reality he works with. This is ordinarily that of the present society as it is centered on specific tasks of science. Why do they not give him bigger dividends? Because the concept of reality that dominates historical science allows no room for other results. The historian of our day is stuck with this kind of rule of thumb: if the historian should apply his criteria to the story of Minerva's birth from

---

[56] By "open" we mean not limited by a predetermined canon of what is possible for experience.

Jupiter and is not permitted to ascribe historical reality to the story, the application of the same criteria to the resurrection of Christ can give only the same results—no historical reality could be allowed it.

Now, there is hardly a Christian who will let the message of the resurrection get lost in this way. The New Testament witnesses to it as the very heart of salvation. But what is one to do with historical science in this regard if, on its own premises, it can accord to the resurrection no genuine reality? There are, in fact, only two main avenues out of this impasse; if one is successfully to persist in holding to the reality of the resurrection as an event of actual history, he must do one of these two things. He can either discover another acceptable concept of reality in which the resurrection can be assimilated, or he can accept the historical event of the resurrection as the event in which one can learn for the first time what reality is.[57]

The first avenue is closed off to us. The whole direction that modern theology has taken is precisely the opposite of this. It is a way that makes God and His acts adjusted to a structure of being that coincides with man's rational structure. In a word, it is a theology built on a metaphysical structure for which truth is constitutionally rooted in the conformity between the thing known and the knowing mind. For it a thing is true because it cannot be otherwise thought of. But the resurrection of Jesus makes clear that theology cannot rely on this metaphysically defined notion. The resurrection is not a rational requirement inherent within a general truth. This first route leads into a morass.

The second avenue leads us into a very different kind of problem. One could argue that the resurrection *tells us* what reality is. With this, theology not only digs up a concept of reality for itself, but threatens to dominate other sciences with that concept. The price we would pay for this unique concept of reality need not be a way between theology and the other sciences, but it does tend to alienate theology from the rest of our scientific tasks. A clear example of this is found in Karl Barth's theology. For many Barth's theology has become a building without doors.[58] And what is true of his theological approach would, if pursued, be true

[57] Cf. Jürgen Moltmann, *Theologie der Hoffnung* (1965), pp. 156ff.
[58] A characterization used by J. Sperna Weiland, "Er is iets aan het gebeuren," *Wending*, XX (1965), 617-622.

of the Christian community as well. If the resurrection of Jesus is preached in terms that have no relationship to the reality in which people ordinarily live and think, the Christian community too would be a building without doors. And this would be a good deal more offensive than if it were true only of theology.

We raise these problems here in order to spare ourselves the temptation of creating instant answers that lead only up theological blind alleys. There *are* answers to the problems. In the first place, practical theology provides the possibility; preaching, pastoral work, counseling, and dialogue offer very realistic settings for answers. The translation of the gospel into the vocabulary of our time comes off best in these practical situations; anyway, it is more likely to be done well here than in the theologian's study. But theologians have to work at it too, if only to support or criticize the practical efforts. There are as many theological answers as there are ways out of the dilemma. This is our bailiwick: we want to understand the answers given by existentialist theologians, who on one hand accommodate to the concept of reality that is part of the Western intellectual heritage, and so declare the resurrection to be a historical impossibility, but on the other hand, in a very different way, by using a wedge in the same concept of reality,[59] seek to hold to the resurrection as an expression of a reality that lies on the other side of ordinary nature and history—the reality of living faith. This transfer of the resurrection from an event in time and space to an event that can escape the categories of causality common to space and time can be described as an existentializing of the resurrection; that is, it turns the resurrection from an event back there to that which says something or does something to us.[60] With this, it is clearer than ever how the existentializing of the resurrection involves the creation of a new space for faith that

[59] Cf. Moltmann, *op. cit.,* pp. 168ff.

[60] A similar effort to cut through the categories of space and time is found in the use made of the term superhistorical. For example, Wilhelm Knevels, *Die Wirklichkeit Gottes* (1964), sees Jesus' resurrection as history, but then as history in a "supernatural-superhistorical" sense. That is, it is not historical in the sense of a "historically observable event within the reality of time and space." One could compare this with Barth's position in 1938 when he abandoned the terms *Urgeschichte* and *Übergeschichte* because, he said, revelation begins and ends with God's revealing Himself in our space and our time. Cf. his treatment of the resurrection in the same vein, as occurring in our time and space, *Kirchliche Dogmatik,* IV/1, pp. 368ff.

not only delivers it from the scientific method but from anything that science can ever offer as its accepted results. Any alternative, it is said, would mean that the most intelligent and capable scientist would be best qualified to be the best believer;[61] and, what is worse, Christian faith would exist only by the grace of science, which would mean in effect that it would never have its own right to exist.

Existentialist theology, thus, is a response to a specific notion of nature and history. Formed by an unbroken nexus of cause and effect, nature and history form a closed circuit. What makes nature nature, and what makes history history is this causally determined closedness. There is no exit, no break-through. Any effort to restore the possibility of a break-through must mean a return to supernaturalism.

It would be possible to show that existentialist theology is guilty of confusing a "methodological interpretation" of history and nature for history and nature themselves. Moreover, the terms nature and history are given a meaning by a prior decision that men have made about the world around them. But, for our narrower purpose, we wish only to point out that the existentializing of the resurrection is a by-product of the causality principles of natural science, which control for the most part our understanding of things in time and space. Faith itself cannot breathe in this climate, and it tends to exile the "facts" of redemptive kerygma to the outer edges of history. The opposite movement is also clear: nature and history, in their hard factuality, shove faith out of time and space into a factless world; that is, the facts of time and space are sliced off faith, leaving it with its own untouchable factuality, the factuality of its own self-expression. We have noted this before, and are here only approaching it—centripetally—from another side. The haven for faith consists in this, reality is not determined by metaphysical or positivistic criteria. In these senses, the resurrection is not a reality. The reality of the resurrection is not a matter of universally valid truth. It is real, even though its reality is not that of an event of past time. Were it set in past time, we would run head on against natural and historical sciences. The

---

[61] The same was true of Schleiermacher. Ebeling underscores the same thought; "faith," he says, "is not a matter of knowledge." But he muddles his thought by adding that by "knowledge" he means that which is "scientifically verifiable" (*Wort und Glaube,* p. 404).

resurrection is a reality insofar as my faith comes to expression today in a form that *says*: resurrection. The resurrection is a way of saying that I am as "committed as Jesus was."[62] Faith is real *as faith;* its reality is nothing else and nothing more than faith itself.

The questions about the resurrection, as we have seen, focus on the problem of what reality is. Existentialist theology tries to break through the problem by changing the concept of reality. At least it circumvents it by lifting it from the old setting of time and space and making it a matter of "what is significant" for our present existence as persons. Under pressure from scientific method— especially as used by historical criticism—it takes the phrase "something happened," which used to refer to an event of the past, and translates it as a "happening" in the sense of an event, or experience in the present. This redesign of reality is a brilliant way out of the embarrassment that one faces when his culture accepts a premise about reality that has no room in it for the resurrection of Jesus Christ.[63]

The Christian church simply has to respect the existentialist undertaking; it has to find a way to wedge itself into the concept of reality held by the culture to which it seeks to bring the Word. It can and may do nothing less. But we are also obliged to say that existentialist theology has ignored the most crucial factor of all in the proclamation of Christ's resurrection. The resurrection cannot be made to fit our going concepts of reality. And this is not because God's actions fall outside of human concepts of reality just because they are acts of God. This ancient heresy is still as wrong-headed as always. What sets God and man against one another is not their respective divinity and humanity; what divides them is man's stubborn pursuit of disobedience, his refusal to be God's partner on earth. Thanks to "us men" six million Jews were offered as sheep to slaughter; thanks to "us men" millions of people are hungry in a world that has more than enough for everyone; thanks to "us men" the world hangs under the threat of nuclear destruction that no one can guarantee will not happen.

[62] The previous gives the terminology of Fuchs and Ebeling in this connection.

[63] The presuppositions at ferment in concepts of reality are so dispropor-tionate that we are tempted to call the whole question of reality a pseudo-question. H. Berkhof says that existentialist theology provides an evasive answer to the modern problem of secularization, "God in Nature and History," *Study Encounter,* I (1965), 142-160.

There is not a single reason to suppose that God has to accept *this* world of "us men." He does not accept it either; this is what the cross teaches us. He renews it. Better, He re-creates it. And Jesus Christ in His resurrection is the beginning of the re-creation. He is the start of a new world, of the eschaton that is not adjustable to this old world any more than guilt can be adjusted to innocence, curse to blessing, re-creation to destruction. The message of Jesus' resurrection is "thanks be to God," the message of an event for which our ordinary design of reality has no analogy. Yet, it is a reality within our reality. This is why the resurrection of Jesus Christ, wherever and whenever it is spoken of, is on a collision course with the design of reality conceived by *every* culture. The message of the resurrection is the announcement of a new creation, the eschaton, and for this same reason, it comes as a critique, a disqualification of our obsolescent designs of reality.[64]

There is more to the encounter between the resurrection message and our concepts of reality than a tragic misunderstanding, more too than the difference between the changes in concepts of reality that occur from one generation to another. We cannot sever the reality of the resurrection from the reality of the new creation that the resurrection represents in our old world. Nor can we dissociate our modern culture's discovery that the resurrection is impossible from the dark riddle of how a culture can exist under conditions that have no room for Christ's resurrection.[65] This is the background of many current theological questions: How can the resurrection of Jesus be believed as really having happened? How can it be proclaimed in a culture that holds a concept of reality dogmatically excluding the possibility of the resurrection event?[66]

It may be objected that the original message of the resurrection comes to us in verbal clothing that is not suitable for the reality as it must be proclaimed today, and it may then plausibly be argued that the very historical description of the redemptive event is part

[64] Moltmann, *op. cit.,* pp. 156ff.

[65] Gerhard Noller rightly calls attention to this. See his *Sein und Existenz. Die Ueberwindung des Subjekt-Objektschemas in der Philosophie Heideggers und in der Theologie der Entmythologisierung* (1962).

[66] From this we see that the profoundest problem of "theological address" is not a scientific theological problem, but that it is part of the scandal of the gospel; when we theologize about guilt and redemption, we are giving words to our guilt and our redemption.

of that alien verbal clothing, and that we—precisely in order to keep the reality of the resurrection—ought to dissociate ourselves from the historical garments in which the message originated and stick to the anthropological category of human existence.[67] There is an element, a large one, of truth in this method of putting the case. The apostolic witness does come to us in a form given it by a specific culture that is foreign to our own. There is a sense in which we have to distinguish between "what is said" and "what is intended" (*das Gesagte* and *das Gemeinte*).[68] The last chapter of this book will be devoted to this distinction. To this point we have only wanted to show how existentialist theology's decision that faith and revelation must not be sought in nature or history was really made by way of a predecision concerning what reality is and can be.

The New Testament places the great events of salvation on a map (Palestine) and on the calendar (in the first third of the first century A.D.). This is questioned by no one, including existentialist theologians. Though one may stubbornly insist that the historical picture the New Testament gives belongs to a culturally antiquated view of reality, he must still argue that Paul and the rest of the New Testament writers place Jesus' resurrection as an actual event in history, even though the writers were not in fact interested in the historicity of Jesus' resurrection. This is an improper way to approach any writer, and thus a wrong way to approach the New Testament. It is wrong on two counts. First, one may claim that he understands better than did the author what that author really intended by his words, but he cannot justify a claim that the author's *expressed intentions* were not really his. When a writer tells us what his words mean, we hardly have a right to claim that the writer is wrong about his own intentions. To claim this right is to make an end of all reasoned interpretation of any document whatsoever. Second, what the New Testament, and Paul in partic-

---

[67] This is, in fact, the position taken by existentialist theologians. Bultmann has tried to give this thesis an exegetical as well as an anthropologico-philosophical defense. Whatever in Paul does not serve to prove the point is disqualified as misunderstanding or inconsistency in the apostle. See Bultmann's *Theology of the New Testament* for a discussion of I Cor. 15; also, *Glauben und Verstehen*, II, 179.

[68] On this terminology, derived from Bultmann, and the related question of how we can get behind the intention of the words—the question of the hermeneutical circle—see the collection of essays by J. Moltmann, *Anfänge der dialektischen Theologie*, II (1963), 50ff.

ular, spells out as its meaning is that the cross and resurrection of Jesus Christ form an event that took place decisively "out
there" (*extra nos*) for us here (*pro nobis*).[69] The unmerited,
gracious dimension of the message of salvation *pro nobis* rests on
this event that took place *extra nos*. What falls away in the process
of existentializing the gospel is not the form of Jesus Himself, but
the *extra nos,* the "out-there-ness" of His saving work.

Walter Kreck puts it as a question: Is the New Testament
message that we are saved "by means of Christ" not watered down
to a matter of "after the fashion of Christ" if the act of Jesus on
our behalf—the cross and resurrection—is no longer relevant to
our faith?[70] In our judgment, all the questions that we can put to
existentialist theology concentrate on this one point. Is the unique
character of biblical salvation, distinguished from all other messages of redemption, found in the fact that we are saved "by
means of Christ" as a "once-for-all" event? Can the uniqueness of
New Testament salvation be discovered in a satisfying measure
within existentialist theology and its definition of the message of
salvation (the kerygma)? Is it not true that it is only as the
"by-means-of-Christ" dimension remains at the heart of the gospel
that the gospel will arouse the offense that the New Testament calls
the scandal of the gospel?

Perhaps our analysis has been able to bring to light sufficient
material to justify the question marks that we have placed behind
existentialist theology on this point. Existentialist theology, in spite
of what it claims, stands at a crossroads. As long as it refuses to
take history seriously as part of the gospel—the "once for all" as
the corollary of Christ's significance—it can accept two consequences: (1) With respect to salvation itself, it can choke on the
dualism that is implicit in its starting point, and so recommend an
escape from the world as the real salvation of man; this is to say
that it can swallow a gnostic, world-despising concept of what
salvation is; and (2) with respect to the means of salvation, it can
be content with an ethical humanism—with roots in the historical
Jesus—such as is sometimes encountered in Anglo-Saxon theology. Both salvation and the means to it are thus watered down into

[69] Notice the obviously important role of the ἐφάπαξ in Paul (Rom.
6:10); also, κατὰ καιρόν (Rom. 5:6).
[70] "Die Christologie Gogartens," *Evangelische Theologie,* XXIII (1963),
169-197.

something other than what is offered in the New Testament. And this very discrepancy with the New Testament betrays that the message of the New Testament has not been translated, but has been radically revised once it is reshaped in the conceptual apparatus of existentialist theology. The introduction of modern concepts of reality and their use as hermeneutical molds for the interpretation of the New Testament—or, better, the accommodation of the New Testament to the limits defined by modern concepts of reality—serves to silence the New Testament at its most crucial juncture.[71]

This leaves us with one conclusion: a canon for interpretation that prohibits the text from being itself is disqualified from service. If the New Testament claims no more for itself than to be a testimony of human religious sentiments, and if we can listen to Paul in the same way we hear a bird sing, the existentialist theologians are on the right track. It would also open the door to any other way of listening to the religious language of the Bible; there could never be a "wrong" interpretation. But if the New Testament, according to its own writers, does have a meaning that is bound to what is said, an interpreter is duty-bound to cull the meaning out of the thing said. He has to deal with the meaning that the author himself intends. A key to the interpretation of the Bible that cannot do this has become a subjectivistic prejudice. And it can keep its respect only if it puts its cards on the table and admits that it is not trying to get the author's meaning, but that it is using the author to elicit the inner thoughts of the interpreter.

Reality and language

Can we solve the problem of reality by means of language? One can only be thankful for the new perspectives opened up for us by linguistics. Philosophical and anthropological work on language has also been helpful. These studies have made one thing undeniably clear: one's language and one's concept of reality are of one piece. The function to which people put language mirrors the way

---

[71] Again one can see here how dependent the existentialist theologians want to make the question of the so-called "point of contact." But with them, the point of contact threatens to devour the real matter. Karl Barth has been accused of the opposite; with him the real matter (grace) is said to devour the point of contact (creation).

they have oriented themselves to their culture. Therefore, the broadest context of a given text is the culture in which this text originally functioned. But this very interlocking of language use and reality concepts makes it impossible to resolve the problem of reality by a simple research into language. The language scholar himself uses ordinary language; he has no super-language or para-language at his disposal. This is why he can recognize the concept of reality that protrudes from language, but at the same time he cannot escape the fact that his own language is bound to a given concept of reality, which he in turn uses to set up criteria for the examination of the language of a given text.

In other words, a study of language can expose the concept of reality that is betrayed in that language, but it can do no more than that. It cannot make a judgment on that concept; nor can it change it.[72] This is how it is that the collision between the reality of God's acts in Jesus Christ and our own design of what reality is comes to light in language. We are not able simply to say, to put in words, what God actually did in Jesus Christ. Paradoxically, if we could put the matter simply, we would lose what God actually did in our world to redeem and re-create it. A deeper investigation into the nature of language only makes the tension between *our* notion of reality and *God's* reality in the resurrection of Christ the more violent. The tension can be removed only if we set up our notion of reality as the norm for all that can be called real, and thus make the language of the New Testament fit our norm. If we turn the language of the New Testament into an expression of self-interpretation, if we reduce it to existence-language, we solve the problem. But at what cost?

Existentialist theology consistently works with language in this way. It does not pretend to be an *analysis* of language, as does the kind of theology inspired by neo-positivism, but it does mean to offer a theory of language. This sounds like a more modest claim. But it could hardly do anything else. For the *proton pseudos* of existentialist theology is woven into its view of language: the language of objectivity *cannot* be authentic language. One must

---

[72] Unless language is revelation, which it is, if we recall that classical theology reckoned man among the media of revelation. But then we are talking about general revelation, and this in Reformed theology is not revelation of man's salvation.

recognize language as an objectification of the self. Only as we manage this can we be rescued out of mere history and nature and set again within the subjectivity of our personal existence; only as we are able to see through language can we become authentic persons. Clearly, existentialist theology has adapted its view of language to its view of man and thus to its concept of reality.

A theology based on linguistic analysis helps us even less. Inspired as it is by neo-positivism, its understanding of language betrays the same sort of prejudgments we found in existentialist theology. The difference is that these prejudgments filter the Christian tradition even more finely than does existentialist theology. Paul van Buren is a case in point. In his case, we may better say that prejudgment transforms rather than filters the tradition. If we define reality as "that which I find significant for my existence as a person," we still have something outside of ourselves which has significance for us. Let it be true that this reality outside of myself is found only in the total situation of my sense experience, there is still something "out there." But in neo-positivist theology, the remnant of objectivity, whatever there is outside myself that triggers my experience, evaporates. The subject is left to himself. If Bultmann's theology can be described as "qualified subjectivism," we could justly call this theology "radical subjectivism."[73] There is a jump from subjectivity to subjectivism here. Subjectivity is intended, subjectivism is not, but the latter is the necessary result. The jump is taken by Van Buren as he reshapes the function of language to accommodate the view of reality that he has elected.[74]

Taking his place in line with Hume and the British empiricists, Van Buren gives language no more to do than to express reality that is *empirically* verifiable.[75] This truly fences language in; it tells us why the predecessors to analytical philosophy were called positivists. Neo-positivistic linguistic analysis deserves to be distinguished from the old positivism. It is, to be sure, faithful to the

---

[73] P. R. Baelz, *Faith, Fact, and Fantasy* (1964), pp. 52ff.

[74] Quotations below are from Van Buren's *The Secular Meaning of the Gospel* (1963).

[75] There are, of course, other kinds of verification than empirical. We would still be involved in the misunderstanding of faith as "holding something to be true" were we to subject faith to the positivistic verification principle. Since faith is not identical with "holding to be true," the content of faith must be verified in another way.

rule that a statement must be verifiable if it is to deserve the adjective meaningful. Unverifiable statements—statements about God, for example—cannot be accounted for by it. And so they cannot be taken either as truth or falsehood. As far as factual content is concerned, they are empty.

But this does not mean that, as religious statements, they are absolute nonsense. There is a significance to statements about God, but a significance about something other than God. We *seem* to be saying something about a reality out there when we say things about God, but *actually* we are dealing with something very different from factual reality. We are certainly expressing our feelings, revealing our outlook on life, demonstrating our engagement with certain matters; a great variety of possibilities is open here; and linguistic analysis can enlighten us on the meaning of our religious language. But one thing statements of a religious nature do not do for us is to provide information about God or His acts. For God is plainly unverifiable, and the word "God" is empty, without meaning by itself. Religious statements have sense, or meaning, as responses or attitudes that people experience within and over against the verifiable world and which they in turn recommend to others. Religious statements are "the language of discernment and commitment,"[76] the language in which believers reveal the "blik" that they have of the world.[77] The Christian's "blik" is very much related to the person of Jesus, whose way of life is the inspiration for his engagement in the world.[78] Jesus is the model for men—not to be imitated, for the world has changed too much to allow for imitation; but for the pattern of being engaged with the world as He was.

The Christology involved here is one that moralizes Jesus of Nazareth into a model for a "way of life." The focus on Jesus is drastically simplified in comparison to the model that the existentialist theologians see in Jesus. But Van Buren makes Him a

[76] Van Buren, *op. cit.*, p. 105.

[77] Van Buren borrows the term from Hare, and considers it to be serviceable because it is able to provide "a noncognitive conception of faith, rather than a cognitive conception." Faith does not exclude commitment; it *is* commitment.

[78] For Van Buren Jesus' way of life is contagious primarily because of His freedom.

model no less than they do. And there is no clear reason why a simple model will not do as well as a complex one.[79]

But we are concerned with the reality toward which faith points. And for this the question of Van Buren's several levels of language is important. That there are different levels of language is obvious enough. A chemical formula is a different kind of statement from a philosophical theory; "I love you" different from "God is my song." But what kind of language is the last statement? When one says "God is my song," does he convey information about God? The word "is" cannot have the same sense in "God is my song" as it does in "The wall is ten feet high." But it is something like the statement, "John is made of iron." No one would be tempted to verify the last statement with a physical analysis. But the statement does tell us something about John. It tells us something real about him, though by way of metaphor.

In the same way, the way of metaphor, "God is my song" tells us something about God. Metaphors and images move in the field of inexact language. But they perform well in telling us about something outside of ourselves. Is it not in fact a very common way of conveying descriptions of things and people? Why, then, is Van Buren sure that a sentence like "God is my song" is unable to convey any information about God? It is not because of its metaphorical character. Just as John can be a man of iron in truth without having any metal content in his body, God can be a "song" without having any actual musical content in His being. The language itself gives us no reason at all for insisting that "God is my song" provides no factual information about God. The reason for saying that such language tells us nothing about God lies with convictions that have nothing to do with linguistic analysis. It lies in a code or canon of meaning. A decision has been made about meaning prior to any analysis of language. The decision is this: only verifiable statements have meaning. This is what convinces Van Buren that a sentence like "God is my song" cannot possibly give us any truth about God. This is why he insists that such language tells us something only about the person who

[79] Jesus functions as a "model" not only for Van Buren, but for John Wren-Lewis, Manfred Punge, Manfred Mezger, Herbert Braun, Fuchs, Ebeling, J. A. T. Robinson, and J. M. Robinson. What is objectionable in all these men is that Jesus tends to be swallowed up in the notion of His being an example, more or less ethically conceived.

makes the statement. In this case, when I say "God is my song" I am only saying "I sing."

Of course this is what I am saying. Van Buren is not wrong in calling our attention to the verifiable element in Christian faith. I could hardly say "God is my song" had I never lifted my voice in song. God enters our lives, our experience, our discoveries, our emotions in ways that are verifiable indeed. (This, of course, is not to say that God is verifiable by means of the experiences.) But if we accept the meaning of "God is my song" according to the canon of verifiability, and let it mean only "I sing," we have made two extremely important prior decisions which land us in a subjectivistic camp.

The first of these decisions is that it is legitimate to interpret an author contrary to his own intentions. Here we enter hermeneutics again. The man who says "God is my song" patently intends to tell us something more than that he sings. He intends to tell us something about the God of Israel.[80] And when Jesus says "He who hath seen me hath seen the Father," He is clearly saying much more than: "Stop looking for the Father."[81] Van Buren reads Jesus in a manner that plainly contradicts Jesus' intentions, as a superficial reading of the context of the statement reveals. But he is sure that the word "Father" *cannot* tell us anything at all about God.[82] Once we agree that an interpretation that contradicts the intention of the speaker is a valid interpretation, we have jettisoned the whole business of interpreting language. If interpretation does not mean getting at the speaker's meaning, every interpreter is right and no one is wrong. But this is really to say that there is no right interpretation, and therefore no interpretation.

[80] Naturally, there is a religious language that can be explained as the language of commitment on a horizontal plane. To say "God damn" is not to utter a terrible prayer to God; it only says that the speaker is terribly angry. So the pious phrase "God is good" may only mean that the speaker is happy. We have chosen these rather rough examples on purpose, for they demonstrate that Van Buren's views about religious language and its content assume a very superficial sense of religion. That is, he brings on speakers for whom, if shown that their words are in fact without content, it would make no difference at all.

[81] Van Buren, *op. cit.*, pp. 146ff.

[82] "Simple literal theism is wrong and qualified literal theism is meaningless" (*ibid.*, p. 99; cf. also pp. 103 and 146ff.). Behind Van Buren's radicalism lurks not only the conviction that the word "God" is worn too thin for it still to be serviceable, but more, that modern science has made such statements as "God speaks" or "God acts" obsolete.

The second decision involved here concerns the basis of this strange hermeneutics: the acceptance of the positivistic concept of reality that lurks in the shadows of the verification principle. No one denies the need for logical-empirical verification, any more than the demand for personal involvement in reality. Theology *has* been known to get away with considerable nonsense. But by applying the verification principle consistently, we would be putting up a fence around a section of reality and demanding that everyone recognize only what is inside the fence as real, before so much as an investigation is made of things outside the fence. The verifying person becomes the judge of what can be given the name reality. With this, the verification principle sins against the primal mark of all reality, that reality is autonomous. It need not beg the right to exist; it is there just because it is there in its own right. Theology does well to shun any temptation to attach itself to any theory of reality other than this primordial one. Once it gives up on reality's own inherent right to be, it falls victim to subjectivism.

Van Buren leaves us with the impression that he is bent on driving theology into the philosophical prison of subjectivism. His subjectivism is of the post-Kantian kind, which trades in reason for "verifying understanding." That which cannot stand up under the "verifying understanding" is considered nonsense.[83] Speech about God cannot be verified beyond the fact of the speaker's commitment in life. This is why such speech lacks sense. The only sense we can impute to it is the sense of the speaker's engagement in life, the speaker's own "blik." Religious language is the language of a man's "blik."

This entire line of thought has no basis at all in language analysis.[84] Why cannot religious language provide information

[83] Cf. John Wren-Lewis' question, "Does Science Destroy Belief?" in *Faith, Fact, and Fantasy*, pp. 11ff. He says that we have learned from Freud to understand religion as a "paranoid fantasy obsession" (p. 28). In spite of this, he says, faith is necessary; but he means faith in the endless possibilities open to creative men in the physical world. "There is a real possibility, in other words, that the idea of resurrection might well be an expression of the ultimate achievements of technology" (p. 43).

[84] It rests in a prior decision that the word "is" cannot apply to God. As an example, though not a parallel, the exclamation "Coffee!" may mean not only that I desire coffee, but that there is coffee to be had. I owe this illustration to my colleague G. E. Meuleman.

about God and also be a testimony to my own engagement with life? When Van Buren allows religious language to say something only about the speaker, he has made language a prisoner of his neo-positivistic prejudice. Language does not prove the point Van Buren makes in *The Secular Meaning*; language is forced into the service of his point of view. And he gained his point of view from a philosophical pretension.[85]

Does Van Buren keep faith with his own presuppositions? Or does a real theological content break through his neo-positivist fences? We can at least entertain some questions on the matter. For instance, what role does Jesus of Nazareth play in his theology? If we take Van Buren at his word, that religious language is the "language of discernment and commitment" and is not a pointer to religious reality, we have to suppose that religious language pointing to Jesus of Nazareth does not really point to a historical person named Jesus, but only betrays a certain "way of life" accepted by the speaker. Van Buren's insistence that there must have been a historical Jesus if Christian faith is to make any sense at all would appear to hang in the air at this point. An actual Jesus in Galilee is not needed to provide for the experience of freedom's allure. Does this suggest that Van Buren still demands a real Jesus in history because he believes a unique revelation of God took place in Him? We are almost inclined to suppose this to be the case; otherwise, why is Jesus important historically? But if it is the case, the gospel has a dimension much less "secular" than Van Buren wants us to suppose.

It is not clear whether Van Buren denies God's existence or whether he only wants us to recognize that the *word* "God" has become "meaningless." That is, does he admit that there "is" something more than man, while he questions whether that "something more" can be meaningfully talked about? If the latter possibility is true of Van Buren, we could describe his theology as a rather crude negative theology; if the former, we shall have to call

[85] "God loves me" means the same as "I feel secure, wanted, of value." Since only the second statement is verifiable—"can be paid in cash"—the first statement has no meaning; it can only be the troubled waters in which mystery fishers fish. This is all very coarse and rough, and only shows how exaggerated Van Buren's reasoning from his own predecisions becomes.

his a crude form of neo-positivistic criticism of religion. There are strong hints in Van Buren that could take us to either position.[86]

The question of how to interpret Van Buren is not as profound an issue as it may seem to be. Using his neo-positivist criticism, Van Buren supports his negative theology; and, vice versa, his negative theology is used to establish his neo-positivistic prejudices. If we begin with the verification principle, we are obliged to insist that what the understanding cannot verify does not exist. At least we must insist on this unless we are willing to admit that reason can accept statements that are meaningless. And this we obviously cannot admit. Since all speech must have meaning— which is to say, must be verifiable—nothing exists beyond that which our understanding can identify as existing.[87] With this, we are linked up with the approach of negative theology. All we are capable of is a this-worldly experience; but a this-worldly God is a contradiction in terms, for God is by definition other-worldly. We cannot speak meaningfully of God, for we cannot speak of God in a this-worldly manner. And since only meaningful speech is real speech, speech about God is nonsense.[88]

We shall have to get back to the question of negative theology that we touched on a moment ago. At this point we must distinguish between Van Buren's neo-positivist theology and existentialist theology. The two have this much in common: both are rooted in a decision as to the place of man as a subject within the reality that surrounds him. But a theology inspired by neo-positivism does not think man's place as subject is problematical; it does not feel the need to chisel a place for man in nature and history. The job of mastering life is accepted by Anglo-Saxons more calmly than it can be by Teutonics; for the former life seems a puzzle to be solved, for the latter a cataract to be survived. This is a psycholog-

[86] Van Buren's negative theology is explicit in this sentence: "Silence is the first and best answer to questions concerning the 'Father'" (ibid., p. 146). "Negative theology" is a classic method of speaking about God in which He is described in terms that "negate" traces of finitude in Him. He is, for instance, unlimited and unconditioned; this is a way of saying what one cannot say of God.

[87] Not to deny the existence of God means nothing as long as one also says that every statement about God is meaningless. For the latter is to say that God can play no role in human life.

[88] Van Buren, op. cit., p. 65. Putting negative theology to an apologetic use ("this Unknown is the true God") is a device that has been employed by Christian theology since the third century.

ical response, and it admittedly adds little weight to the argument. But we do mean to suggest that in respect to the place of man as a subject the two theological streams do not cross one another. The major difference is that existentialist theology is not prepared to call talk of a human encounter with God "nonsense" language. On the contrary, it declares this encounter to be the real source of human-beingness as existence. But we must add that the correlation of revelation and existence sets the encounter with God outside the sphere of nature and history. Here the two streams of theology meet again. That is, the centripetal movement, which we called the second facet of existentialist theology, moves in the same direction as neo-positivistic theology.

Under pressure from natural science and history, neo-positivist theology pushes God outside of time and space; but since there is nothing beyond time and space, it pushes God out of consideration altogether. Van Buren reminds existentialist theology of its half-way-house position. Experience of a nonobjective reality is, from a neo-positivist viewpoint, utter nonsense. Horizontal reality is all the reality there is.[89] Van Buren's complaint is understandable; he focuses on the positivistic element of existentialist theology and keeps asking why this element should, at the last moment, be sidelined. But this touches on the very heart of existentialist theology, as we have already seen. It *needs* a positivistic component over against which man—as freedom—is truly man. And, on the other side, it *needs* a free man—the person—over against which nature is truly nature. In this balance of polarities the whole thought pattern is maintained. It is responsible for the strong anthropological bent of existentialist theology: everything centers on the maintenance of man's authentic humanity in and over against this world of nature.

Neo-positivistic theology is doubtless a good deal more optimistic, perhaps more superficial, and even more humanistically attractive than is existentialist theology.[90] It misses something of the drama that existentialist theology feels, man's struggle against the powers. It misses the heroics of man's futile resistance to the

[89] Van Buren, *op. cit.,* p. 65.

[90] P. R. Baelz makes this judgment (*op. cit.,* p. 60). It is accurate in view of Van Buren's reduction of Christian faith to a moral disposition without any cognitive components. "There is no arguing about 'bliks' " after all, because they have no intention of conveying knowable content (Van Buren, *op. cit.,* p. 155).

powers and the excitement of his successful bid against them at the moment of God's gracious revelation. But both theologies miss still another drama, the drama between God and man. And this lapse unites them. In neither are God and man seen as at odds with one another (guilt). And so in neither theology does anything have to happen to bring them together (reconciliation). As long as both are blind to this drama, they are not at odds with one another. The existentialists interiorize revelation and the neo-positivists "horizontalize" it. One existentializes and the other ethicizes the tradition of faith. But there is no real conflict between these. And there is no significant option between them either.

Looking over all that has been said, a couple of points should be made in summary.

Existentialist theology—and the same can be said for a theology oriented around neo-positivism—makes its appeal as a theological project constructed on the ground provided by modern, post-Kantian subjectivity. It offers itself as an alternative to metaphysical theology, which made its appeal as a theology constructed with the aid of a thought apparatus that assumed an objective ontological structure of being. It was a theology built without much regard for the subject, and therefore could make a claim for universal validity. The entire metaphysical thought apparatus was put in use in order to set forth statements about God and His acts as scientifically valid. Theology, in this sense, proved itself again to be a child of its time.

In its bid to be scientific existentialist theology turns itself toward subjectivity. To be a man implies speaking about God, whether one thinks of God in terms of the categorical imperative that man experiences as a *given* of his humanness, or whether he thinks of God in terms of the ground or depth experiences that every man has by virtue of being man (Schleiermacher).

This does not demonstrate the notion that one can build a theology on the basis of subjectivity; that is, it does not show that one can begin with anthropology and end with a legitimate theology. The final chapter will give us a chance to raise this question again. But we must come to the conclusion here, I think, that *this* subjectivity—the subjectivity rooted in existentialist theology's definition of man—can offer us no basis at all for a theology that lets the biblical witness come into its own.

Existentialist theology—and this applies even more forcefully to

theology inspired by neo-positivism—addresses itself to man under
the "powers," to modern man who no longer can be addressed by
metaphysical theologies. It is a theology with intense "concern for
understanding," as Van Buren puts it.[91] And as long as orthodox
Protestant theology shows itself lacking in this concern—and here
we must think of theological deeds, not merely professions of
intent—existentialist theology will have a greater hearing precisely
because of its concern. But the price that existentialist theology
pays for this open ear is very high. It sacrifices nature and history
to the "powers" in order to pose as the theology that plucks the
brand of human existence from their burning. God is exiled from
nature and history. And we have seen what this implies. Existentialist theology in this respect is a product of the "powers" from
which the gospel seeks to rescue men; this, in fact, we share with
existentialist theology. It is a theology that is eager to be under the
powers and at the same time wants to be *theology,* indeed a God-
and Christ-confessing theology. This invests it with heroic appeal.
But does it not stand closer to Greek drama with its tragic man
than it does to the biblical speech about man and his covenant
partnership with God on earth and in time?

Existential interpretation has its limits, we are told.[92] This is
fine. It is also true that it has made an interesting, although not
extremely original, contribution. It does seek to give the subject its
rightful place, and it tries to provide that place by using a new
hermeneutic. We agree that the subject *must* be recognized as
having a significant role. There can be no argument with existentialist theology here. But what is at issue is the definition of the
subject. Who and what is man? This is the decisive question in
theology.[93] If anyone talks merely about the limits of existential
interpretation of the New Testament, he means to say that he
agrees with its strategic stress on the acting subject as a legitimate

[91] Van Buren, *op. cit.,* p. 57.
[92] George Eichholz, "Die Grenze der existentialen Interpretation," *Evangelische Theologie,* XXII (1962), 565-579.
[93] Not only in hermeneutics. One can hardly be too insistent in asking
about the role of anthropology in theology. The concept of man that one
has frequently determines the kind of theology one constructs, or Christology, as we can note in such new Roman Catholic constructions as those of
Rahner, Schillebeeckx, Schoonenberg, and Fiolet. Anthropological constructs determine one's Christology in a striking way. This was true from
the days of the early christological confessions; but we have gotten so used
to these that we hardly notice their anthropological backgrounds.

factor in theology, but does not agree with its definition of that subject. At least this is the way we chose to speak of its limits. The subject that existentialist theology posits is the subject who thrusts himself forward and who can maintain himself as a subject by thrusting himself forward as a person; that is, he can be a subject only by maintaining himself in isolation. Turning theology into this kind of anthropology is an acute threat to genuine theological formation.

Does God, in terms of this definition of man and his existence, become a mere "as if" proposition, a kind of limiting concept?[94] When Robinson, and Van Buren too, though more cautiously, speak of love as the be-all and end-all, with no need felt for talking about God at all, do they leave the theological door wide open to the charge that God is merely a predicate of a creaturely phenomenon, a kind of pious adjective to lend special dignity to the love of man for man? Is there a real difference between God as an "as if" postulate and the fuzzy adjective "divine" applied to man and his existence in love?[95] Can we really speak of God in any other way than as the He (subject) who addresses us as You.[96] And does not any other way of talking about God leave us right where Feuerbach left us?[97]

But we must stop asking questions. Our purpose in raising them is only to register the objections that can be brought against the concept of subject used by existentialist theologians. This subject never gets beyond itself; at least it provides no possibility for corrections of its own definition.

If this concept of man commits us so decisively to anthropological theology, we want to ask whether we are indeed stuck with it.

[94] On this danger see Albrecht Peters, "Betrachtungen zum sittlich-personal geprägten Gottes- und Christusbild des 19. Jahrhunderts," *Kirche und Dogma*, IX (1963), 122-166. The heavy emphasis on God's transcendence offers no guarantee of a fruitful doctrine of God.

[95] We are forced to wonder about this when we hear Van Buren say that linguistically speaking there is no need for the word God, since whatever is intended by the word can be put into other words as well (*op. cit.*, pp. 67f.).

[96] K. Barth, *Kirchliche Dogmatik*, II/1, p. 291. Barth speaks of God's perfections in order to indicate that God is subject. As protection against predicative, objective talk about God, this phrase is a useful one, though we prefer a less formal terminology and choose to speak of the names of God.

[97] Cf. Rudolf Lorenz, "Zum Ursprung der Religionstheorie Ludwig Feuerbachs," *Evangelische Theologie*, XVII (1957), 171-188.

Existentialist theology holds that we are, as a self-evident truth, and proceeds on this assumption. It insists that it is the only scientific way. But this says considerably too much in our judgment. Acceptance of this definition of man is a matter of a free decision. There is nothing about it that constrains us to accept it. It is not a scientific datum; it is a choice that one can make or reject without so much as touching on the question of the scientific respectability of theology.

The last remark can be strengthened by another argument. Is the self-projection of man as freedom over against the world of nature and history—the world, that is, of force and unfreedom—a primeval human experience? Or is this "experience" rather an unverified postulate? We think that a good defense can be made for the latter. The freedom versus nature scheme is really an emergency escape from man's experience of unfreedom. Taking refuge in existence as the place where freedom, and thus personhood, is preserved is really a philosophico-anthropological response to man's actual experience of the absence of freedom; it is a response with soteriological overtones.

We cannot deny the factuality of the situation to which existentialist theology seeks an answer. Present-day Western man is hemmed in by the threat to his personal freedom that comes from the powers of science and technology. The answer of the freedom versus nature scheme is one answer. This does not only mean that it is one among others, including better ones perhaps. It also means that the freedom versus nature scheme is not an original given, but is a product of West European philosophy, which has accustomed itself to thinking in terms of freedom and, from this habit, has developed the freedom-nature polarity in order to help man create the possibility for his own self-determination. One must keep in mind, then, that only a fraction of Western culture is spiritually in condition to develop itself in freedom. The project of free self-development has the mark of the elite on it. There is something uncharitable about it. It smacks more of Greek philosophical ideals for the aristocracy than of the Christian ideal for everyman.

Another remark follows from the last. A phenomenological study of Western man does not suggest that people generally can size up the whole human situation and create a place for themselves within it. By a strange coincidence, an age that talks more about man having come of age is also the age that has witnessed the mass man, the lonely crowd, and the depersonalization of men. Again, we suggest that the appeal to freedom must be seen as an escape from our cultural situation. It is not a basic anthropological given discovered through scientific analysis of man; it is an escape from a dilemma. Without doubt, man's experience of himself as something alien to himself belongs to the fundamental human experience. But to experience oneself as "other than" history and nature, and as freedom over against these powers, is not a universal experience. What that experience is we shall seek to explain in the following chapter.

Chapter Four

REVELATION WITHIN THE MOLD OF HISTORY

- Beginning with tradition
- Tradition and history
- A history that says and does something
- Faith and reality

REVELATION WITHIN
THE MOLD OF HISTORY

The assault on metaphysical theology has ended in a *cul-de-sac*. A justified protest against one way of doing theology created a new way of doing theology that leaves more question marks than did the theology against which it rose in protest.[1] Existentialist theology stakes everything on a view of man that leaves it defenseless against a radical anthropological conquest of theology. Its capitulation to anthropology resulted from a theory of reality implied within the existentialist view of man, the theory that reality is limited to what man accepts as real in free responsible decision (in the case of existentialist theology) and to what can be verified by proper scientific method (in the case of neo-positivist theology). But our task is not completed with this negative judgment. If theological dialogue is to be fruitful it cannot end with negative assessments. Hence, we must ask, where do we go from here?

There is no way back to metaphysical theology. Orthodox Protestantism may be tempted to seek the way back, but it is really closed off, not only because the presuppositions on which the traditional metaphysic must function are foreign to modern thought and life, but also because the crusade of modern theology has not been without good fruits that we must thankfully accept. As to the fact that the presuppositions of metaphysical theology have evaporated, we can be brief. We feel no demand to construct a rational system in the style of the great medieval system builders and the brilliant Protestant scholastics. The reason for this is

[1] Hans Georg Geijer criticizes metaphysical theology from quite another point of view. Answering W. Weischedel's attempts to construct a new metaphysics, Geijer claims—perhaps correctly—that God is the predicate in *every* metaphysics; God or the divine is the ultimate ground of the totality of being. The limited self is central, and in the course of time the predicate was dropped without being missed. Cf. Geijer, "Theologie des Nihilismus," *Evangelische Theologie,* XXIII (1963), 89-104.

simple: people no longer make use of the traditional, metaphysically rooted, rational concepts. For Christian faith to go back to these
would be tantamount to adopting the language of a ghetto or the
esoteric language of art. All of modern theology, from Bultmann
to Van Buren, alerts us to the fact that the church can make itself
a museum piece in the modern world.

The rationality of faith, which once fit into an entire world-and-
life view, was a kind of rationality that was maintained in harmony with the thought system of Aristotelian science and philosophy.
But if we assume that this concept of rationality is obsolete, we
cannot use it to demonstrate the rationality of faith.[2] No one
would be served by such an effort, and a motive for faith cannot be
distilled from it for anyone at all. If we seek motivations for belief,
we must seek them in the direction of the functional power of
Christian faith or in the observable and experiential reality of it.

In this respect we are obliged to respect the modern theological
structure. Certainly, one might object that there are conceptions in
modern theology that smack of the modern *Zeitgeist,* but in the
first place the *Zeitgeist* possessed our orthodox fathers as much as
it does modern theologians, though in a different way (without
Aristotle there would have been no Reformed orthodoxy), and
secondly we are not given the luxury of a timeless theology nor the
right to desire one. Something more must be said about this last
remark. But now we want only to support the thesis that the
rational and philosophical framework in which metaphysical theology must fit can no longer be used (at least in that form) and that
for this reason alone a metaphysical reconstruction of theology is
out of the question. History shows that the Christian faith can be
shed of its Thomistic framework without losing its Christian character. Did not the Protestant Reformation help to shake off the
medieval philosophical garments in which the gospel had been
clothed? In fact, the very abandoning of Aristotelian metaphysics
opened the door for the rise of the scientific method.[3]

Our remark that existentialist theology has given us a fruitful
harvest needs some explaining. The imbalance between the num-

[2] Note well that it is *this* concept of rationality that is obsolete. To
abandon it does not necessitate accepting irrationality. Christianity would
gain nothing by jumping from the frying pan of a certain kind of rational-
ism into the fire of irrationalism.

[3] Cf. P. O. Kristeller, *Renaissance Thought,* (1961), pp. 44ff.

ber of questions we have raised about existentialist theology and the number of answers we shall provide in this chapter will require defense. In this chapter we shall sift the harvest of theology described in the previous chapters. We can begin with the preliminary gesture of saying that modern developments of theology have set hermeneutics in the center of the theological enterprise, and have done this with sound insight and intuition. A theology that pretends to be Scriptural—and does reformational theology want to be anything else?—can only be grateful for this modern development.[4] It is a separate question whether existentialist theology has, in fact, practiced hermeneutics, or whether it has been content merely to develop a hermeneutical theory. In any case we have learned from it that reformational theology demonstrates its reformational character when it makes hermeneutics its chief concern. For hermeneutics is simply a way of solving the problem of the Ethiopian eunuch: how must we read the Scriptures in a way that brings us *understanding* of them?

A further consideration intrudes at this point. Theology since Schleiermacher has set hermeneutics off against metaphysical pretensions in theology. We must not be offended by this. On the contrary, the whole hermeneutical attack against metaphysical theology must be recognized as an effort not only to put the Bible in the center of things but also to provide a proper place and role for the believing subject in the process of understanding. It seeks to set this subjective function within the whole of theology, not merely to give it legitimacy but to keep it under control. The objections that we have registered against the existentialist use of hermeneutics apply specifically to that particular use, not to the demand that hermeneutics be central to theology in general. The mistake of existentialist theology is not its demand that man be recognized as the horizon within which the biblical text must speak. What other horizon could we imagine? Our objection is against the view of man that controls existentialist thought and defines that horizon. Hermeneutics must not be shoved aside or minimized, but it must be rescued from theological fruitlessness[5] by bringing it in at a point other than that to which existentialist

[4] Ebeling correctly notes this, *Wort und Glaube,* pp. 22ff.

[5] Existentialist theology raises many questions of understanding, but it submits little dogmatic material.

theology leads us. One's conception of truth must not be hemmed
in by the criterion of what he can understand. As we have seen,
existentialist theology made its decision on this when it decided on
the nature of understanding and on what, therefore, *can* be understood.

How must we go about the creation of a more fruitful theological approach? We should like to have a try at providing theology
with a foundation—in rough format—that will not be handi-
capped by such dilemmas as personalism versus ontology or existential interpretation versus metaphysics. For one thing, dilemmas
like these are too inexact to be of much help to theology; for
another, they set up the problem in a one-sided and distorted form.
We can best proceed in a quite new direction, hoping thereby to
find a way that stays clear of metaphysical theology without laps-
ing into existentialist theology. We must follow theology's *own
way*—not merely a third way. Theology has every right to develop
itself scientifically *sui generis*, and so keep its own character. It
ought to be able, for instance, to speak in a personalist as well as
an ontological way. That is, it ought to be able to extract the
elements from both existential interpretation and metaphysical theology that belong to the inalienable province of theology.

The discussion that follows, then, is an effort to sketch roughly
how theology's own way ought to run.

Beginning with tradition

The protest against metaphysical theology had its beginnings in a
growing appreciation for subjectivity. In fact, the entire theological
development discussed in this book could be described as a struggle for the claims that subjectivity has on objectivity, a struggle
that ended in a complete conquest of objectivity by the subjective.
There is a tragic element in this history; needless and unintentional
casualties have been suffered. But every struggle between objectivity and subjectivity is abortive, and always leads to a debacle. One
of the two parties is always virtually eliminated. If we substitute
the word "God" for objectivity and the word "man" for subjectivity, which is really the case in the final analysis, we can see how
futile any competition between the two is. Putting them in opposition, it appears that God, if He really does exist, exists to the
disadvantage of man, while man, if we wish to speak of genuine

manhood, exists at a cost to God and His honor. It is clear that neither man nor God can be his genuine self in this relationship. Each negates the other. And this is more pronounced to the degree that one stresses one or the other of the false polarities. Theological and philosophical balancing devices have frequently been devised in an effort to find the right relationship between subject and object, which Herman Bavinck once called "the heart of a good theology."

The question is whether any relationship or balance can ever be freed from this latent tension that seems always to be present within theology. Past efforts have not succeeded in this. Nor is the problem a new one. What we often refer to as modern subjectivity was not invented by Kant or Descartes (the man usually branded as the culprit). Certainly both men were tremendously significant for the rise of modern subjectivity. But both of them upset the balance between subjectivity and objectivity as part of a traditional problematic that had long occupied the European mind, a problematic that was felt precisely because of the tension between objectivity and subjectivity. Modern subjectivism is part of a heritage as well as a product of it.

This consideration helps to illuminate the tragic side of modern thought. Metaphysical theology cannot simply be explained as a desire to objectify that which cannot be objective, namely, God. Even less can modern subjectivity be dismissed as a desire to eliminate God. From this, as will be elaborated later in the chapter, it is clear that we cannot simply choose the one or the other. Both objectivity and subjectivity have roots in a deeper background than this. Here we shall point to one part of the background, which has fermented in both ways of doing theology and which, in each case, is quite legitimate: each came to the defense of what had been neglected by the other.[6]

To get to the problem: there are theologians who, in reaction to the antimetaphysical prejudice of contemporary theology, are tempted to fall back into another metaphysical theology. This amounts to a rejection of the light that Calvin and Luther have given us. Others, aware that theology has to do with something

[6] In the Western cultural situation, the objectivistic and subjectivistic views of the world cancel each other out continually. Consider, for example, the revival of positivism in the form of neo-positivism, or the *nouvelle vague* and the *roman nouveau* in the world of films and books, as an indication of how objectivism is gaining new vogue.

other than metaphysics (an insight they may have gained from the
Reformers), fall into the hands of an existentialism that denies
Reformation theology as much as does metaphysical theology. For
this reason—and we must be perfectly clear on this—the tension
or opposition between objectivity and subjectivity can only bring
us into theological frustration. Existentialist theology—which in its
way tried to overcome this problematic—serves as a lighthouse for
us.

Concretely, this means that the last thing we must set against
modern subjectivity is the very objectivity that gave rise to it.[7] To
do so would leave the discussion stalemated. But what is more
important, it would cut us off from a very legitimate subjectivity,
one that lives and breathes by another power than does objectivity.
This subjectivity cannot live by itself; it cannot, in the end, stand
by itself. But we must attempt to demonstrate that such a subjectivity really is possible.[8]

To achieve a point of view that is not trapped in this kind of
vicious circle, theology must begin with tradition, that is, with the
material of faith that has been handed down to it. This gives us a
new hermeneutical point of departure. The basic question asked by
hermeneutics is not "what can I understand?" but "what is the
meaning and scope of the material of faith that is handed down to
me prior to all my own reflection and, for that matter, my own
existence?"[9] We could use the word canon instead of tradition
here, but the word canon suggests a rather limited notion of the
authority of the books of Scripture. And this authority is what is at
issue. For this reason, we prefer the more phenomenologically
tinted word "tradition," in the sense defined above. Concretely,
what we mean by this is the biblical witness.[10]

[7] Pannenberg's *Offenbarung als Geschichte* does not avoid this mistake.

[8] In saying this, we are in line with H. Bavinck and Berkouwer. That is,
we are concerned to assert that subjectivity has a legitimate place in the
large arena of revelation and faith.

[9] A similar point of view is expressed by Herman Diem, *Sine vi sed
verbo. Aufsätze Vorträge Voten* (1965), pp. 246-270.

[10] A. A. Van Ruler remarks about the "shamefully exaggerated fear of
the tradition idea in reformational Christianity" (*Reformatorische Opmer-
kingen in de Ontmoeting met Rome* [1965], p. 46). His entire chapter on
tradition is most instructive. On the large role that the tradition idea played
in Paul's thought, see H. Ridderbos, *Heilsgeschiedenis en Heilige Schrift*
(1955), pp. 40ff.; L. Goppelt, "Tradition nach Paulus," *Kirche und Dogmatik*, IV (1958), 213-233; Klaus Wegenast, *Das Verständnis der Tradition
bei Paulus und in den Deuteropaulinen* (1962).

There are three things that recommend beginning with tradition. (1) Tradition binds dogmatics to the Christian church. To be sure, making dogmatics a function of the church can raise questions too; church and dogmatics ought to be relatively independent of one another if they are to serve each other. But they should not be separated so far that theology forgets its service to the church. Where theology is being done for the church, the tradition of the church is what it is occupied with. When theology defines its own task, it is obligated to reckon with this fact.

(2) By beginning with tradition, theology is also recognizing a specific claim that tradition makes, namely, that understanding of tradition calls for something more than hermeneutics. This claim does not disqualify the hermeneutical approach of modern theology. Tradition, after all, has to be interpreted. But it does tell us that the question "what can *I* understand?" is not the proper starting point for an understanding of *this* tradition. The subjectivistic question of modern theology makes a pretension that runs amok over the claims that this tradition makes concerning itself.

(3) There is also a logical reason for beginning with tradition. Christian tradition has, through history and until the present time, claimed and received men's fidelity. The continuity of that tradition must be explained either as an enormous error or as the result of the powerful claim that its content has on men. If Christian theology decides for the latter reason, of course—as it has—it must reckon with this dynamic influence of tradition. Theology must begin with that which was handed down originally, that which the church has carried through the ages and which is therefore the content of its preaching. To begin with tradition is to accept the premise that preaching has a content that is meant to be taught us.[11]

The last argument leads to the methodological question of the approach that a hermeneutically oriented dogmatics must make. That it gets us into this question is not accidental. Methodological questions are never *merely* methodological. The method one uses

---

[11] Goppelt (*op. cit.*) sees Paul's notion of the kerygma as being not only "actual preaching" but also "a declaration with permanent content" (pp. 218, 219). Wolfgang Schrage, *Die konkreten Einzelgebote in den paulinischen Verkündigung* (1961), speaks of "the teachable and transmittable aspect of the apostolic enterprise" (pp. 129ff.). To speak about a kerygma without the specific content that belongs to it makes the Word mere general revelation.

to get hold of the material reflects the view that one has of the material, at least at the beginning. This does not bring the question of method into doubt. Every method has to demonstrate its usefulness to the material at hand. Any approach to the subject is shown to be a sound method only in terms of its function. The method that is chosen must prove itself by *serving* the material rather than mastering it.

The advantage of starting with tradition is, as we have said, that it forces us to pay attention to the role of history within theology. It forces us to give due weight to a problem that theology has never been able to solve since Lessing's famous difficulties with it. We are faced here with the most critical point of all theology, but also the most promising. This issue forces us to face great questions with which theology has wrestled in the past, but it also promises us answers insofar as theology is capable of giving them.

To begin with the most obvious: tradition tells us that the material with which theology works comes to us by way of history. A heritage implies the existence of former generations. (It also implies future descendants, but more of that later.) The mention of history and antecedents raises a series of questions. To list a few of them randomly: how did this tradition begin? who are the people who handed it down? why did the tradition not die? what kind of history does the tradition itself have? Questions like these are part of the approach that the Christian church makes to the content of faith when it respects the traditional character of that faith. They are all questions about historical states of affairs or about historical processes; they are all questions that belong to the sphere of the scientific discipline called historical research. A tradition must be looked into—in awareness of all the problems involved—with historical criticism. This is why we call it tradition, that is, a handing down.[12]

Thus theology cannot and may not remain aloof from historical-critical research, because every tradition offers itself as an object for historical research, and for theology to try to exempt itself from this would be for it to sacrifice scientific responsibility. Theology may—indeed it must—demand that historical research be some-

[12] An excellent critique of the historical-critical method is given by Jürgen Moltmann, "Exegese und Eschatologie der Geschichte," *Evangelische Theologie*, XXII (1962), 31-66.

thing that has nothing to do with a subjectivization of tradition; for the same reason, historical criticism may not be identified with liberal theology.[13] Moreover, theology must cooperate in the continuing attempt to form a serviceable historical-critical method. For example, it must insist that historical criticism make no other pronouncements than those that apply to the situation that it can approach with its own methods. That is, it must prevent historical criticism from pronouncing that those unique situations that its method does not cover are not real situations. It must insist that the historical-critical net be big enough to include unique situations.[14] We are not making a decision at this point, nor are we approving of any method; what we are doing is merely orienting ourselves to existing efforts to pursue historical-critical research properly.[15] Meanwhile, we need not conceal the fact that even when done properly, with a concept of history that is not reduced to cause and effect, historical-critical research can create many problems for Christian theology. We shall also see how, and in what degree, the historical character of Christian tradition remains the greatest stumbling block for every attempt to subjectify or existentialize Christian faith. But honesty compels us to admit that its very strength is also its weakness.

We have mentioned what is fundamentally implied by tradition: the material of faith comes to us by the route of history. The second thing that must be said is directly related to it: the question of the significance that this tradition has for me, its bearing on my life, and whether a matter that comes to me from the past *can* have bearing on my life. The fundamental implication of tradition is that it claims to have a bearing on us, but for the present we shall leave the matter in question form. This will give us more room to work into an answer.

---

[13] For the same thought, see Betti, *Die Hermeneutik als allgemeine Methodik der Geisteswissenschaften*, pp. 31ff.; and Ebeling, *Wort und Glaube*, p. 48.

[14] That it is possible to pursue historical-critical research in a way that is not determined by a prejudgment as to what can and cannot be true is demonstrated by Günter Bornkamm, *Jesus von Nazareth* (1956). The resurrection of Jesus is an example of a unique event, in the strictest sense.

[15] See, for example, the discussion between Pannenberg (in *Offenbarung als Geschichte* [1961]) and Günter Klein (in *Theologie des Wortes Gottes und die Hypothese der Universalgeschichte* [1964]).

Tradition and history

The heritage that the Christian church has received from previous
generations and which it must in turn pass on to following ones
serves as a witness to the historical partnership Israel had with
God which culminated in a partnership with Jesus Christ as the
unique representative of this same God. The tentative character of
this christological formula must be underscored. That the Christian tradition has the character of a witness to a partnership that
took place in the past, a witness that uses the words and concepts
of the past, rests finally with how Israel's God reveals Himself. He
is the God who, as a covenant partner, goes with, speaks with, and
works with Israel. He is the God who reveals His covenant partnership in Jesus Christ, albeit in a unique way. *What* is handed
down is essentially this: the story of what Israel experienced in
partnership with God.

This accounts for the elements of confession and praise in the
language Israel uses as it witnesses to its partnership with its God.
In this sense, we may call biblical speech subjective. The speaker
does not extract himself from his report. Quite otherwise. He
confesses himself as involved wholly in what he has to say. He
cannot speak of Israel's God in any other way; to speak of this
God without being involved would be to speak of another than the
God who enters into partnership. But this is to say that the
subjectivity we meet in the Christian tradition is unique, and is of
another sort than is ordinarily met in the subjective-objective
dilemma. It stems from another source; it is part of the unique
character of biblical experience. The uniqueness of the God about
whom Israel's spokesmen write demands that a witness to Him
come through the subjective experience of Israel, its prophets, and
its apostles. The tradition that the Christian church carries through
history flows out of Israel's knowledge of God; it springs from a
partnership with God in time past, which was told to others,
handed on, and made into a tradition so that successive generations can be summoned to partnership with the same God.[16]

We have been emphasizing the Israelitish-Jewish character of
the biblical images, expressions, concepts, and stories, and calling
attention to the historical associations of this material. This is the

[16] For a more extensive treatment of this fundamental idea, see the
author's *De Mensvormigheid Gods,* especially pp. 289ff.

premise from which we approach the entire problem. Because of
the difficulty of this theological problem, what follows should be
considered as only a suggestion that is open to improvement, that
indeed is very much in need of improvement. It is put down here
only to help advance the dialogue within orthodox Protestant
circles.

We proceed from the thesis, then, that the tradition—or, if you
will, the *fides quae* (the faith that is believed)—is historically
generated, historically formed, with all that goes with this fact as
far as concerns world views, cultural contexts, historical conditionedness, and the like, because faith—the *fides qua* (the faith
that believes)—is historical (that is, it rises at a certain point in the
history in which partnership with Israel's God occurs). The very
notion of partnership carries history with it. We must insist here
that the so-called historicity of Christian truth—it exists, after all,
only in historical form—is not a conclusion forced on us by some
kind of spirit of the times, and is even less a lapse into the morass
of relativism.[17] It is a given of God's self-revelation. God's revelation occurred in a historical way in His partnership with people
of definite historical limitations. Hence, the knowledge of God is
historically formed for us within the inheritance of faith.

For a theology that has grown up with the aid of concepts
provided by Aristotelian metaphysics, appreciation of the historical character of the Christian tradition is hard. But this historical
dimension must be acknowledged if justice is to be done to the
Bible itself; any other approach to the Bible fails to honor the
Bible as it comes to us. Not only in the Bible, but in the history of
the Bible itself—the faith history of the church—the knowledge of
God is and has to be historically formulated. Christian truth
cannot afford to sacrifice the mark of history if it wishes to retain
its specifically Christian character. It is essential to Christian truth
that it cannot be incarnate in unchangeable formulas.

The historicity of Christian truth is rooted in the historical
manner of human existence. Man exists historically; this is why we
have to pass the truth on from generation to generation.[18] But

[17] Christian truth means Christian doctrine as the "doctrine of truth." We
read this genitive as an explanatory genitive: the doctrine that is truth.

[18] This is the current way of establishing the necessity of tradition. Cf.
Ebeling, *Wort und Glaube*, pp. 33ff. It is also common in Catholic circles.
Cf., for example, E. Schillebeeckx, "Exegese, Dogmatik und Dogmentwick-
lung," in H. Vorgrimler (ed.), *Exegese und Dogmatik* (1962), pp. 91-114.

there is a second and more basic ground for it: God Himself calls forth and effects the historicity of truth in His very self-revelation. We must insist on this if we are to be true to the trinitarian way of talking about God. To try to rise above the time-bound character of human formulas is to fail to admit human limitations by trying to invest man's formulations with the quality of eternity. But even more important, it is to fail to appreciate the trinitarian manner of God's existence, to enclose God's revelation in the past, and to eliminate the Spirit as the power by which Israel's God comes to man today in a revitalizing and liberating companionship. In a word, if we refuse to see that the biblical tradition is typically Hebraic and fail to honor it as such, instead turning it into something timeless, we will be forcing today's reader to set himself back into the cultural situation of two to three thousand years ago (we shall all have to become Israelites). This would turn Israel's God into a God who rules only over Israel instead of the Lord over the universe.

To speak of God in His self-revelation in the trinitarian manner—Israel's God, who showed Himself as God in Christ, goes with us in the Spirit—prevents the Christian faith from being converted into the acceptance of a set of principles for the construction of a philosophy of life, even a philosophy that is painted Christian. Christian faith is something else; it is partnership with God. Only by speaking in a trinitarian way can we satisfy this essential definition of faith. The hermeneutical question must have a trinitarian answer.

Having laid down the historicity of Christian truth as a trinitarian premise, we immediately face this important question: does its historicity negate the possibility of unchanging truth? How can Christian doctrine be final truth if it is at the same time historical? This, in a sense, is the heart of the problem that concerns us here.[19] It requires as much care as candor. The great concern of us all for the certainty and security of faith forms the very real background to our discussion. It is in this concern that we take up the problem.

First of all, the historicity of Christian truth does not imply that it is on that account less reliable and trustworthy. The reliability of

---

[19] The extraordinarily complicated role these questions play in Catholic thought is illuminated by Berkouwer, *The Second Vatican Council and the New Catholicism* (1965).

Christian truth is the spiritual heart of the Christian tradition, both within the canon of Scripture and after it. The variety of ways in which the New Testament talks about the foundation of faith carries with it an affirmation of the certainty of what is believed; faith is not a gesture of insecurity; it is not a substitute for certainty. Faith is a synonym for certainty.[20] Were Christian truth assumed to be less than certain, being a Christian would make little sense. But the question of Christian truth is this: how can we express it theologically and at the same time embrace the fact of its historical character? How can we avoid a short-circuit between the certainty of Christian truth and the historicity of faith? How can we speak about Christian truth in a way that best reveals its own unique nature?

The certainty of Christian truth does not rest with timeless or eternal propositions. Christian truth is not called "truth" in the sense of consisting of many timeless, eternal formulas. The biblical vocabulary for "truth" in general, but especially the specific (and more particularly, the later) New Testament passages that speak of the "teaching of the truth," clearly point in a direction other than to eternal abstractions.[21] In the quest for security, we must not look for unhistorical, timeless formulations in the Christian tradition, which we can then hold on to with certainty because they are eternal. This has often been used as the solution to the problem; but this method always betrays what it seeks to achieve. It seeks to escape uncertainty by declaring that what it believes is "superhistorical," and thus it refuses to take seriously the historical character of Christian faith. It does not dare believe that faith can survive within history. This kind of faith requires "eternal truth" for its certainty. But the same can be said about existentialist theologians, who also seem afraid to believe that the historical character of Christian faith is a blessing. The escape from the historicity of faith for them is not by a metaphysical route but by the avenue of existentialism. They require eternity, although they call it "eternity here and now."

[20] Christ is called "foundation" in Rom. 15:20; I Cor. 3:11 (cf. Eph. 2:20). This foundation is powerful enough (II Tim. 2:19ff.) to secure the building of God (the church) (I Tim. 3:15). It is remarkable how personally the New Testament tends to speak of the foundation.

[21] This is not accidental. On the many meanings of the word truth, depending on the context in which it functions, see C. A. van Peursen, *Waarheid en de Taal der Wetenschap* (1963).

We must dare to relate ourselves to God's own method of self-revelation. We must not seek our certainty by demanding that it belong to a super-historical or timeless category, but by holding on to the historicity of faith in all its dimensions, without fearing that doing so will necessarily take something away from the certainty of truth.

Our thought must be led by God's concrete self-revelation, which comes to us in history and summons a response in history. The response summoned by revelation creates the historical "material" of faith. We must keep in mind the role that man plays in the event of divine revelation. We achieve a workable grasp of the problem only as we wholeheartedly admit the historicity of all responses of faith. We must not too quickly ask whether some elements of faith are not exempted from historicity. There will be no such elements as long as God's revelation summons human beings to pass on to others faith in Israel's God and His Christ.

There is, however, what we may call the *continuity* of faith formulations. The certainty of Christian truth, faith in its foundational dimension, does not reveal itself in the category of timeless truths, but in the form of *historical continuity*. Christian faith speaks of God in no other than human ways, which is to say in no other than historical ways. Christian faith and its talk about God is never in conflict with God's historical partnership with man; nor does the continuity of the historical statements of faith conflict with the historical character of God's way with men. On the contrary, this continuity—amid the discontinuity of life in general— is felt and heard throughout the tradition. The continuity of faith and truth is as much a part of Christian tradition as the historicity of faith and truth. Therefore, we must search into the background of this continuity.

The background or efficient cause of this continuity lies in God Himself, the knowledge of whom is passed on by tradition. He is continuous, that is, He is the same through the ages. His attitude and benevolent will do not change (Ps. 102:28; Mal. 3:6). He is the same yesterday, today, and forever (Heb. 13:8). This is why, in all the responses of faith that rise from partnership with this God, continuity always exists alongside of discontinuity. And it is within this dimension of continuity that (speaking now very tentatively) Christian truth arises in its trustworthy constancy. Only in this way does the trustworthiness, the certainty of Christian truth remain a matter of faith, in contrast to sound reasoning, which feels no need of faith at all. We must keep in mind that the continuity of faith does not diminish the historicity of faith. Continuity is not unhistorical; the historical need not be discontinuous. The permanence of the knowledge of faith as well as its changeability is the fruit of the *historical partnership* in which God reveals Himself to man. Faith confesses that continuity does exist in this historical situation. That we can speak of continuity rests on a knowledge of and trust in Israel's God; without trust, we cannot know the continuity of the truth of faith. Continuity of Christian truth, then, is an article of faith.

With this approach we are able to accept the full weight of the historical and (most important for our discussion) we are in a position to see the real significance of the human contribution of language and point of view. Of course, orthodoxy has always confessed a certain human contribution to the truth of faith; but our theological task is to indicate the true role and scope of this human dimension. The theology of orthodox Protestantism has not always managed this. Its own point of view, understandably enough, usually prevented it from giving the respect due to the human factor.

We must now indicate how important it is for faith itself that the human element not be filtered out. For this, we shall use three theological themes that illustrate clearly the human element, which themselves are understood only as the human role is adequately acknowledged in them. We shall begin with a brief discussion of the theological doctrine of knowledge; then we shall discuss a few problems of hermeneutics; and finally something about the nature of faith statements.

(1) We are now in a position to speak about the mechanism by which we make images.[22] We could do this only after we had established the human or subjective contribution to all faith statements, a contribution required by the very way that God reveals Himself to men. Now, the forming of images is an integral part of our everyday knowledge and our making of judgments. But it is *also* part of our relationship to God.[23]

[22] By concepts we understand—to use the language of homeopathy—a D-quantity refinement of *images,* a refinement achieved by abstraction. The background of this remark is the idea that language as used in ordinary communication serves, not to define, but to point to things.

[23] The word "also" here is important; one should not read it as "only."

church has formed images of salvation, of the Messiah,
Christ, His person and His work, and the fruits of His work,
of God Himself. These images are always put into words. In
fact, the formulations we give to our faith are concepts of God,
His work, His salvation, and His future as they are set in words.
This is what is meant by image-forming. This process goes on
constantly. Words like "God," "salvation," "grace," "redemption,"
all bring forth images; otherwise they would not have the power to
speak to us. We can only tell *what* they say to us by using pictures
that are given to us by our cultural and physical environment. We
can talk about "reconciliation" only if we have a *picture* of conflict. But this is why "grace" does not in fact speak to many
Christians; they are not able to make images of it.

What about the word "God"? When Van Buren says that the
word "God" does not have meaning for many and that it therefore
does not have the power to signify anything, he has a basis in fact.
But how has this situation come about? Theological tradition,
including the orthodox tradition, is not free of blame. Theology
has consistently frowned on making images of God; to make an
image of God appeared to violate His invisible essence. We can see
the results of this taboo all around us. After centuries in which any
representation of God was disqualified as a mere anthropomorphism, the word "God" really has no concrete or vital content for
many people, including Christians. In this respect, Van Buren's
theological project is an outgrowth of traditional negative theology.
In this tradition the subject-object problem had gotten horribly
tangled—a problem that was haunting theology long before Descartes disturbed the exquisite balance between subject and object
that medieval theology had achieved. Looked at from the perspective of this problem, God is considered too great to be portrayed as
an object. He is transcendent, and a mere man must not make
images of Him. A man does not have the mental reach to make
representations of God. As a result, image-forming came to be
mistrusted in Christian theology. And the suspicion of image-
making can be laid at the feet of the problem of subject and
object, man as the subject over against God who is transcendent
and therefore unthinkable as a representable object.

Provided that we keep in mind the unique character of the
subjectivity that theology is concerned about, we can insist that

image-making is indeed a genuine ingredient in faith and a legitimate part of our knowledge of God. The primary biblical illustration of this is the anthropomorphic character of God.[24] Every
biblical writer presents God in the image and likeness of man, the
Hebrew man in particular. From this Feuerbach concluded that
God is merely a projection of man: we create God in our own
image. And what was orthodoxy's standard reply? Theologians
dug their defenses more deeply in the theology of negation; that is,
they used Feuerbach as a new reason to say that God can have no
theologically valid representation. But this was all wrong! Of
course, not every image of God is adequate, nor can it be certain
in advance that any given image of God will escape the judgment
implied in the Second Commandment. What is prohibited in this
commandment is putting God on the same level with the gods of
the world and thus robbing Him of His freedom to be who He in
essence wills to be, Israel's covenant partner.

But Christian theology will be well served if it, in response to
Feuerbach, not only admits to forming images of God, but demands that images form a necessary part of our knowledge of
God.[25] The writer of Genesis 1:26ff. stresses the theomorphic
dimension of man; he says that being a creature of God means to
look like God. We must either disqualify a great deal of biblical
language, including that passage, or we must recognize the legitimacy of forming images of God. Images form part of the question
of who God is, because He in reality corresponds to some images,
though not to all. The images of God and anthropomorphisms
that biblical writers use are adequate ones. Men are prone in this
area as in others to distort their own understanding of themselves
and thereby make false images of God on the basis of their false
images of themselves. But even when distorted, all anthropomorphic speech about God contains a kernel of truth. The Second
Commandment does not attack image-making as such, but it does
attack images, especially cultic images, in which Israel's God is not
honored as the covenant partner that He is and wants to be, the

---

[24] See the author's *De Mensvormigheid Gods*, pp. 277ff., for an elaboration of this.

[25] If anyone is fearful of this, he should recall that the *reality* to which
images and concepts are related is independent, since it does not originate
from the ordinary mechanism by which images are formed. This requires
everyone to be critical of all imagery, even images that he does not reject.

He who desires to become a You in our response to Him.[26]

Do our images of God have a correspondence in reality? We ought not to answer this question with a dialectical Yes *and* No about images in general. Rather, we must answer by a critique of concrete images. The question must always be: "Can *this* image serve?" This is what orthodox Protestantism has tried to do: its failure was in attacking not just certain images, but *all* of them, including the concrete anthropomorphic images presented by biblical writers. In this orthodoxy has been a poor guide. For it is precisely to these images—in which the humanity of man is mirrored—that reality corresponds. God is that concrete He who becomes a You in our response to Him; He is the You to whose faithfulness each generation anew must trust itself (Ps. 78:1-4). Knowing Him, we must maintain a critical reserve toward all possible images of God, including those that are claimed to be biblical. This critical reservation is the only proof theology has that it takes the Second Commandment seriously; the only proof, that is, that it really wishes to let God be God.

(2) The role that historicity, and thus the human factor in faith, plays in hermeneutics leads to one of the central questions of the entire hermeneutical problem. Since tradition is wrapped, so to speak, in history, we are obliged to make a distinction in the body of this tradition—including Holy Scripture—between the witness of revelation on one hand and the cultural situation in which this witness finds a sounding board at particular times. That is, we must distinguish between witness and its historical sounding board. To make this distinction is only to conform to the manner in which God's self-revelation comes to men. Scripture gives us God's self-revelation in the form of Israel's own knowledge of that

[26] The creation of man as the only legitimate image of God has always been the basis for interpersonal relationships. In this sense, Braun, Robinson, and Van Buren are certainly right: God puts a claim on us in the claim that our neighbor has on us. But insofar as they identify God Himself with this claim, they are forcing God into the frame of general revelation. Van Buren denies any sympathy with general revelation and brands natural theology as the seedbed of all theological sins. When we say that Van Buren forces God into the frame of general revelation we are not, of course, saying that Van Buren works with Thomistic categories; we are saying that he confines God's revelation to a revelation of our fellow man's claim on us, a revelation other than that witnessed to in preaching. In this sense, it is true, I think, that Van Buren's concept of God is a concept limited to general revelation.

revelation. That is, revelation comes in a form that is inseparably bound up with a specific cultural and historical context.

Failure to make this distinction leads to biblicism, a fact that is apparent in the history of orthodox Protestantism. Despite its worthy motives, biblicism is an aborted hermeneutics. Its most prominent characteristic is a refusal to distinguish between the biblical witness and its sounding board. It is driven by a fear lest truth be lost to historical relativity, a fear, however, that gives rise to a typically fundamentalistic rejection of any critical analysis of the problems of faith. It grounds its rejection of critical understanding in this area on a suspicion that critical understanding is always wedded to unbelief. Biblicism, especially when it is rooted in fundamentalistic fears, is disastrous for faith in these revolutionary times. It demands that the Christian assert that both the biblical witness and its cultural sounding board, together and inseparably, are absolute. This is why Christians were sometimes obliged, at cost of their orthodoxy, to accept the notion that the world is 6,000 years old. And this is also why, in reaction, other Christians have concluded that the biblical witness and its cultural sounding board are relative. Each theological position evokes the other.

Orthodox Protestantism has asked with good reason: Is there a criterion by which to distinguish unfailingly between elements of the sounding board into which the witness was given and the biblical witness itself? It is essentially this question that is being asked in efforts to pinpoint what particular message a passage of Scripture is concerned to get across to us. How one goes about determining what that message is need not occupy us here. In general, the particular message of the text depends on the scope that the text is thought to have or that the interpreter thinks he must define in order to get at the text's real message. But the notion of a text's scope is ambiguous; and the whole hermeneutical problem gets involved in this ambiguity. Defining the scope of the text is a way of making the distinction between the witness given and the sounding board of the witness. But at the same time, when we raise this problem we are already indicating that we know the particular purpose that a given passage has, a purpose that gives us a lead in understanding Scripture. In this way, defining the scope of the text in reference to the intent or matter of the text becomes an impossible task. Or, looking at it from the other side, one could say that it becomes far too simple, for one is trying to verify the scope that the text has in reference to its message, while in fact it has been predetermined what the message is in order to define what the scope is. At any rate, the definition of the text's scope must answer to this circular verification if it is to be considered an acceptably delineated scope.

How then can we proceed? We must admit that the church at work need not have nearly as much difficulty with this problem as theology does. When Luther, and for that matter all reformational Protestantism, insisted that the biblical witness to Christ is the real message of Scripture, and that Scripture must be read in terms of this message, he was generally correct. But how can this view be defended if one refuses to base it in the church tradition that has always read Scripture as a whole in terms of its witness to Christ? And, to focus on a very immediate problem, when does Scripture witness to Christ? Does it witness to Christ only when it actually speaks to *me* or works on *me*? Must the intent of Scripture become actual here and now, to my humanity, in order to be its real intent?

This last suggestion has already been disqualified as a *cul-de-sac*. It is surely not the idea that would suggest itself first. If the essential message of Scripture is reduced to my own actual encounter or experience with Christ, that to which the tradition (in the sense of Holy Scripture) owes its origin and continuity is lost. Tradition owes itself not to my present "history" (experience), but to history as an event of the past, an event that is transmitted precisely because of its implicit significance. Any other reason for transmitting history is unthinkable; as a historical event it must have been important enough for each generation to pass the story of it on to the next generation. Thus, we must say that history *in* its significance is that which gives rise to and keeps tradition going. This is the only answer to the question about the message of Scripture. The message of Scripture is that which commends itself as that which has kept the tradition alive until now as the transmission of history *in* its significance.

On the basis of the foregoing, we can say that the search for a workable distinction between the biblical witness and its sounding board must take seriously the fact that the witness must be recognized as a witness of a historical event that happened in time past, but then that event must be seen *in* its meaning and implications. We must reflect further on what the last clause of the preceding sentence implies. We want to insist that *history* is the message of the tradition, in particular the history of Israel as it is led by its God, which culminates in the history of Jesus Christ as the representative of Israel's God in Israel's midst. This has wide implications for hermeneutics and for dogmatics in its hermeneutical concern.

First, we must insist that history as an event, or series of events, that took place in past time has an irreducible factuality about it. What has once happened can never be treated as though it did not happen. Whether the fact that it happened in past time makes it passé and irrelevant to us is another question. But history cannot be melted away into dimensions of subjectivity. It successfully resists subjectivistic reduction; it is not amenable to existentializing. Whoever attempts to subjectify history has no respect for history. It must be emphasized, to be sure, that it is significant history that is transmitted. In asking what gives a past event its significance, one ought not to confuse the *significance* of that event with a merely human *interpretation* of it.

We are often reminded in this connection that two witnesses of a single event—consider the case of an automobile accident—seldom give exactly the same account of it. This is suggested as proof of the subjective factor of interpretation present in every witness of an event. This is true, but the illustration has definite limits. The eyewitness accounts of two people who have seen an automobile accident may differ, but neither of them is likely to inform the police that he saw two bicycles or two trains collide. Nor is either likely to phone the police that an accident really did not take place. The fact that there is no such thing as an unattested event does not entail that attested events are not really events but only attestations *of* events. Dealing with actual events, we have only human witnesses of those events. Who other than men can talk about things that happen? Witness takes place in human form; in what other form could it take place? But the temptation involved here is clear: in view of the human character of the witness, we are tempted to conclude that what we have is the self-expression of the witness rather than a report of an event. But this is a temptation we must resist. It is like saying that the report of two witnesses of an automobile accident tells us only what happened in the minds of the witnesses and not what happened on the street.

One could defend this by saying that he is interested in the witnesses and not in the accident. But our peculiar interest cannot undo what happened to the two cars that collided. Nor can it undo the fact that people were injured in the crash, and that the witnesses would have witnessed to nothing at all had there been no accident. Moreover, witnesses are not at all interesting *as witnesses* if nothing happened to which they gave witness. Without an event, our interest in the witnesses would be limited to a psychological interest in them as persons. The event witnessed to makes the witness *and his testimony* interesting. It is not the other way around.

No matter which way we turn it, history as an event of past time has something about it that resists existentializing of itself. Existentialist interpretation reaches an insurmountable wall in the past time dimension of events. Reaching this wall of the once-for-all historical past, it must stop there or eliminate this aspect of history and corrupt the whole character of history as event. The character of the biblical witness as history preserves an element in the text and its content that remains external to us. It signifies that something has happened outside of ourselves. As long as the biblical text is not robbed of its historical character, revelation and religion will be distinct from each other, no matter how closely related they may be within the Bible.

We must now say something further about the nature of past time. Past time must be respected as past time. Abraham is not our contemporary, and he must not be tortured into being interpreted as our contemporary. The cultural context that Abraham needs in order to be Abraham is too far removed from us to allow him to leap over it into our time. Lessing's "nasty big ditch" is indeed very broad. But need it be nasty? There is no reason at all to think so. We need not lament the chasm between present and past; we must let the past be what it is. Historical distance is historical distance, and it must be kept that way. The temptation to do away with it rises from a kind of panic in the face of the historical nature of human existence. Efforts to erase the distance between present and past are really attempts to rescue us from what seems to be a threat to our being.

But theology cannot work with this kind of rescue effort, which mixes everything up and, instead of offering clear lines between present and past, throws all existence into a jumbled mass. Past is past; and we must not tamper with this fact, especially if we wish to keep hermeneutics on the right track in understanding the message of salvation. The witness to salvation is historical in the sense that it is carried to us by former generations, but it is also historical in the sense that it reports a history that did not occur in our time. To restrict ourselves to the most salient example, Jesus of Nazareth is—besides being much else—a historical figure, and must be seen as such. To attempt to escape from the historical or incidental character of Jesus is to desert the basis of Christian faith—the Christ for us and outside of us. Jesus once lived in a place and time that is not our time and not our place. Whatever else we must say about Jesus—and that is a great deal—we must begin here. The "nasty big ditch" is given with tradition and is as such inexpendable for Christian faith. Christian faith is vitally bound to the "accidental historical truths" that Lessing found so frustrating. Nothing can wash away the fact that the evangelists meant to give us reports of events that were confined to past time.[27] It is just as impossible to avoid the fact that Paul also meant to convey the death, burial, and resurrection of Jesus as events of the past, and understood their pastness to be the source of power for his gospel message (I Cor. 15:1-11).

The past eventfulness of the resurrection is our special concern, just as it is obviously the center of Paul's concern in I Corinthians 15. When Bultmann insists that the Gospel record of Jesus' resurrection is the early Christians' way of expressing their faith in the cross, he is obviously viewing the situation differently than Paul did.[28] For Paul, Jesus' resurrection is an event of the same order, in the same historical sense, as the crucifixion (I Cor. 15:4).[29] To

[27] Without prejudice to the form-critical method of exegesis, we can say that the first Christians surely had an (apologetic) interest in the how and what of the events surrounding Jesus, and that the Gospel writers in that sense are reconstructions of how it all began. Not every author in the New Testament has the same interest in history; but in Luke we see it in its best form. Cf. C. F. D. Moule, *The Birth of the New Testament* (1962), p. 211.

[28] Cf. the previous chapter; also Bultmann, *Theologie des Neuen Testament*, p. 295.

[29] The focus is on "in the same order" and "in the same sense." Barth insists that the gospel message of the New Testament stands or falls with this (*Kirchliche Dogmatik*, IV/1, p. 328). If Fuchs means by "objective facts" scientifically discernible facts, his rule makes some sense. For the cross is scientifically available only in its poly-interpretable exterior sense —just as is the empty tomb; it is not available in this sense according to its unique significance—just as the resurrection is not.

its own hurt, orthodox Protestantism has frequently been fearful of the historical dimension of Christianity, as though the firmness of its truth would be jeopardized by the acknowledgment of its roots in history. It has in fact occasioned various kinds of idealistic and existentialistic reconstructions of the gospel message. Against any temptation to lift Christianity out of history, we must stubbornly hold that historical events form the hard core of the biblical witness. They are historical in the full sense; they belong to past time. This facet of Christian truth cannot be undone nor escaped.

The historical character of the biblical witness establishes the legitimacy of historical-critical research. This was also implied by the fact that the biblical witness is carried to us on the waves of tradition. Here it is implied by the fact that Christian truth is framed in *past* history. That which is transmitted by tradition is no less historical than tradition itself. This makes historical research unavoidable. Moreover, it is required for the self-criticism that Christianity must make of its own manners of speech and its own conceptual forms. An orthodoxy that fears historical research or shuns the history of its tradition—the history that is given by the content of the tradition—and seeks to set its faith in an exclusive haven outside of history, no matter what means of assurances it uses, does no service to Christian faith at all. One is inclined to ask orthodoxy of this sort whether it really believes what it wants others to hear and believe.

This does not mean that historical research provides the basis for Christian faith. One does not pursue historical questions vigorously in order to guarantee Christian truth through scientific research.[30] If orthodoxy were to do this, it would fall victim to the same presuppositions as does the very historicism that it abhors. Both would proceed from the conviction that scientific research is able to demonstrate the truth of Christian faith and, for the same reason, is able to prove its untruth. Science cannot do this without transgressing its own character beyond all reason. This, once again, does not mean that Christian faith is disinterested in his-

[30] Bultmann has often accused those who want to anchor salvation in history of being victims of this mistake. Cf. Bornkamm's criticism of Bultmann on this score in "Geschichte und Glaube im Neuen Testament," *Evangelische Theologie*, XXII (1962), 1-15. Günter Klein sees the beginnings of this mistake in Luke ("Lukas 1:1-4 als theologisches Program," in *Zeit und Geschichte*, pp. 193-216).

tory, especially *this* history. On the contrary, faith stands or falls with the real eventfulness of this history. Historical research is pursued as historical science, not as disguised theology. And as long as it is true to itself, without going beyond its own scope, it can prove to be of great service to both the church and its theology.

Not every method of doing research is acceptable to theology, of course. Nor is every concept of history a viable option. Nothing contains more important, and more hidden, presuppositions than does a person's view of history, for one's concept of history determines what one supposes can or cannot have happened in history. We would be taken too far afield to go into an analysis of various concepts of history, but we do wish to point out that the conflict between theology and certain forms of historical criticism and their results exists at the point of the concept of history implicit in them. Thus contemporary theology cannot avoid the responsibility of making a judicious analysis of the nature of history.

We must investigate one aspect of the concept of history a bit further, namely, that involving the relationship between the *interpretation* of an event that is implied in the witness one gives of that event and the *event itself*. The necessity of making this distinction has been demonstrated above. The heart of the problem is this: what is the real source of the significance that the witness ascribes to the event that he reports? There is no such thing as history without significance. To speak of nonsignificant history not only does injustice to the nature of history itself, but, what is more important, it tends to isolate us from the past and raises the suspicion that one wants to cut himself off from the past.[31] Positivistic notions of history are especially susceptible to this temptation whenever positivism does more than merely isolate historical events as a methodological device, and instead passes off that which its own critical research is able to ascertain as the only *real* past history.

The question of the historical Jesus may illustrate what we mean. Without doubt, the historical Jesus refers to Jesus of Nazareth who lived, died and—according to the tradition—arose again at the beginning of our era. But the so-called historical Jesus is

[31] Cf. Jürgen Moltmann, *op. cit.,* pp. 32ff.

only an *extract* of the *real* Jesus.[32] To reject this is to fall victim to the positivistic notion of history. Nonsignificant history, we repeat, does not exist. Theology has been right in demanding that history *is* always significant. The history of Jesus is Jesus in His significance.

But this does not solve the problem. What gives significance to an event or series of events? What invests Jesus with the significance that tradition ascribes to Him? There is no doubt that it is a significance that *men ascribe to Him*. To fight subjectivism by denying the role of the subjective is to fall on one's own sword. Seen from the vantage point of God's self-revelation, the tradition begins with a subject answering to revelation. We should not hesitate to pay full respect to the role of men, in this instance of the human biblical witnesses. Who else but these witnesses transmit to us the significance of the person and work of Jesus?

The real issue is this: is the significance of Jesus given to Him or received from Him? We judge that only the latter is an acceptable way of putting the matter. Pannenberg's suggestion has a good deal in its favor: the matter does not reside in its significance, as Bultmann would have it, but the significance resides in the matter itself. If this means to refrain from saying what the matter is that the witnesses transmitted to us *in* its significance, however, we must go beyond Pannenberg. For Pannenberg is open to the suggestion that the significance of the event is swallowed up in its *interpretation*; his concept of history carries the suggestion that real history is its interpretation. But the matter that we are concerned with here is too specific and special to allow for this. It is not approachable as an ordinary event, nor as an irrational affair, but as a unique history.

The witnesses with one voice insist that this history is a *credendum,* a thing to be believed. That is, the witnesses not only report it, but in reporting it they also confess it as a matter of faith, and in reporting it they call on others to make a faith commitment. In the event of Jesus something happens for the salvation of guilty mankind. And in the salvation of mankind man's responsibility for the chaos that prevails in our world is also exposed. Therefore, this

---

[32] This means Jesus as He walked in Palestine. Cf. Walter Kreck, "Die Frage nach dem historischen Jesus als dogmatisches Problem," *Evangelische Theologie,* XXII (1962), 474; and J. R. Geiselmann, *Die Frage nach dem historischen Jesus* (1965), p. 44.

history is not approachable in a neutral, uninvolved, superficially intellectual manner. One is saying far too little if all he can report of this history is its historicity. A reporter of this history must betray the fact that it is a scandal; he must convey the impression that what he reports is the "foolishness of the cross." Failing to do this, he fails to convey this history in its genuine significance. The best transmitter is never the unbiased reporter. The content of the tradition allows for no neutrality. The witness of this history must choose sides in the controversy that is decisively settled by this very history and its transmission to others.[33]

How does this explanation of the events arise? It stems from the first witnesses, as we have seen, but the witnesses receive their interpretation from the event itself, which demands a decision before a true account of it can be given. The affair itself and its significance are interwoven; the event does not stand apart from its significance. The interpretation of Jesus, His way, and His work as the way of salvation and the saving work comes from Jesus Himself.[34] This is a dogmatic assertion. Exegesis has the task of establishing and refining it, and it is able to do this job.

Paul did not damage what Jesus accomplished. In his own way—and his way is different from that of John or the writer of Hebrews, and is more explicit than that of Jesus Himself—Paul illuminated Jesus in His person and work by means of the person and work itself. That Paul did it in his own way is interesting enough, since it touches the question of the historically conditioned character of the tradition. The limits of subjectivity were set by the events of history themselves; they are transmitted in their significance, not merely along with (but apart from) their significance.

[33] This agrees with Helmut Gollwitzer, "Der Glaube an Jesus Christus und der sogenannte historische Jesus," in Ristow-Matthiae, *Der historische Jesus und der kerygmatische Christus,* pp. 110-114.

[34] This is not the same thing as to trace the kerygma back to the *verba ipsissima* of Jesus (Jeremias). The continuity between Jesus before and after His death was underscored by Jesus Himself after His death, and it was also understood by the disciples after the Passion. As an unsubtle example, we can mention Paul (cf. I Cor. 11:23: "I received from the Lord"), but the same is true of other New Testament writers. The Jesus of pre-Passion days cannot be neatly peeled away from the picture of the whole Jesus (the Jesus of before *and* after the Passion). This is, of course, not our intention at all, for the message of salvation takes the whole picture as one, and only as such is it the saving message. Still, Jesus before the Passion is the same person as Jesus after the Passion. The gospel stands or falls with this continuity; the crucified one is the risen one.

The events are the hard core. But the diversity of the New Testament confronts us with the subjective factor in the transmission of the events. If one rejects the subjective factor, he is cut loose from the content of the New Testament; for the content is handed down only in this diversity of witness.

We must therefore conclude that in broad lines we can distinguish between the witness and its sounding board; but we can do this only as we see that the matter which forms the content of the witness resides in the history of Jesus Christ as it is transmitted to us in its significance. This matter is the foundation of the Christian church. But the phrase "in its significance" necessarily implies the subjective role of the witnesses and the existence of a verbal package that the witness uses to hand down the "matter," but which is not the same thing as the matter itself. The inseparable connection in which the witness and its sounding board or "packaging" are given to us makes it possible for us to distinguish between them only in rough outline, and not in precision. The border clashes will have to be watched by theology, because an invulnerable line of demarcation cannot be built. To demand an unmistakable border line—in order to render uncertainty or mistakes all but impossible—is prohibited by the character of the biblical witness. The Christian church has no choice but to go its way, in wisdom and care, keeping its lines of communication open, and led by diligent theological labors. Only in this way, and not by assuming that God keeps His truth "untouched by human hands," does the church need to or have the right to pray for the guiding presence of the Holy Spirit to lead it into all truth (John 16:13).

(3) We now come to the third dimension of the historical—its relationship to faith statements. What kind of statements are the faith utterances formulated by the church and its theology? We have seen that the truth of the Christian faith has the dimension of continuity. The firmness or trustworthiness of truth is enhanced by its continuity. We saw that the continuity of the truth of faith is sustained by the hard core of faith's utterances as they point to that which happened and was spoken. That is, they were passed on as *history*, and therefore as *significant event*. We can now add to this that the adequate definition of this hard core—concretely, the events involving Jesus—is possible only as we together with the whole community ("with all the saints," Eph. 3:18) see it in its full

significance. That is, its adequate definition comes in the fullness of times, in the eschaton.

The eschaton does not signal the dissolving of the historical perspective. Even less does it imply a summing up of all previous but partial attempts to grasp the truth.[35] The extent to which these elements must be included when we try to describe the nature of dogmatic statements and faith utterances, we need not attempt to say. We are concerned with a prior question. It has a bearing on the incompleteness of all utterances of faith—the "in part" of I Corinthians 13:12. It is associated with history in its continuity, and with the life of the church in this history, a life that is on the way toward the fullness. Why does this being in history, being on the way toward the end, imply the incompleteness of every Christian faith utterance and every dogmatic statement? We want to approach our answer from two different avenues.

In the first place, the reason we are always seeking new images, representations, and concepts to bring the content of tradition into words lies in the church's very mandate to transmit its message. The church is a transmitting center. Its mission is transmission.[36] This is why its message is called a tradition: it must be handed down to coming generations over and over again. This fits the nature of its content. Since the tradition consists of dated events in their significance, the transmission of the message cannot be a mechanical transmission of texts that report certain events; the transmission includes a constantly renewed unfolding of the significance of the events. This is the example we find in the biblical witness; the biblical witness gives a report that is at the same time the original proclamation of the gospel message.[37] Not only in the canonical report given by the early church, but in the whole history of the tradition, we see that new unfoldings of the faith are happening constantly. This, in turn, shows that the task of transmission implies the tentative character of all formulations of the faith. This makes it clear how closely related are the

[35] Pannenberg, *Offenbarung als Geschichte,* pp. 95ff.

[36] The term transmission is used in the *Constitution on Revelation* of Vatican II. Reformed thought can feel quite at home with the word.

[37] Cf. C. H. Ratschow, "Das Christentum als denkende Religion," *Neue Zeitschrift für Theologie und Religion,* V (1963), 16-33, who rightly says that the incarnation—as an event in a given space and time—makes Christianity a transmitting religion.

mission, transmission, and theological work of the church. Mission in the form of transmission is the genesis of all reformulations of Christian faith, whether they are made purposely or unwittingly.[38] Mission is therefore the genesis of all theology.

But this is only half the truth. It answers only in part the question of why Christian faith can never stand still at a formulation once given. The tradition, the message the church hands down, is not only history at its hard core. It does not only have a history of transmission behind it, but it also requires history in order to come into its own. The tradition, in the sense of the message that the church passes down, carries within it a promise, implied in the coming and the work—in short the resurrection—of Jesus Christ. The confession "He is Lord of all" (Acts 10:36) is perhaps the shortest form in which we meet the tradition in the form of promise. More extended forms are found in Philippians 2:5-11 and I Corinthians 15. The promise is implicit in the tradition. Every knee shall bow before Jesus as Lord: the promise is part of the message that the church hands down.

To say "promise," however, is to speak of time, and the course of history. Without the passage of time, the idea of promise loses its sense. Of course, it is also true that without the promise time loses its meaning (clearly the meaning of I Pet. 3:9). The church's mission—the transmission of the tradition—is thus the genesis of all theology, but the promise that is implicit in Jesus and His resurrection is the genesis of the church's mission.

As long as the promise inherent in the tradition is not yet fulfilled, as long as every knee does not yet bow before Jesus as Lord and every tongue does not yet confess that He is Lord, the Christian church keeps the tradition alive in ever renewed formulations. It speaks in the images and concepts that new cultures arising in new times offer the church as vehicles for witness to the saving significance of Jesus Christ, as this significance is passed on to each new generation. The tentative character of Christian truth

---

[38] Reformulation is quite another thing than demythologizing. The former has reference to the history of interpretation, and consists of a constantly renewed confrontation of a transmitted interpretation of the tradition with the tradition itself—the tradition which is called the canon because it is the touchstone of all interpretations. Reformulation is not the same as a reinterpretation of previous expositions. Catholic theologians are confined to such reinterpretation. Reformed theology can go further (whether it does or not is another question); it can reformulate antiquated and erroneous doctrinal decisions.

can perhaps be put in this way: Christian truth exists among us only as it is both appropriated and passed along; we possess the truth only in the form in which it is at once received and then passed on. This is the reason for the unfulfillment peculiar to the church and its tradition; it is implicit in the method of God's self-revelation.[39] Revelation is always given, appropriated, and transmitted.

Christian truth is trustworthiness itself. But it is incomplete, unfinished. This is why complete truth is an eschatological matter. It is not here as yet, but the Spirit will lead us toward it (John 16:13).[40] Truth is not something we discover, but something that is going to be given in the final verification of all the promises, which is to say, in the eschaton. As long as faith lives by faith and not by verification (cf. John 20:29; II Cor. 5:7) it confesses that Christian truth is not yet final.[41] The other side of the eschatological fulfillment is the partial character of all Christian knowledge in the present time.[42] The church that refuses to negotiate on the basis that the church by the very nature of the situation possesses the truth only as it both appropriates it and passes it on, instead insisting that the truth is not open to reformulation, is liable to sin against one of the most essential characteristics of the tradition.[43] To fail to recognize that Christian truth cannot exist in unchangeable, eternal formulations, is to put oneself under the law again and to forfeit grace (Rom. 6:14). This is the gambit that tempts orthodoxy.

The fierce fidelity to the tradition that orthodoxy exemplifies can be twisted into a legalism that violates its own best intentions whenever orthodoxy loses sight of the unique nature of its own tradition and forgets that tradition is kept alive in transmission to the next generation. Orthodoxy must beware that its predilection

[39] Cf. Ernst Kinder, "Dogmatik und Dogma," in *Dogma und Denkstrukturen* (1963), pp. 9-29.

[40] The future tense—$\dot{o}\delta\eta\gamma\dot{\eta}\sigma\epsilon\iota$—is essential.

[41] It finally does come to verification, even in a tangible sense. Believing without seeing is an exceptional situation.

[42] The historicity of Christian truth makes ecumenical dialogue a required program.

[43] We mean by the above to describe the heritage of the Reformation in a practical sense: the free Bible, the Bible free from bondage to historically defined interpretations, implies that none of us may set any human words above the Bible. That is, the Christian remains free only as long as the Bible is free. This entire chapter may be read as a further suggestion as to the way in which biblical authority actually functions.

for unchangeable formulations does not—as Bonhoeffer reminded us—tempt it to preach circumcision instead of Christ. It must be on guard lest its commitment to the very dogmatic concepts and formulas given it by previous generations prevent it from passing the tradition on afresh to generations to come.[44]

Once again, we are dealing with the difficult question of how the real matter of faith is related to the packaging in which that matter is passed on. We do not wish to underestimate the problem involved here. Abortive solutions to this problem have been discussed earlier in this study. But to reject other solutions is not to satisfy the demand to keep working with the problem. A legalistic Christianity—that is, a Christianity that legalistically holds on to stated formulations—is as potent a threat to the faith of the believing community as is a liberal Christianity that rejects doctrinal formulations. The sense of liberation that many orthodox people experienced, to their own surprise, at the reading of *Honest to God* speaks volumes. The success of this little book cannot be explained by its contents so much as by the endorsement it gives to Christians to let go of yesterday's language for the sake of a new language of faith.

One would hope that the appearance of Robinson's book, along with the furor that it created, would open our eyes to the fact that we have really accomplished nothing at all by a mere rejection of it, granted that it is wide open to the severest criticism. We do gain a step if we can see that there need be no contradiction—indeed, that there may not be a contradiction—between faith as a discovery on one hand and faith as the received tradition on the other. In fact, the truth demands appropriation by us, and only as we appropriate it in our times and express it in a form possible to us in our times can we in turn hand it down to others. This peculiarity of Christian truth must be apparent in the formulations into which the truth is poured.

Still further, we must test our formulations by asking about their ability to function. Dogmatic formulations too—if they really share in the truth that sets men free—must function as liberators, not as straitjackets.[45] They can liberate only as we fully accept the

---

[44] See Bonhoeffer, *Widerstand und Ergebung,* pp. 180ff.
[45] The phrase "Luther as language event" that Ebeling uses tends to sloganize the liberation from legalism. The liberation was the "event" of the Reformation. Still, Ebeling touches on a vital aspect of the Reformation.

promissory aspect of truth that is implicit in its tentative character. We must spurn the temptation to argue this aspect away, a temptation that stems from a fear of the historically conditioned nature of every human formulation.[46] We must pay unqualified respect to this promise aspect—and its tentative character—as "promise" *and* as "tentativeness"—because all formulations are efforts to clothe truth in words that are still on the way toward triumph.[47] Only as we do, will our dogmatics have a liberating function.

A history that says and does something

We must still ask how the past that comes to us in the form of tradition can and does really affect us. We must ask whether historical events of time long past can actually touch us today. Can the past really awaken faith? Can it summon authentic experience? Can it function as a liberation today? Or must a Christianity that points back to the past content itself with a faith that merely demands that we "hold as true" things that lie outside of our own human existence?

A few preliminary remarks are in order before we hazard our answer to these questions. First, a word on behalf of Reformed and Lutheran scholastic theology. To say that these theologies understood faith as an arid intellectual "holding as true" is to caricature them. Protestant scholastics generally realized that faith was not completely captured by this intellectualist definition, and they attempted to point out the more profound dimensions of Christian belief. The distinctions that were created between these different dimensions of faith—for example, between historical faith and saving faith—are poignant examples of the difficulty the scholastics experienced.[48] But one can understand such distinc-

---

[46] We cannot escape the temptation of turning the gospel into a new law by shedding faith statements and dogmatic propositions; we can only do it by accepting the gospel as an invitation to the proclamation of salvation and not as a demand to believe certain things to be true. The temptation happens to a preacher especially when his listeners appear to turn away; seeing someone reject the gospel, he is tempted to lay it on him as a sheer obligation. This is quite another style from what Paul uses in II Cor. 5:20ff.

[47] If we are able to recognize the fact that Christian truth is always en route, we will be able also to appreciate some of the motives of modern theology, for instance, the conviction that we must listen to the gospel with our own ears, in our own time.

[48] Ebeling makes this point in *Wort und Glaube*, pp. 205ff.

tions in a positive sense. Historical faith was understood as an inadequate faith. The Heidelberg Catechism is a good example of this, for here (Question 21) faith is specifically not "only a sure knowledge whereby I hold for truth . . . but also a firm confidence. . . ." The Catechism makes a distinction that takes us out of the objective into the personal sphere. Even so, as we conclude that faith is neither created nor served by a mere pointing to things gone by, we must add that traditional orthodoxy was not satisfied with such a notion either.

Secondly, traditional orthodoxy's refusal to be satisfied with a faith that merely holds certain things about past time to be true, and its desire to add an element of experience inseparable to faith, reminds us that there is a legitimate motive in the efforts of existentialist theology. Faith is something more than acceptance of texts that tell us about God and His acts in time past. If faith has to do with God in the present time, however, we must ask how a text that tells us about God in past time can be the means of His speaking to us today. How can faith be established by another man's story of his liberation long ago, when in the last analysis what is an issue is our faith and our authentic liberation today?

The third observation is meant to put the previous one in a perspective that, without taking anything away from it, will try to keep it in proportion. Doubtless, the demand for authenticity that marks existentialist theology is justified if it is understood as a demand that our expressions of faith be honest and genuine in contrast to forced or faked ones. The demand for authenticity is simply a demand for integrity; this is the way we are using the word authenticity. But can we go further with the notion of authenticity and say that each person must confirm himself in real freedom if he is to be an authentic person? Phrased in this way, the demand may seem to require too much of a man. It smacks perhaps of the absolute demands put down by the Moral Rearmament movement and like groups. Can a man know for sure whether he is being an authentic person or not? We must remember how ambiguous a person is in his own eyes, and how few of his motives are really clear to him. Exaggerated demands for authenticity can be unrealistic in view of the realities of human nature.

Another objection may be that one can get rather far with the demand that a person must realize himself as an authentic person, as long as one has a clear view of the goal of self-realization. Otherwise he may end with nothing but the abstraction of pure freedom, which would be setting up a being-less man as the goal of authenticity. But can man be being-less in this strict sense? Abstractions are theologically unpromising; faith at least knows that one thing must precede self-realization in freedom: one's recognition of his own past in the pregnant sense of his guilt. Faith also knows the riddle of sin, which is seen in the bewildering fact that horrible evil as well as virtue rises from the human heart (Mark 7:21). Faith is notably aware of both guilt and sin. But these are just the factors of human life of which the modern concentration on being-less freedom appears to be unaware.

Having said this, we must go further and ask what it is in relationship to which we are guilty sinners. The view of man entertained by those who accept pure freedom as the human goal seems to take no stock of the covenant partnership that defines the essence of personhood. (The reader is referred to the previous chapter for an elaboration of this objection to existentialist theology.) The term authenticity needs a number of restrictions in order to demonstrate that theology does not propagate a notion of authenticity that can fit a murderer as well as his victim. In other words, authenticity is a meaningless word until it is given at least a minimal definition by one's view of man and the relationships that form the background to his being as sinner.

With this background we can turn to our real question: is faith established or vitalized by means of a tradition that witnesses to historical events that took place in a time long past?

We have seen the serious effort that Bultmann's disciples have made (in contrast to Bultmann himself) to restore the Jesus of history to a significant role for faith. That is, unlike himself, Bultmann's students have tried to find a place in faith for past time. Their solution was that Jesus, though belonging to the past, has genuine bearing on faith insofar as the ground of our human being came "to expression" in Him. He interpreted His own selfhood and thus revealed our true humanity. He is our teacher, our example, who creates in Himself a model of true existence.

Though this probing into the past provides more historical foundation for faith than Bultmann was able to give, it offers little in comparison to the role Jesus and His work plays in tradition. A legitimate question is whether Fuchs and Ebeling have given

Christian faith a basically different historical framework than did nineteenth-century liberalism, and whether they do not stand in closer affinity with the old liberalism than Bultmann does. What can "historical" possibly mean for them other than a stimulating example in history?

The construction given by Fuchs and Ebeling is still plagued by the notion that past time in the true sense of the word is passé and must remain passé if man is to give full significance to the achievement of his own genuine existence. Existence cannot be touched by the past; it demands a revelation in the present; it needs "eternity of the moment." Two observations must be made on this point, both of which have penetrating importance for our whole question.

In the first place, the notion that man is existence is incompatible with the historical character of the tradition and with the human work of handing that tradition down. The intention of Bultmann and his successors was in fact to invest the historical existence of man with genuine significance (recall Bultmann's efforts to interpret faith as an actuality). But in spite of his good intentions, his attempt to make faith a historical actuality has led to a new flight from history by means of faith.[49] Inasmuch as existentialist theology appeals to human-*being* as Existence, we are left within the idealistic tradition, which sought to rescue the core of human-*being* from the surging stream of history and, as it were, to set it high and dry on the banks of eternity. Existentialist theology sees this core in the actuality of freedom in which man lifts himself above historical conditionedness. In the freedom into which man realizes himself, man lifts himself above history and temporality. With this, as we have remarked before, we are set with both feet in metaphysics. The genuine human-*being* is something above history, and is therefore metaphysical.[50]

This view of man is in tension with the Christian tradition, which sees man as completely historical. The historicity of tradition points to this fact; more precisely, the historical definition of tradition, including its historical origins, points to man as through and through historical. We have pointed to the ultimate foundation

[49] Moltmann correctly observes this, *Prädestination und Perserveranz* (1961), p. 177.

[50] Moltmann remarks that to lift the real self out of history comes down to a process of cutting oneself from history in the sense of past events (*Exegese und Eschatologie der Geschichte*, pp. 38ff.).

of this fact: this historicity is not a concession to some sort of *Zeitgeist,* but is an acknowledgment of the way in which Israel's God demonstrates Himself as God, in the historical partnership He takes up with Israel.

But this is not the only indication we have of man's historical nature. Why is tradition necessary except because man lives wholly within the stream of history and because the tradition must go with him there from one generation to the next? Tradition presupposes the historical mode of human existence. Now we must take another step along the way suggested by this thought: tradition not only presupposes everything that we have mentioned, including the chain of generations that helps define the character of man as man, but it also presupposes that what is handed down is itself the reward for the trouble it takes to hand it down. In the concrete instance of the Christian tradition, the very fact that the tradition lives must tell us that the past time that the tradition carries over to us is *not* passé. On the contrary, the tradition occurs in the firm conviction that if, indeed, any past time has ever been passé, the past time of Israel's experience with its God up to and including the events that happened in Jesus Christ is decidedly not passé.

We cannot go off into the question of the canon. But we offer a few remarks on the subject to indicate at least that canon formation is an element in the tradition as transmission. The formation of the canon comes into right perspective if we associate the concept of canon with the history of the tradition. The fact that men handed down the message lay—and still lies—in the fact that the message was needed. That is, the tradition as an act (transmission) is explained by the tradition as content (message). The tradition became canon for the sake of transmitting the gospel message to following generations. What we call the canon (the Old and New Testaments) is no less a form of appropriation and passing on—no less, that is, a form of faith—than all the appropriating and passing on that has been done since the canon was accepted. There is no structural difference; at least we are unable to see any as long as we remain true to the nature of God's self-revelation. There is a difference in authority; it is the difference between what the first ear- and eyewitnesses noted and reported and all the other witnesses who depended on theirs.[51]

[51] Unrepeatable events imply irreplaceable witnesses. With this the canonicity of the biblical witness is implied.

Our second observation regarding the question of how the past can be respected as really past and yet not passé requires us to turn to the events of the past themselves, as the tradition urges us to do. The content of the reports must tell us how and why this past concerns us now. So we must not seek our own methods of applying the past to the present in order to demonstrate its possibilities for relevance in the present. The application of the tradition is not something added to the tradition itself; the tradition must do its own work. We are dealing with a tradition that has something important to say; it does not have to be invested with relevance. This is why tradition has another name—proclamation. It makes an appeal to its listeners. But how does that appeal make itself heard?

The tradition does not make a hortatory appeal to its hearers. The reportorial style of the evangelists illustrates this. Tradition in this sense tells us a story about something in the past tense; it lets the past itself speak (to use Ebeling's terminology). In the telling of the story as something that took place in the past and not in the present lies the secret of how the story is able to "speak to us" now. We must underscore the fact that only one such story exists: the history of Jesus Christ. His history we have learned to listen to as "inclusive history" (Barth) and therefore a history that we must tell to others.[52] The story of His cross and resurrection is told as our story: we are buried and risen with Him (Rom. 6:4). The inclusiveness of Jesus' person and work determines everything for us. We are not dealing with an application of something that is really external to the application made as well as to the thing to which it is applied. We should not try to make Jesus' story significant for us by applying His life to ours in a moral sense. His story is a fundamental given of the apostolic preaching, and is therefore repeatedly recalled. It has its significance in itself as history.

The church has used a variety of terms to indicate this fundamental aspect of the tradition; it has talked of Christ's "inclusive history," of Him as our "substitute" and as a "public person." These are ways to say that, by the power of His loving identification with us, *His* story can now be told as *our* story, a story to be understood ever anew and passed on again and again. This is the way the early church—via the first eyewitnesses—understood

52 Cf. *Kirchliche Dogmatik*, IV/1, pp. 16ff.

Jesus Himself. He was preached as a "public person" because He understood Himself in this way before God and made this clear to His disciples.[53] The "for me" dimension is implicit in the gospel; indeed, it is inherent there because Jesus wanted Himself understood as He willed Himself to be, and was—*for us*.[54]

This means that we who live in the present do come to expression in the tradition, and in a very specific way. We come to expression in a way that we may not approve of. The "for us" aspect of the tradition puts us in the context of the cross, the "offense" and the "foolishness" (I Cor. 1:18ff.). But whether we like it or not, we do indeed come to expression in the tradition in this way. This helps explain why a story of a past event can concern us in a profound and unique way.

But this brings us to a border line. This history of Jesus "for us" can be told again only as a believed and obeyed story. Obedience in discipleship is a precondition for the transmission of the tradition. And this observation implies much more than that a witness to this story has an edge on a mere historian. It also implies that tradition and church belong together. The story of Jesus Christ is the tradition of the Christian church; that is, it can be dealt with only in faith.

This is the border line we mentioned. In all our thought there must come a point where we make the implicit faith decision *explicit*; that is, we must account for the fact that Christian theology speaks from the circle of faith, the believing community, or church. We do not have to posit this fact at the beginning, as though we have to start the story by warning the reader that the story is going to demand a decision of faith. Nor do we need to hold it back until the last moment, as though we want it to come as a surprise. Rather, we ought to provide a proper place for the demand of faith within the entire prolegomena; we must give it a place where the appeal to a faith decision cannot be thinned down to a formal matter, such as an appeal to the canon, but kept

[53] It only serves to complicate the question to assume that Jesus' "messianic self-consciousness" is merely the theology of the early church. Furthermore, this assumption leaves the question of how Christianity ever arose hanging in the air.

[54] Cf. Hans-Joachim Iwand, "Wider den Missbrauch des 'pro me' als methodisches Prinzip in der Theologie," *Evangelische Theologie*, XIV (1954), 120ff.

materially directed to Jesus Christ Himself as the content of the whole tradition. This point is relevant here, where we are discussing the meaning and content of theological statements, because we are invited to recognize the history of Jesus Christ as a history that concerns us in the most intense way, a history that urges us to *remember* with thanks and to *anticipate* with hope.

The words "remember" and "anticipate" provide for modern men without a history a history in which they can truly participate. But these words are part of the tradition, not from the history of Jesus Himself, but from the history of the handing down of His special history. In the Old and New Testaments, the handing down or transmitting of the history belongs to the history itself as it took place in past time; the transmitting of the story is part of God's liberating action. This is true, even though the history and its proclamation are not one and the same thing, a fact that must be stressed in opposition to Bultmann.

The words "remember" and "anticipate" are the warp and woof of the history that reveals how the tradition functions as transmission and proclamation. They indicate—in a variety of tones and colors—how the story speaks to the hearer in a decisive way. The tradition "says something" and "does something" to us. This is why the act of transmitting is only one aspect of tradition. Tradition "says something" and is therefore a message, a gospel, and a kerygma. What the message says and does is perhaps best epitomized in the words "remember" and "anticipate." Both words suggest an authentically human action. They demonstrate most clearly that faith can never exist on the arid plateau of holding something to be true as long as it is directed to *this* message of Jesus and His "inclusive history."

Furthermore, the words "remember" and "anticipate" cannot be separated. Anticipation is another word for Christian hope. The redemptive message opens a window to the future; it takes a bead on the salvation that is coming to man and his world; the message is a promise, and carries us along in our expectation—the risk of hope—to the fact that something is going to happen. Faith does not exhaust what there is to be said. In contrast to what existentialist theology tells us, faith and salvation are not one and the same thing (Rom. 13:11). To say that faith and salvation are identical catches hold of the fact that faith is an event, as Paul indicates it to be (Gal. 3:25), but it cuts faith off from the future as promise.[55] And this is not Paul!

We cannot cut anticipation loose from memory. On the contrary, anticipation is dependent on memory. Our knowledge of the future, in the form of hope, is dependent on our knowledge of the past, in the form of faith in Jesus and His saving work.[56] In this sense, "remembering" is as authentic a Christian experience as is "anticipating." In memory, one celebrates the past in its significance for the present and future, rejoices in it as the basis for his freedom, and insinuates the past into his own life as the fuel for his hope. This is how Israel remembered God's past acts (Ps. 77:12; 78:35). And this is how the church remembers by way of sacrament His superb act in Jesus Christ (I Cor. 11:25). The Lord's Supper is a celebration; it is an emotional event *par excellence*.[57]

It is not easy to describe how various emotions can summon remembrances and the sort of relations into which they can put a person. We sometimes remember things in order to recall them; that is, we can do things that recall by act what we are to remember with our inner selves. Everything depends on what is to be remembered. When we remember God's covenant, that is, His promises, recollection is not much different from calling on God in prayer; that is, we call on God by means of our act of recalling.[58]

There is another form of "recollection" that demonstrates the

[55] The loss of hope as anticipation of the future is a consequence of existentializing the message of salvation. H. Berkhof suggests that Berkouwer's theological method—the correlation of faith and revelation—tends toward this kind of existentializing of redemption. But this is obviously a misreading, as is clear from the very book from which Berkhof draws his suggestion. Berkouwer, *De Wederkomst van Christus,* vols. I and II (1961 and 1963). Both volumes begin with an affirmation of future anticipation. Cf. H. Berkhof, "De Methode van Berkouwer's Theologie," in *Ex Auditu Verbi* (1966), pp. 37-55.

[56] Gerhard Sauter, *Zukunft und Verheissung* (1965), pp. 46ff., makes clear how unique the Christian knowledge of the future is, especially in view of the complexity of a word like *kainos.*

[57] For the role that remembering plays in the Old and New Testaments, see P. A. H. de Boer, *Gedenken und Gedächtnis in der Welt des Alten Testaments* (1962); Willy Schottroff, *Gedenken im alten Orient und im Alten Testament* (1964); M. Noth, "Die Vergegenwärtigung des Alten Testaments in der Verkündigung," *Evangelische Theologie,* XII (1952), 6-17.

[58] Cf. Rudolf Bohren, *Predigt und Gemeinde* (1963), p. 105. He says that preaching is recollection in the sense that preaching *recalls* and, in a real sense, appeals to God's own memory. For an example, see Luke 23:42.

pregnant sense of remembering. Hollanders, for example, recall the past to each other in its fundamental significance and scope for our lives here and now when they celebrate days like the fourth of May, the anniversary of the liberation of Holland in 1945. Hollanders who refuse to participate in this remembrance are outcasts in the eyes of their patriotic countrymen. To refuse to remember along with the community is to despise the sacrifices made at that past time for the life of people today. It is thus not only their pregnant significance for the future that leads us to celebrate the great acts of God in the past. This is surely an aspect of our remembrance; we do celebrate the past act of God because of its power for the future. But *this* past—that of the mighty acts culminating in Jesus Christ—is distinguished (without being separated) from all others in that it is celebrated for what these events signified back there in the liberation of many, and thus also of myself. Remembering carries with it the intention of celebrating the genuine effectuation of salvation in Jesus Christ. This is also a fundamental aspect of the celebration of the Lord's Supper.

A third observation can be made by way of uniting the previous two. Remembering and anticipating are words that point respectively to the past and the future, both of which are the substrata for genuine humanity.[59] A man stands somewhere on the line of history; this makes him a genuine man. But he stands on a point of history today. How does the saving effect of the message of salvation actually work itself into the present? It becomes present in the concrete experience of remembering and anticipating. We could say that remembering and anticipating are the two inseparably united ways in which salvation is present here and now in history.

To be more concrete, redemption, which happened "once for all" in the past, is present among us in the remembrance of the vicarious act of Jesus Christ. That is, it is present in the constantly new receiving and giving of forgiveness (cf. Matt. 18:23-25), practiced in everyday life as "existence *for* others" and celebrated each

[59] Past and future underscore the fact that the historical man is not an *acosmic* man. If he were not bound to this world, what point would there be to his anticipation? Man is covenant partner of God in time and on earth. To be unworldly is to be unhistorical, and vice versa. Peter Stuhlmacher rightly reminds Bultmann that, for Paul, "God's faithfulness is never experienced except along with God's world" (*Gerechtigkeit Gottes bei Paulus,* p. 242).

Sunday at the Lord's Supper.[60] The eschaton is present among us in our anticipation of the future, in the living hope to which the Christian church is born again into a concretely new life (I Pet. 1:3), and which she answers for intellectually in her theology (I Pet. 3:15).[61]

We must neither underestimate nor overestimate these two words in their relation to reality. Remembering lets the past remain past, where it belongs. Past time must be kept in its place; everything depends on this. But remembering is at the same time a calling back (recollection) of the past in praise, prayer, and rejoicing at what happened back there. In thankfulness, to put it briefly, the past becomes living reality. The burden of the Heidelberg Catechism is how very real thankfulness must be if it is, in this recollective power, to be true thankfulness.[62]

The same is true of anticipation. It lets the future remain future. It allows that which is to come to be talked about the way the past is talked about, as something that is not here and now. At the same time, anticipation sets the future within the reality of hope. Both words, with all they imply, describe the way a man exists in history. He remembers, along with the whole Christian community, in more ways than sacramentally, the "death of the Lord" (I Cor. 11:25). And again, with the whole Christian community, he is "born again to a living hope" (I Pet. 1:3).

The Christian's new mode of existence begins where the message of salvation—*this* message of the events in which Jesus Christ is the actor—speaks to and does something to us. The tradition, as it is transmitted by the Christian church to each new generation, is the means by which that which is inscripturated is able to speak to us. It is that means because He speaks to us in it. The tradition speaks and does something to men of today; it is a tradition that intensely concerns us. The reason is clear. He who is recited in the tradition seeks to be of concern to us. He seeks to grasp us. He seeks to speak to and act on us. And He does these things through the transmission, in a variety of ways, of the transmitted and

[60] The phrase "practicing Christian" should not be limited to someone who regularly takes the sacrament.

[61] Cf. Sauter, *op. cit.,* p. 70, for a fascinating effort to invest the word "logos" with a new ontology of hope, in reference to I Pet. 3:15 and its demand that we be able to give a reason ($\lambda\acute{o}\gamma o s$) for the hope that is in us.

[62] The Catechism treats good works and prayer together under the heading of gratitude.

to-be-transmitted material of faith. He does these things, not only
through the Scriptures as the canon of tradition, but also through
men as those who are assigned in full responsibility to be transmitters.[63] Obversely, He does these things not only through men,
without whom no transmission can occur, but also through the
canon of the tradition, Holy Scripture. But in all this, it remains
true that He Himself speaks to us and acts on us through the living
proclamation, the concrete and actual transmission of the tradition.

Jesus Christ, who is proclaimed as past time in the tradition, is
the only one who becomes more than past time by means of an
unrepeatable event in the past.[64] By His resurrection from the
dead, He became the living Lord of the present. Thus, we ask, can
an event of the past be relevant for faith? We must answer that,
since the past event is the resurrection of Jesus Christ, we not only
remember and anticipate the living Lord, on whom faith rests its
hope for the world, but we see that remembering and anticipating
are themselves the works of the Lord; they are signs of our having
been born again to a new hope, which is our new mode of
authentic human existence.

The New Testament tells us about the effective power of the
Lord in terms of the Spirit.[65] In one sense, the Spirit stresses the
fact that Jesus is the Jesus of past time, the Jesus of events that
took place in an era other than our own. In another sense, the
Spirit represents the fact that Jesus, by His resurrection, has become the effective Lord of the present time. Paul means nothing
other by the word Spirit than Jesus in His recreating and liberating
power in this world (II Cor. 3:17). How, then, can the tradition
that comes to us so insinuated within history create and vitalize
faith? It is through the Spirit that He who is witnessed to is the
Christ present by means of the Spirit. He creates that historically
permeated witness and through it awakens faith unto obedience.

Words like "foundation" or "ground" of faith do not even

[63] Naturally, this responsibility implies that we must keep a sharp eye on
every new translation. *Traditores* (transmitters) and *tradutores* (traitors)
differ by only one letter!

[64] "His history (*Geschichte*) is not mere history (*Historie*)" (Barth,
Kirchliche Dogmatik, IV/1, p. 346).

[65] Cf. E. Schweizer on *spirit, Theologisches Wörterbuch zum Neuen
Testament,* VI, 330ff., and especially the passage captioned "The Relation-
ship of the Spirit to Christ." See also H. Berkhof, *The Doctrine of the Holy
Spirit* (1964), especially the first and last chapters.

scratch the surface of the significance of Jesus for faith. Existentialist theologians get by with terms like these only as long as their meaning remains fuzzy; and they are indeed vague as alternatives to the "content" of faith. Jesus, they say, is not the *content* but rather the "ground" or the "foundation" of faith. No matter how one twists and turns, the words "ground" and "foundation" are meaningless if they do not also indicate a "content" of faith, "content" in the sense of a material something to which faith is directed. We saw that theologians whose lines go back to Ritschl (via Herrmann) tried to clear up this problem by making the content of faith—the *fides quae*—a value judgment about Jesus' person and work. Now we must take care lest we call Jesus Lord because we make Him our Lord; this notion is as ridiculous as the idea that He becomes Lord only when we discover Him as our Lord.

Jesus can, without doubt, be *called* the ground of faith because we experience Him as such. But this hardly says enough. The historical character of the tradition tells us that the content of faith, the *fides quae*, is not captured by talk about "ground-experiences"; the content—the historically executed saving work of Christ—was created by what went on before any believing, and it has *provoked* all experiences of faith.[66] Jesus is not called the ground of faith simply because we find our firm foundation in Him; He is called the ground of faith because He was the "one foundation" before we experienced Him as such.

Ebeling uses the term homology to indicate the subjective involvement that is present in all faith statements. It is a good word: believing is in fact nothing but *homologein*, agreement with the community's immense respect for the person of Jesus. We have tried to show all due appreciation for this inexpendable and very normally Christian side of the whole issue. The issue between orthodox theology and existentialist theology cannot possibly be that the one understands *homologein* as a "take it or leave it" proposition while the other understands it as a value judgment of the heart. The controversy is closer to this: does *homologein* indicate agreement with the immense respect that the evangelists and apostles had for the Jesus of the tradition (only then does *homo* get any meaning), or with the extract that Fuchs and Ebeling draw

---

[66] Cf. H. Diem, "Theologie als kirchliche Wissenschaft," *Dogmatik*, II, 30.

from the Gospels and present as the so-called historical Jesus? *Homologein* is a pregnant word as long as it suggests the act of faith (the *fides qua*)—the respect or admiration—that is summoned by the message of salvation (the *fides quae*), which precedes all admiration that any men have had for Jesus. In brief, *homologein* implies *fides quae* as well as *fides qua*.

We touch here on a possible antinomy in existentialist theology that we have met earlier: faith never exists without at least a minimal content. Is this a real antinomy or is it consistent with the basic intentions of this theology? We think that a good argument can be made for the latter. To put forth Jesus as the "ground" of faith instead of the content of faith is consistent as long as Jesus means nothing more than what Fuchs and Ebeling suggest: a Jesus of whom all hints of saving facts are crossed out. There is indeed no reason for making *this* so-called historical Jesus the content of faith.

The distinction between "ground" and "content" arose when historical criticism first whittled Jesus down to the so-called historical Jesus in contrast to the so-called dogmatical Jesus. The dogmatical Jesus, it was said, could not be the content of faith on the ground of sound reason. But the so-called historical Jesus can be that even less, on strictly religious grounds. Existentialist theology discerned this quite accurately, and so it tried to rescue the word "ground." But, as we have seen, a content is always implied in the notion of ground. Strictly speaking, the notion of ground implies too much. This is why Ebeling talked about the "foundation" that faith finds in the historical Jesus. Perhaps this expresses better than any other word the place that Jesus has and can have in existentialist theology. The "historical Jesus" can never be a real "ground" in the sense of something that truly gives to faith roots in something deeper than itself. If the resurrection of Jesus means no more than a value judgment made by the early Christians about the cross and the crucified, Jesus remains past time and He cannot become present with us through the Holy Spirit. He cannot be the person of the present time who awakens faith and keeps it alive.

The dissension within existentialist theology occurs at this point. On one hand, one wants to stress the actuality of the Christ-experience. Jesus must be somehow involved with that which gives certainty to faith. On the other hand, faith appears to possess no content; that which would qualify Jesus to be the source of my faith today—that is, His resurrection—is purposely eliminated on behalf of man in his authentic existence. Jesus is isolated from the *source* of faith's certainty. This is why the question of truth is not only exhausted by the question of certainty, but is in fact eliminated as the ground of certainty; existentialist theology has nothing left to say about the ground of certainty. To have faith means to be certain. Certain of what? Existentialist theology refuses to make any dogmatic statement about the content of faith at this point. It can only talk in the terms of a general revelation, in the sense meant by traditional theology. But this is too meager to recommend this theology as a Christian theology. Christian theology stands or falls with Jesus Christ as the living Lord, to whom faith today is still directed. Existentialist theology cannot solve the hermeneutical problem; the so-called "historical Jesus" cannot substitute for the Holy Spirit. It presents as a Christocentric theology what looks more like a "cryptic personalism."[67]

Faith and reality

We have said enough to indicate the way out of the maze of questions that is created when we object equally to a theology built on metaphysics and to the way existentialist theology defends its antimetaphysical bias. This promising discovery was found in history and (at least if one takes history seriously) the historicity of man and the historicity of all his verbal formulations. Due to its metaphysical needs, orthodox theology had far too little eye for historicity and history. To put it more strongly, it denied (as much as it was able) the historical element in the representations, formulations, and concepts in which the message of salvation was transmitted. It did this in order to preserve an incontrovertible, eternally unchanging, universal validity for faith. This antihistorical tendency, coupled with a strong metaphysical penchant, has cost theology dearly. With its denial of the genuinely historical element, it also lost the unique subjectivity that truly belongs to Christian faith, the subjectivity that is involved in the way God in history deals with us. And with the loss of the subjectivity of faith, the character of the Christian truth as promise is also threatened.

---

[67] Otto Weber, *Grundlagen der Dogmatik*, II (1962), 13.

Formulations and general concepts bring us under the law rather than grace whenever their human limitations are ignored.

There is, we believe, a very promising perspective in this way of stating the situation. The denial of the historical moment is the result of a philosophical choice, the choice of a metaphysically constructed theology. Resistance to historicity has never been the real intention of orthodoxy. It is a necessary by-product of the attempt to construct a theology in a certain philosophical manner. This means that there is no reason on earth why orthodoxy should canonize its antihistorical position as though salvation might depend on so doing. There is, in fact, good reason why we should, for the sake of the continuing task of transmitting the faith, forsake this antihistorical position once and for all. It may just be that its antihistorical bias is what has prevented orthodoxy from being fully successful in transmitting the message to the new generation.

In conclusion, we can accept existentialist theology's indictment of the shortcomings of metaphysical theology. To identify theological statements with metaphysical statements rules out the unique kind of subjectivity that the origin of theological statements presupposes. It opens the door for anyone to make theological statements without actually making a confession. It ignores the appropriation factor in statements of faith made in the past. And it demotes the liberating message of salvation to a new law. Where existentialist theology went wrong was in its total war against all kinds of "is"-statements, against statements such as "Jesus is God's Son," "Jesus is risen" and even, "God 'is.' "[68]

One thing becomes clear from the preceding argument: the historicity of our faith statements provides support for the "is"-character of dogmatics, that is, for the reality to which appropriation and transmission is bound. One is bound to say that without the reality indicated by the word "is," transmission is either nonsense or genuine creativity—and the last thing we want to say of Christian faith is that it is creative in this sense. The historicity of "is"-statements does not refer to the "is"-character of the statements; the historicity of these statements refers to our way of appropriating

---

[68] The quotation marks around the word "is" here only indicate that the word implies a predication; they are not intended to suggest a double meaning.

and passing on the content to which the "is"-statements refer. When we say that all faith statements are historical, we mean that they are meant to be appropriated and passed on. The "is"-character of the reality that dogmatics affirms is such that it is not destroyed by our constant reappropriation and transmission of them. In fact, our appropriation and transmission of them reaffirms the genuine "is"-character of the statements. The reality that faith statements affirm—God's reality—is of a unique sort, in that it resists polarization into either subjective or objective statements. The "is" in the statement "God is" is never truly understood if we turn it into either a general metaphysical assertion or a mere witness to our own subjective, existential reality. We do justice to the word "is" only if we persist in saying that theology's speech about God is speech about a completely unique reality that demands a wholly unique order of speech.

To get back to the antimetaphysical penchant of existentialist theology, we can agree that if the word "is" in the message about Israel's God and Israel's Messiah means merely that one holds a certain thing about that God to be true, without himself being involved, the word "is" has failed to convey its real significance. For this insight, we owe existentialist theology a debt of gratitude. But we must not disown the word "is" in theology; to cancel out the real sense of the "is" in theological statements does not help to bring commitment or involvement back into religion. What we must do is recognize the unique way in which the word "is" functions in statements about the God who speaks and acts in history. True commitment is born when the true meaning of "God is" is grasped. When a man says "God is," he puts on his lips a truth that contains a song and a life. If it does not mean that to the person who says it, he has not spoken truth.

But we must now ask still another question. Are these great statements—"God is" and "Jesus is risen"—true outside of the presence of faith? One must not too quickly take flight into subjectivism in answering such questions. The threat of subjectivism is very real. The notion that the truth is true only for believers opens up a bottomless pit of subjectivity. To this, we would counter that to speak of God without faith can provide the theoretical correctness of an objective statement, and thus appear to express a knowledge of God, while in fact there is no greater affront to

Israel's God and His Christ than correctness without personal appropriation.[69]

This does not provide an answer to the question of the universal validity of the "is"-statements of faith. What is claimed is that statements about God and His acts in Christ are by nature—that is, according to the manner in which Israel's God *is* God—confessions of faith; they presuppose a speaking subject who could not be substituted with an anonymous or universal subject making accurate scientific statements. The man who speaks truthfully about God is a person who lives in a believing, trusting, obedient, thankful relationship with God. If this relationship is lacking, an ingredient so vital to the truth of these matters is absent that a person who speaks about God's being and salvation without it has lost his profoundest right to speak of them. He loses his right because, speaking with so-called objectivity, he is not speaking of the God whose very "being" and "salvation" is always "for me"; this "for me" belongs to the "being" of God in His revelation. It was not something added, as Bultmann insists, *by us*. When this involved knowledge is not apparent in the statement itself, it is no longer evident that the statement is one that must be believed, in the full and broad sense which we mean by belief. The "is" that the tradition carries, and which dogmatics has given a name about which it speaks in a critical manner, is an "is" that, in an extra-intellectual sense, *has to be believed*. It is not created by faith, nor by personal evaluation, encounter, or experience. Were the "is-ness" of God a result of a creative experience, we would fall head over heels into subjectivism. Nonetheless, this "is" must be brought into speech in the manner of a confession of faith. To neglect this is to miss the nature of the reality of God, and to revert to an objectivism that is as serious an error as is subjectivism.

The reality of faith is a reality toward which faith is directed. The genitive "the reality of *faith*" is an objective genitive. But this reality—God in His relationship with man and the world—demands a subjective genitive, a true and genuine act of faith, if reality is to come into its own according to its own nature. Thus, we see again, no matter how we consider the reality of "is"-state-

[69] That God can strike cleanly with a crooked stick shows His greatness. The scribes told about in Matt. 2:1-12, though themselves unbelieving, could still teach others (the Magi). This does not suggest, however, that unbelief does not really matter.

ments in theology, it comes down to the unique nature of this
particular "is." Christian theology cannot forfeit its "is"-language.
Nor can it allow it to become involved in a dialectic of special and
ordinary being. We must not fall into the trap of saying that God
is and at the same time is not because He is God.[70] Even less
should we let the word "is" be turned into a value judgment; we
must remember that in the word "is" the universal validity of
language is involved. Dogmatics is concerned with statements of
universal validity. This is true, even though this universal validity
has its own brand and origin.

Metaphysically based theology also wanted to defend the universal validity of dogmatic statements and faith concepts, but it
failed to do justice to the unique character of the universal validity
of Christian faith because of the philosophical system into which it
fitted its theological statements. Its construction of universal validity—as necessary rational truths—was not able to do justice to the
serving and liberating character of Christian truth. Metaphysical
theology is a theology of mastery instead of a servant theology.[71]
Though it once had a place in a Christendom defined by the
medieval social structure and governed by the church, it is out of
place in the modern world.

But can Christian truth be a *serving* truth and yet insist on
pretensions of universal validity?

Christian truth can. Its validity has the form of a confession of
faith and a summons to obedience that is rooted in the faith itself:
the valid and universal claim that God has on His people and His
world. Since the Christian church confesses that God is the universal God-for-men, it also claims that the word "is" has general, or
universal validity.[72] The Lord is merciful and gracious (Ex. 34:6;

[70] Gollwitzer speaks, on one hand, of the "*un*usefulness of the 'is' statements" and, on the other hand, of "the necessity of 'is' statements" (*Die
Existenz Gottes,* pp. 162, 169), leaving the reader unsure of his meaning.

[71] Rossouw is quite right in saying that the Reformers' principle of the
clarity of Holy Scripture was essentially a break through the metaphysical
concept of authority that was fostered in medieval church and theology.
Cf. his *Klaarheid en Interpretasie,* p. 340.

[72] On the claim of universal validity and the basis for certainty implied
in it, see Lothar Steiger, *Die Hermeneutik als dogmatisches Problem,* pp.
7ff. An article that is as exciting as it is instructive is Heinrich Vogel's
"Wann is eine theologische Satz Wahr?", *Kirche und Dogma,* IV (1958),
176-190. Vogel wrestles with the mystery of truth (the *Herrengeheimnis*)
concerning the Lord as over against the universal validity of theological
language, managing to do justice to both.

Num. 14:8); this is a general statement of universal validity which carries its universality in the form of confession and a summons to faith.

This description of the universal validity of faith statements also clarifies the kind of knowledge that is expressed in the "is"-statements of faith. Theology is an effort to express and develop our knowledge. It has to do with statements that contain more than individualistic expressions of individual emotions that imply no duty at all that another share them. Theology maintains the reality of its "is"-statements because it understands that they are statements of knowledge.[73] In theology, as in every other supposedly "objective" field of knowledge, we assume that the knowing subject was creatively involved in the *origin* of statements about God. But theology goes further. The knowing subject is also vitally involved in the statements themselves. He makes the statement only as a subjectively involved confessor; for him, the "objective" knowledge is a confession. Statements in theology, then, are always made in the faith that, while they are now unverified, they will one day be verified, and that they will then not only *be*, but will *obviously* be, statements of knowledge.[74]

Further than this we cannot go, either in Christianity generally or in theology particularly: that there is a reality corresponding to our statements about God is a fact that Christians believe. In this sense, in which the whole Christian mode of existence by faith can be a genuine challenge to the world, and conversely, the world can become an enormous resistance to Christian faith, the knowledge conveyed by theology is faith knowledge. It must remain this if the true nature of its universality is to be made evident by its appeal and its summons to faith.

---

[73] On the necessity of either holding dogmatic statements to be expressions of genuine knowledge or giving up on dogmatic statements altogether, see Gerhard Stammler, "Von Erkenntnis-Charakter der theologischen Aussagen," *Kirche und Dogma,* IX (1963), 259-315.

[74] We have no vocabulary by which we can discuss the possibility of verifying eschatological statements. This does not, however, disprove the reality of the eschaton, contrary to Van Buren, *The Secular Meaning of the Gospel,* p. 98.

AN UNSCIENTIFIC
POSTSCRIPT

AN UNSCIENTIFIC POSTSCRIPT

The modest question as to the reality of faith has turned out to be as troublesome as it is modest. Why is this? Why should we moderns, after all this time, be bothered by the question of whether faith actually attests to a reality outside of itself?

The answer is twofold. A simple answer is impossible, partly because of the nature of the Christian faith, and partly because of our own times. Christian faith is a faith that is handed down, that is passed from one generation to another. The heritage of faith involves a process of new developments as faith passes from one situation into another, into ever new cultures. Today, we are experiencing a departure from one world and an entrance into a new world in a more dramatic manner than has any previous generation. Our life-situation is changing. And the change of our world of experience and thought forces the church to face the challenge of translating the gospel into language understood by the new world.

We are not able to digest the many characterizations of our changed and changing world that insightful people have made. Nor shall we add another to the list. Every person must make his own discovery of the change. And he will indeed make it if he merely stops to compare the things that occupy his attention and force him to be concerned with what another person in his same station was concerned about four hundred years ago. I mention this number of years because it takes us back to the time when the Reformation creeds came into being.

Not everyone is as deeply involved in the rapid changes of our time as others are. The citizens of Amsterdam are much further into the modern world than are the provincial residents of Friesland. Perhaps the word "further" betrays a bias, as though we are saying that the metropolitan is better integrated into real life.

195

Use the word "differently" then, and say the city dweller is differently involved. He lives in another world. But, if this other world is said to be the world of the future, and by that token a better world, the provincial would indeed be skeptical. Let anyone try to convince the townsman of the province that the life of the metropolis is the better life and he would be laughed out of town. The villager would tell him that a single week in the chaos called city would drive him mad. So, the question of value is a matter of opinion. At any rate, the villager must know that 800,000 city dwellers *do* manage to live in this madness, this stench, this frenetic tempo, this howling din—this city—and do make the best of it without going berserk.

This ought to say something to the Christian in this time of whirling change. The changed world is with us; it is not going to be unchanged. The readiness with which Christian people are able to adjust to it varies from person to person and group to group. Some Christians have their eye on the year 2000. They wonder about the problems that it is going to set before their children, and are asking what direction they should take now to be ready for that strange new world. But others are scarcely feeling the change even now, partly because it has passed them by and partly because they are in a situation to arrange their affairs so that it cannot touch them.

The differences in response to change are partly a matter of geography; they are determined in part by where one lives, in the country or in the city. But this is a very rough distinction. In reality the boundaries are fluid. The distinction between the younger and older generation is equally fluid. We have to be on guard against neat classifications. The young are soon old; and how they will manage with change then is always unpredictable. Besides, some young men talk like old men while our fathers often have enough vitality to face the new with a vigor that makes young men look old. Be this as it may, the fact is that a tangible difference exists among Christians when it comes to breadth of vision, openness to information, and ability to understand, and that this difference plays a role in the confusions of Christendom as it tries to reorient itself into a new world. Some Christians have dug much further into the problematics of modern life than others, and— whether because of their rearing, interest, or social position—are a good deal more at ease than the others in this world. And this difference does more than create a marked tension and breakdown of communication between the two types of Christians; it also creates a sense of uncertainty about the answers that today's Christians ought to give to the problems of today.

No one, I suppose, is against any change. Whether on the extreme right or extreme left, all agree that some changes in our ways of expressing the Christian faith are inevitable. But the question is how far we can go with these changes. Theologian A sets the teeth of group B on edge because his theological language is different from the familiar language of their fathers. But theologian A is nervous as a cat when he listens to theologian C, whose methods and manners, theologically speaking, are even further out in left field. Everyone who thinks theologically—and who does not?—sometimes feels like theologian A. He too discovers that he upsets people and, to his sorrow, creates anxiety in them. But he is just as likely to feel someone close behind who creates uneasiness in him and who makes him wonder where in the world theology is heading.

All this is hardly surprising. It should not inflict a burden of anxiety on our generation. For we are only experiencing a little more bluntly what people have always had to go through. We are a step ahead of the generation just past; and another generation is around the corner who will be two steps ahead of us. The difference today is one of tempo. The boundaries are shifting very fast. Speed is the difference. What once happened in a gradual succession of generations is now happening simultaneously; that is, developments that used to be associated with successive generations are now happening all at once. Many boundaries of thought are being opened up all at once. They are opened, not successively, but alongside one another. Everything is up for grabs. What used to take a century's history now happens simultaneously.

The speed with which boundaries of thought are opened complicates the whole situation. But, even more, rapid shifts of thought horizons invite us to be radical. They *demand* that we be radical. We have to be *with it*, lest we find ourselves talking in terms of a thought pattern that has already become obsolete. We have to be *radically* with it, lest our being in this period of rapid change has no point. We have to be with it or there is no point of being in it. When boundaries shift as rapidly as they do today, rapid response has to be radical response.

This is notably true of today's theology. If we do not look on today's theologians as charlatans, if we do not assume that they are either fools or knaves in their revision of theological projects and their rethinking of Christian faith, we have only one point of view left to us: modern theologians have made a crucial decision to be "with it." They have decided to keep pace with the opening up of the world to human knowledge. They have determined not to have to catch up a hundred years later. And so they have made radical decisions; they have jumped in with the same direct address to the situation that characterizes all radicals, but which is typical especially of the radical who rejects the patterns of our culture. That this radical theology is less original than it is radical, that it smacks more of the nineteenth century than the twenty-first century, can perhaps be attributed to the haste—that matter of speed again—with which it plunges into the questions of our time in order to give an answer to them.

Must we panic? Or should we betray a little less panic than evangelicals tend to engender? Are the theological novelties—from Bultmann to Van Buren, and the others still to come—not to be taken with bitter seriousness? Is their criticism of traditional forms of Christian faith to be taken in stride? These questions call for others, questions of a somewhat different kind. For instance, why should we take the theology of, let us say, Van Buren, more seriously than the theology of Calvin or Luther? Perhaps this betrays a kind of panic too. Perhaps our entire Christian world is best with a deep insecurity that takes the form of a demand for "fixed and finished" theological systems as well as choleric reactions to them.

Now, theology is not the same thing as faith. We began by saying this, and it needs to be said again. Christian certainty, whether of the whole church or of the individual Christian, is not born of theological labors. Nor is theology the midwife in the birth of certainty. Christian certainty has another secret. Its birth is from the Lord Himself. It is the Lord who "speaks to our condition" and "does something to us" through the preaching of the message that has been handed down to us. To say the same thing another way: the Holy Spirit is the final secret of Christian certainty.

But this is no reason for theologians to hold their peace. We can create no end of trouble for one another by our theologizing. In fact, our noble attempts to be theologians can create a reaction that will put us in a position that we did not really want to take and ought not to take. The same thing can happen if we reject a sound and promising theological project. Theology has brought some Christians into a tragic plight: they find themselves in the middle of a battle of words and have no defense. They are uncertain.

This book is dedicated to uncertain people. I do not mean to teach them a lesson with it; the time for teaching other people lessons is past. We have rediscovered faith for what it is—a reality that is so real and genuine, so large and powerful, and especially so liberating of the soul that we have no compulsion left for setting other people on a chair while we review their primary lessons for them again. Since faith has come, we are no longer under the law—as Paul put it (Gal. 3:25). Nor may we put one another under a law again. Indeed, we all have to learn over for ourselves how to stand firm in the liberty with which Christ set us free, free from the yoke of human traditions (Gal. 5:1 ff.). This is the first word that uncertain people have to hear today: the gospel of Jesus Christ is a gospel that liberates people. If we refuse to listen to this word, and listen to it well, we will use the law instead of the gospel to rid us of our uncertainty. And this is precisely what Paul sets himself against in the letter to the Galatians. We must not seek our certainty in the law, but in Christ.

So, we are not allowed to read the law of right theology to one another. Instead, we have to reach out our hands to one another. This book is a gesture of the hand to others. How can we translate the one, undivided, liberating gospel of Jesus Christ, the gospel that has been handed down through the many generations past? How can we translate it today in a way that demonstrates its significance *for* today? How can we translate the one gospel in a way that "says something" and "does something" to us now? The outstretched hand that this book means to offer can be expressed in three points:

(1) The Christian message that we are called to pass on to coming generations has a content that can be defined and taught to others. This must be said to those who have not been willing to let the content of the message do the speaking—and we are talking, as does all of modern theology, about the speaking God. It must be said to those who, on the contrary, insist that "being spoken to" or "being acted on" is the criterion for the genuineness of the mes-

sage. If it "speaks to me" it is God doing the talking; this is the criterion. What is it that speaks to us decisively? What is it that speaks to us so unmistakably that we are bound to recognize it as the voice of God? A consensus has grown around the answer that theologians like Robinson, Van Buren, Braun and others have given: a man is a man, and because of his humanity he hears the voice of God in the claim that his fellow man, simply because he is fellow man, puts on him. This claim is unconditional and unavoidable. To hear it in its unconditioned and unavoidable demand is to hear God.

Surely this is true. God does put a claim on us, and doubtless makes His claim through the agency of our fellow man. But this is not all we have to say about God. In a sense, we scarcely need to tell the next generation this at all. For this is a claim that all men will feel as long as they are human. The unique content of the Christian message is that which they cannot discover by themselves; it is that which no eye has seen, nor ear heard, nor has risen in the heart of man (I Cor. 2:9). This is why handing the message across to future generations is called preaching. It has a content that we must "hear tell" or else not have it at all. This is the message of the cross and resurrection of Jesus of Nazareth as the end of the old and the beginning of a new world. It is the message of a new creation that began in the history of Christ and goes on in the work of the Spirit. When the church talks Spirit, it means to say that God *is* in action, re-creative action, and that things have made a radical turn, that the ball has been thrown in another direction, that we are not falling anymore, but are climbing up.

God's action is not swallowed up in the anonymous presence He assumes in our fellow man. He is there too, of course. But to concentrate on this will find us leaving crumbs for the hungry generations to come. God has come to grips with our guilt—the six million Jews that we are already conveniently forgetting about—and wants us to know about it. He has created a future for men and their world, and wants us to take a meaningful place in it. In a word, we have to tell the next generations that God has His own face, illuminated as it is by the total witness of the Bible. He is His own He, and He comes to us to let us say You to Him. He is a Re-creator, and He has set a great deal in store for us. He lets us appeal to Him on behalf of our fellow man and our world.

But what if *this* God no longer speaks to us or does something to us?

This question is, in a way, a short circuit. Naturally, God does not say just anything at all to us. Nor does He do anything and everything to us. We distinguish Him, for example, in the claim that our neighbor puts on us. But the Christian tradition goes far beyond this. For the same reason, the tradition exists and is handed down as *gospel*. There is a lot more to say about God than that we experience Him in the demands that other men have on us. This "more" has to be *said* to us. We have to be told this. That we need to be told about it is hardly strange. For what is told us in the cross and resurrection of Jesus is not something that one is likely to come on by intuition or guess. It takes time to get across the things that are proclaimed in the gospel. It takes time to come to terms with God on these things.

(2) The gospel has a content. This is why it can be a tradition. But its content cannot be handed down like a map or a scientific formula. It demands commitment; it requires our engagement. It needs people to stake their lives on it. And it does not show its real face except in these conditions.

Our times run the risk of dividing what is indivisible in the matter of Christian tradition. The heritage of faith is, for many Christians I fear, a matter of perpetuating a kind of *attitude* about things while ignoring the need of a commitment to the *specific content* of the faith that forms the tradition. Other Christians are filled with zeal to keep loyalty alive to specific *formulations* of faith and *concepts* of faith in the conviction that faith is kept alive when the forms are kept intact. Both ways are untenable; there is, in fact, something of the one-track mind in each. One does not go into action without having something concrete that incites one to action. And, on the other hand, concepts that do not inspire their faithful adherents to a new way of life, a new humanity— including Van Buren's new "blik"—waken the suspicion that they are empty and meaningless concepts. Orthodox Protestantism, faithful as it is to the tradition, must consider this latter point candidly. Orthodoxy must never let itself become useless; orthodoxy must not let the church suppose that faith is irrelevant to action. It must make clear that it involves decisions, that it comes down to a personal investment. Christians in a country like this one are tempted to forget this, if only because one can bear the name Christian here without much personal cost. It is possible that, for many, the only real decision one makes, and sometimes the greatest sacrifice one makes, consists in accepting a dogma that has nothing to say or do to them other than a demand for submission to its intellectual content.

These are temptations as great as any the Christian church experiences. Many Christians are really at loose ends when they are faced with the question of what they ought to *do*, where they ought to set about changing. They live on the sidelines of the real action in the world. They do not much experience the expansions of our horizons of knowledge. And so they are not overly bothered with nettlesome questions. But they purchase this luxury at the cost of an atrophied faith that in the long run—contrary to what they had planned—leaves them weakened at precisely the point they wanted to make secure. We cannot meet this challenge merely by reminding one another that orthodox faith also demands works. This would be true, needless to say. "Which of the two *did* the will of the Father?" Jesus asked after telling the story of the two sons, one of whom "said yes" and "did nothing" while the other said "no" and yet acted out a "yes" (Matt. 21:28-32). Warnings like this can hardly be taken too seriously. But orthodox Protestants have another task besides this. We have to help one another see our way clear through this changing world so that we will know *where* we should be now and *what* we should be doing today. It will not do to remind ourselves of what Christian people did a generation ago.

We have never believed that a person could be pure of doctrine and yet a murderer. Certainly, some of those who professed pure doctrine have been known to commit crime. But when they did, an automatic correction was made. Immediately it was assumed that the doctrine was not—could not have been—pure after all.

No one is likely to dispute this rather trite example. But the amazing fact is that orthodox Christians are ready to say a good word for this type of Christianity in reaction to a sloppy and enthusiastic movement within Christendom that despises all talk of fidelity to doctrine. Reaction is always married to shortsightedness. It serves only to compound confusion. For it suggests in spite of everything that a person is a Christian after all by virtue of holding as true that which the generation before him held to be true.

Moreover, it is of no genuine help to a Christian trying to find his way through God's world of this day and this place.

The last matter is the more serious. A great many Christians, convinced that faith and works are inseparable, are nonetheless unable to discover for themselves how to focus this unity on the issues of our own time.

The tragic fact of the matter is that people can be doctrinally orthodox, zealous for the dogmatic formulas of the fathers, and still be anti-Semitic and racist. The history of this century betrays the truth of this statement beyond doubt. And the combination of orthodoxy and racism is still with us. It demonstrates the limited value of the word orthodox when it refers to the intellectual content of Christianity. Regardless of how orthodox he is, the racist has lost any right to the name Christian; his fidelity to sound doctrine makes monstrous mockery of Christian truth. No one *can* be both Christian and racist. The day may come when we will say the same of Christianity and waging war. After all, it took a while for us to see that being Christian and being a slave trader were incompatible.

In any case, speaking biblically, fidelity to truth involves *doing* the truth as well as speaking it (John 3:21; I John 1:6). We need a new and more inclusive definition of orthodoxy. And if we are going to see this biblical requirement function today, we need to know today's world. We have to know the issues, what is at stake in our time and place. It is here and nowhere else that the truth must be done. (Fantastic as it sounds, an orthodoxy exists in the Netherlands that puts a taboo on TV.) If it is not practiced today, the faith of orthodoxy loses its authenticity; its disciples make it unmarketable.

(3) Our words can never validate the gospel. Our confessions do not make it true. Neither does our "doing" of the truth make it true. All our words and actions can do is help make clear what faith is all about. As we try to pass the gospel on to the next generation, our own faithful involvement in faith can at best capture a little of the light of the message.

Every generation of Christians has an almost frightening responsibility here. We are not off the hook if we, for fear of botching the job, try to hand it down without translating it anew. If we try this, we are simply like the man in the gospel who buried his talent for fear of losing it. Like him, we would make ourselves unprofitable stewards. The message that needs passing on demands living people to do the passing; it has to be kept alive as *gospel*, the life-giving truth. But while the job is demanding, it is liberating and comforting too. If it is true that our verbalizing cannot make or break the truth of the gospel, then we can work confidently with all the definitions and formulas that the Christian church has employed in its pilgrimage through history.

The fact is that the church's words are not definitions. Language is not given for defining things; at least defining things is not the prime task of language, and it is surely not the use we put it to in daily communication. The language of communication *points*; it puts its finger out, calls for attention to a piece of reality that the speaker wants another person to share. This applies to the language of faith as well as to any. Perhaps many of us have to relearn that expressions of faith are not meant to be definitions, hard and clear and granting no quarter. In reality, if our confessions of faith were definitions, they would not be hard and clear, and they would have to give quarter to many an argument.

But the language of faith does the same thing as ordinary language does. It points to a reality, the reality of God and His salvation. And it does this job with a touch of creativity; it is not a photograph, but a portrait.

This is why not all words do the job well. A photograph is a mechanical reproduction. But if a man portrays something, he can do it badly and disfigure its reality. This is why it makes sense to pay heed to the doctrine; this is why a Christian ought to be orthodox. But something else makes as much sense. That something else is to see that the function of language, including the language of faith, is not that of encasing intellectual content within formulas, but of pointing to the reality of God, a pointing done with words, a pointing that cannot be entombed in any particular words of any particular time.

INDEXES

INDEX OF PERSONS

INDEX OF SUBJECTS